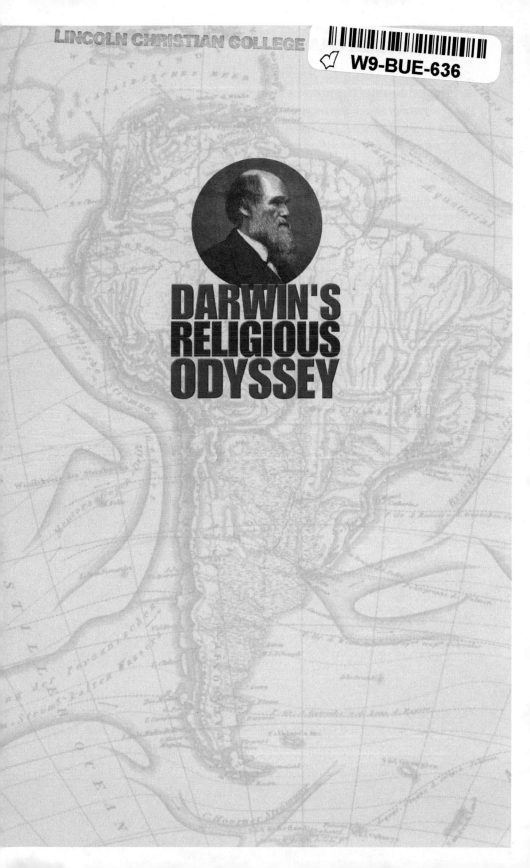

DARWIN'S RELIGIOUS ODYSSEY

DARWIN'S RELIGIOUS ODYSSEY

William E. Phipps

TRINITY PRESS INTERNATIONAL
HARRISBURG, PENNSYLVANIA

To my beloved grandson, Charles Anderson Engh III.

Descended from generations of physicians as was Charles Darwin,

he shares that genius's scientific curiosity and observational keenness.

Trinity Press International, P.O. Box 1321, Harrisburg, PA 17105
Trinity Press International is a division of The Morehouse Group.

Cover art: Portrait entitled *Mr. C. R. Darwin, Author of "The Origin of the Species"* by an anonymous artist. © New York Public Library/Art Resource, NY.

Cover design: Wesley Hoke

Library of Congress Cataloging-in-Publication Data

Phipps, William E., 1930-
  Darwin's religious odyssey / William E. Phipps.
    p. cm.
Includes bibliographical references (p.   ).
  ISBN 1-56338-384-5 (pbk. : alk. paper)
  1. Darwin, Charles, 1809-1882—Religion. 2. Evolution
(Biology)—Religious aspects. 3. Religion and science. I. Title.
  QH31.D2 P55 2002
  576.8'092—dc21

                          2002005401

Printed in the United States of America

02 03 04 05 06 07   10 9 8 7 6 5 4 3 2 1

Contents

109486

Abbreviations

Autobiography   *The Autobiography of Charles Darwin.* Edited by
Nora Barlow. New York: Harcourt, 1958.

Correspondence   *The Correspondence of Charles Darwin.* Edited by
Frederick Burkhardt and Sydney Smith. Cambridge:
Cambridge University Press, 1985-forthcoming.

Descent   Charles Darwin. *The Descent of Man and Selection
in Relation to Sex.* In *Great Books of the Western
World,* edited by Robert Hutchins. Chicago:
Encyclopaedia Britannica, 1952. The text is from
Darwin's second and final edition in 1874.

Diary   *Charles Darwin's Beagle Diary.* Edited by Richard
Keynes. Cambridge: Cambridge University Press, 1988.

LLD   *The Life and Letters of Charles Darwin.* Edited by
Francis Darwin. 2 vols. New York: Appleton, 1888.

MLD   *More Letters of Charles Darwin.* Edited by Francis
Darwin and A. C. Seward. 2 vols. New York:
Appleton, 1903.

Notebooks   *Charles Darwin's Notebooks 1836–44.* Edited by Paul
Barrett et al. Ithaca: Cornell University Press, 1987.

Origin   Charles Darwin. *Origin of Species by Means of
Natural Selection.* In *Great Books of the Western
World,* edited by Robert Hutchins. Chicago:
Encyclopaedia Britannica, 1952. The text is from
Darwin's sixth and final edition in 1872.

Voyage   Charles Darwin. *The Voyage of a Naturalist Round
the World in H.M.S. "Beagle".* London: Routledge, n. d.

Preface

On February 12, 1809, two babies were born who would both become emancipators. Abraham Lincoln would become a leader in liberating American slaves, while Charles Darwin would assist in freeing scientists and theologians from enshackling modes of thinking about nature and nature's God. This bicentennial decade of their birth is a fitting time to recall aspects of the life and thought of each: one the most esteemed president of the United States and the other the most influential scientist in world history. No one has done more than Darwin to challenge cherished self-images engendered by world religions. Indeed, he revolutionized theology as well as science. Darwin's evolutionary theory not only transformed his own religion but, more than any other scientific discovery, has caused ordinary people to deal with issues affecting their core outlook on humankind.

Detesters of Darwin tend to interpret him as anti-religious, determined to undermine the biblical faith. Jesuit Joseph Bayma, who taught at an English college in the nineteenth century, declared, "Mr. Darwin is, we have reason to believe, the mouthpiece or chief trumpeter of that infidel clique whose well-known object is to do away with all idea of a God."[1] Protestant William Jennings Bryan, the anti-evolution prosecutor at the Scopes trial, stated in 1923 that Darwin's "hypothesis destroyed his own religious faith" as well as that of Darwinians.[2] Those Americans who have persistently agitated during the past century for state laws prohibiting the teaching of evolution in public schools have presumed that Darwin's ideas were rooted in atheism.[3] Robert Clark concludes: "[T]he so-called 'evolutionary outlook' is still exactly what Darwin made it—a substitute god."[4]

Admirers of Darwin have also occasionally thought that as an adult, he was against religion. Philosopher Thomas Goudge thinks "the image of Darwin as an enemy of the Bible, the church, and Christianity" that anti-evolutionists have created is "fairly close to the truth."[5] Brandeis professor Silvan Schweber asserts, "By 1839 Darwin was certainly an agnostic."[6] Harvard zoologist Ernst Mayr declares that by that same date, when he was thirty years old, Darwin had become a "materialist," which is "more or less equivalent to an atheist."[7] Richard Dawkins, a distinguished Oxford professor, views Darwin as "an intellectually fulfilled atheist."[8] A biography by John Bowlby contains hundreds of pages about Darwin's bouts with persistent undiagnosable illnesses but virtually nothing about his theological struggles. Bowlby presumes that Darwin lost his religious faith before he married.[9] Michael White and John Gribbin, in another recent biography, state that as a young man Darwin "had little time for orthodox Christianity and even less for Anglicanism." Moreover, from the age of forty-two onward "Darwin was a total, uncompromising atheist."[10] The *Evolution* series on the Public Broadcasting System, first aired in 2001, portrays Darwin as having a patronizing attitude toward religion and its representatives.

Darwin's five-year circumnavigation of the earth on H.M.S. *Beagle* has been painstakingly examined by those interested in the gradual changes in his ideas on geology and biology, but few have studied as carefully his lifelong religious odyssey. Even as adventuresome Odysseus meandered about his Mediterranean world exploring intriguing sites on his way home from war, so Darwin wandered about in both the theological and scientific spheres, struggling with hoary assumptions he found there. The tempestuous issues he encountered often challenged his confidence, so that his mind as well as his stomach was frequently in turmoil through much of his life. His circuitous journey of faith is a captivating one—in part because it mirrors the struggles of other scientists who have endeavored to harmonize their findings with religious worldviews accepted from youth.

Some current biologists seem to project their own secular orientation onto Darwin and discount that he made frequent positive references to God in his private and public writings throughout his life. His life is more accurately viewed through the lens of the nineteenth-century culture of natural theology. Previous treatments of Darwin's religion have usually dealt less with his personal values and social commitments than with his changing theology. Without diminishing the importance of those intellectual issues, there is still need for a full contextual treatment that compares his religious and moral viewpoints with those of his family and associates, as well as with the spirit of the society in which he lived. Darwin was a product of his Victorian culture as well as the shaper of future scientific culture.

The best source for understanding Darwin's religious musings and commitments is the self-portrait that the expectant grandfather sketched for his offspring. A version of that autobiography, from which thousands of words were deleted, was published posthumously in 1887, a decade after he wrote it. Until 1958 when Darwin's granddaughter Nora Barlow published his full autobiography, some members of his family had succeeded in suppressing parts of it from the public for religious reasons.[11] His autobiography makes clear that he did not sail from Christian orthodoxy to atheistic materialism. The 1987 transcription of Darwin's notebooks from 1836–44 discloses his attempts to reconcile his initial evolutionary views with Christian theology.

New material discovered by an intense search of Darwinian archives is resulting in the gradual publication of his voluminous correspondence. When completed, the project will provide five times the 2,845 previously published letters.[12] The unexpurgated autobiography, plus the great quantity of notebooks, journals, drafts, and letters he left, now provide us with the resources for a full-orbed awareness of his religious voyage. This study will use Darwin's own words to state his views on theology and religion, because he usually expressed himself quite clearly. His books that present his theory may be the last major scientific works that can be understood by the common reader.

My fascination with Darwin has resulted from my education in both theology and science. Whereas he prepared to become a priest at his college, I prepared to become a physicist as an undergraduate. But neither he nor I entered careers for which we were initially trained. After graduation he crossed the Atlantic to study science and I crossed that ocean to study religion. For many years I was stimulated by being a member of a team that taught "Emancipators of the Modern Mind," a course organized around readings by Darwin, Stanton, Marx, Nietzsche, Freud, Einstein, and Gandhi. In 1983 I published articles on Darwin and theology in *Bios* and *The Christian Century*. I have produced this book out of my twenty years of research and thinking about Darwin.

Without the resources of research libraries, this project could not have been accomplished. The holdings of the University of Virginia, the College of William and Mary, and Virginia Commonwealth University have been helpful, but I am particularly indebted to the library of Union Theological Seminary / Presbyterian School of Christian Education. Their reference librarian Patsy Verreault was of special assistance in obtaining books on interlibrary loan. Above all, I have been helped by Martha Swezey Phipps, who has brought her training as a scientist to bear on copyediting. Thanks to my arch-critical wife, this study, along with my dozen or so previous books, have been made more logical and readable.

Notes

1. Quoted in Andrew White, *A History of the Warfare of Science with Theology in Christendom* (New York: Appleton, 1898), 1:72.

2. William Jennings Bryan Papers, Library of Congress, General Correspondence, 35.

3. Norman Furniss, *The Fundamentalist Controversy* (New Haven: Yale University Press, 1954), 81–82.

4. Robert Clark, *Darwin* (Exeter: Paternoster, 1966), 187.

5. Paul Edwards, ed., *The Encyclopedia of Philosophy* (New York: Macmillan, 1967), 2:295.

6. Silvan Schweber, "The Origin of the *Origin* Revisited," *Journal of the History of Biology* (fall 1977): 234, 310.

7. Ernst Mayr, *One Long Argument* (Cambridge: Harvard University Press, 1991), 75.

8. Richard Dawkins, *The Blind Watchmaker* (New York: Norton, 1986), 6.

9. John Bowlby, *Charles Darwin* (New York: Norton, 1991), 229.

10. Michael White and John Gribbin, *Darwin* (New York: Dutton, 1995), 23, 156.

11. Nora Barlow, ed., *The Autobiography of Charles Darwin* (New York: Harcourt, 1958), 11–12.

12. Frederick Burkhardt, *A Calendar of Correspondence of Charles Darwin* (New York: Garland, 1985), 7.

Selective Darwin-Wedgwood Genealogy

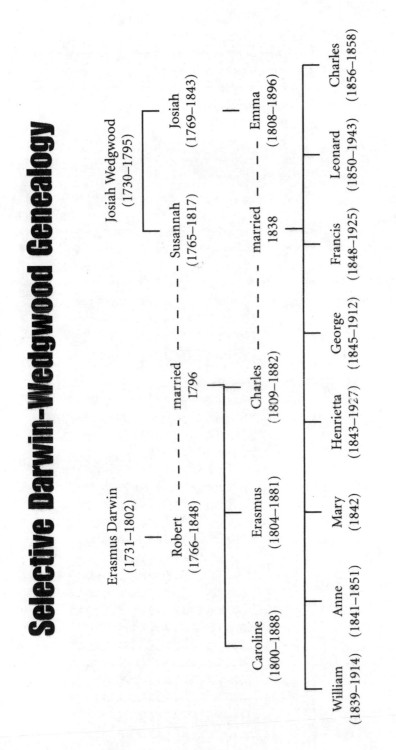

CHAPTER ONE
Growing up Anglican

EARLY RELIGIOUS INFLUENCES

Charles Robert Darwin was born in Shrewsbury at The Mount, an upper-class mansion overlooking the Severn River in the West Midlands of England. He was the fifth child of Dr. Robert Darwin, a successful physician and financier, and Susannah Wedgwood Darwin. She was the daughter of Josiah Wedgwood, the founder of a prosperous pottery firm whose china was to carry his name for centuries. He was also a Unitarian disciple of Rev. Joseph Priestley, the famed discoverer of oxygen, and consulted with him more about theology than chemistry.

Although Priestly had had a Calvinist upbringing, he became a main leader of the Unitarians in England and America. In 1782, while pastor of a church in Birmingham, he wrote *A History of the Corruptions of Christianity*. He argued that Jesus did not advocate Trinitarian or limited atonement doctrines but believed in the "unity of God" and in "free mercy to the penitent." Since Jesus was against superstitions, Priestley reasoned, Christians should never have accepted the belief that baptismal water can wash away sin or that the communion sacrament is somehow magical. He contended that Jesus was not "God Almighty or an superangelic being" and that "rational Christianity" follows the Unitarian belief of its founder.[1]

Charles's grandfathers Josiah Wedgwood and Dr. Erasmus Darwin had been fellow members of Birmingham's Lunar Society, which discussed both scientific and religious issues. They jointly made original contributions on the properties of ice.[2] Erasmus twitted Josiah by remarking that the freethinking Unitarian religion was "only a feather bed to catch a falling Christian."[3] But Unitarians thought they were restoring authentic Christianity by discovering God's design in nature. For example, Priestley viewed oxygen as an expression of God's goodness because it is given off by vegetation to restore air contaminated by breathing.

Susannah, like her father, was committed to liberal Christianity. Not thinking of herself as a fallen Christian, she and her six children worshiped at the Unitarian chapel in Shrewsbury. The children also attended the primary school operated by George Case, the Unitarian minister whom Susannah had helped to bring to town. Charles was enrolled at this day school before his mother died in 1817, and remained there for one term. Eight-year-old Charles was then raised mainly by his sister Caroline, who was nine years his senior.[4] Since Susannah's husband had nominal ties to the Church of England, their children had received an orthodox baptism. Charles attended Anglican services after his mother's death, but he did not become a confirmed member as a boy.

From 1818 to 1825, Charles attended Rev. Samuel Butler's grammar school in his hometown. He resided at the school, which was located about a mile from his home—close enough for him to visit in the evenings before the school doors were locked. He remembered his naïveté: "I often had to run very quickly to be in time, and from being a fleet runner [I] was generally successful; but when in doubt I prayed earnestly to God to help me, and I well remember that I attributed my success to the prayers and not to my quick running, and marvelled how generally I was aided."[5] Pupils were required to attend Sunday morning and evening worship at the school as well as the daily chapel service. During morning chapel, Charles diverted his attention from worship in order to memorize dozens of lines from Virgil or Homer that had been assigned.[6] Students were drilled on the Anglican catechism, biblical history, and theology.[7]

Butler's school had an excellent national reputation, but Charles's main interest was not in the classical curriculum or in the religious training. He confessed that his passion lay elsewhere: "I do not believe that anyone could have shown more zeal for the most holy cause than I did for shooting birds." On observing his mediocre scholarship, his father scolded, "You care for nothing but shooting, dogs, and rat-catching, and you will be a disgrace to yourself and all your family." Fearfully, he tried to be deferential to the patriarch's desires. Even after Charles had grown up he called his father the largest man he had ever known, and that assessment appears to have had reference to more than the man's enormous physical size.[8]

Charles read some important extracurricular books during this period. Rev. C. C. Clarke's *Wonders of the World* stimulated his desire to travel to distant countries. Another of his favorite books exemplifies how the British surpassed all others in searching nature for theological significance. In 1789 Rev. Gilbert White published a well-illustrated study of the wildlife in his parish entitled *The Natural History of*

Selborne.[9] It demonstrates the interdependence of myriad creatures in a small area and the intricate intertwining of nature and religion. Details of nature were shown as invested with mystery, and observing them was treated as a sacred experience. In the words of England's greatest bard, White found "tongues in trees, books in the running brooks, / Sermons in stones, and good in everything."[10] After studying White's popular book, Charles began to record ornithological observations and to appreciate birds as something more than hunting targets.[11]

Like his grandfather, father, uncle, and older brother, Charles enrolled as a dutiful son in the unexcelled medical school of Edinburgh University. At sixteen, he and brother Erasmus traveled the several hundred miles by stagecoach to Scotland to prepare for a physician's career. But Charles found the medical lectures dull, and he rushed out of a grisly surgery demonstration, never to return. He remained haunted for the rest of his life from observing, in that era before anesthesia, the great distress of a child during a bungled operation.[12]

During his two years in Scotland, Charles occasionally attended services at the Church of Scotland. He wrote home that he was relieved to find that one sermon, which he timed at twenty minutes, was not "a soul-cutting discourse of two hours and a half," as his reading of Sir Walter Scott had led him to expect.[13] He was intrigued to observe the Presbyterian pageantry when its General Assembly held its annual gathering in the Scottish capital.

Caroline wrote her brother while he was in Edinburgh, "I hope you read the Bible," and, aware that he had not been confirmed as a church member, she added, "I suppose you do not feel prepared yet to take the sacrament."[14] He replied to his surrogate mother that he had tried to follow her advice on Bible reading and asked, "What part of the Bible do you like best? I like the Gospels." In accord with the perennial favorite of most Christians, he further acknowledged that he most liked the Gospel of John.[15] Darwin's experience in Edinburgh was unlike that of David Hume, recognized then as Scotland's most famous philosopher, who a century earlier had attended the university there and had become a thoroughgoing skeptic.

On realizing that Charles lacked the temperament to become a physician, Dr. Darwin advised him to prepare for the priesthood. Charles described his father as a "free thinker in religious matters,"[16] so he realized that this second vocational directive was not due to his father's wholehearted commitment to Anglicanism. Dr. Darwin was resigned to having his son enter any respectable profession, hoping it would overcome his obsession with hunting and beetle collecting. Charles's half-brother John and his first cousin John Wedgwood were already Anglican priests. His father realized that a Church of England priest could live contentedly without much religious conviction or intellectual ambition. Appointments to parishes could easily be purchased by the wealthy, and endowments guaranteed an ample living as well as plenty of leisure for hobbies. Adrian Desmond and James Moore, the best of the Darwin biographers, plausibly suggest that Dr. Darwin envisioned such a life for Charles:

> Let him be educated for three years as a gentleman, take the Bachelor of Arts degree, and spend another year, if he liked, attending theology lectures to prepare for ordination. He could marry afterwards while apprenticed as a curate, and then be presented to a rural benefice not far from Shrewsbury—the perfect restingplace for a wayward second son.[17]

Moore associates the undemanding life of a country vicar at that time with "a little shooting, a little drinking, a little doubt, and, if one liked, a good deal of natural history."[18] As Karl Marx would observe in England, churchmen were not expected to disturb the tranquility of well-heeled congregants by insisting that they ought to engage in social action to relieve those trampled down by unrestrained capitalism.[19] In a stanza of "All Things Bright and Beautiful," an Anglican hymn writer living in the mid-nineteenth century expressed the economic status quo that her church was reinforcing:

> The rich man in his castle,
> The poor man at his gate,
> God made them, high or lowly,
> And ordered their estate.

The universities of Cambridge and Oxford were integral to providing leadership for England's state church. The core curriculum contained much Anglican theology, and daily chapel attendance was expected of all in the academic community. Before a student could be graduated he was required to accept the Thirty-nine Articles of the Church of England that had been handed down since the reign of Elizabeth I. By way of preparation, Charles received special tutoring to freshen up on ancient Greek. He recovered his ability to translate the Greek New Testament, which he had mostly forgotten during his years in Edinburgh.[20]

For three years, beginning in 1827, the medical school dropout resided in Cambridge and enrolled in undemanding, ordinary degree courses there. Charles chose Christ's College, which was founded in 1505, because that was where his brother had studied a few years earlier. The tedium of the lectures was compensated for by a stimulating life apart from the classroom. He enjoyed friends who "sometimes drank too much, with jolly singing and playing at cards afterwards."[21] He was especially fond of his beetle-catching cousin, William Darwin Fox, who was one year ahead of him at the university. But Charles also had a serious side, and at the death of Fox's sister he wrote a letter of sympathy in which he commented on the comfort afforded by the Bible.[22]

Darwin's friend Fanny Owen wrote him that she was surprised to learn that he had "decided to become a DD instead of an MD."[23] He lacked a sense of divine call, and admitted that he could not honestly affirm to a bishop in the ordination service that he felt "inwardly moved by the Holy Spirit" to become a priest.[24] Late in life, Darwin reflected:

> I had scruples about declaring my belief in all the dogmas of the Church of England; though otherwise I liked the thought of being a country clergyman. . . . As I did not then in the least doubt the strict and literal truth of every word in the Bible, I soon persuaded myself that our Creed must be fully accepted. It never struck me how illogical it was to say that I believed in what I could not understand and what is in fact unintelligible.[25]

The Anglican articles that Darwin found "unintelligible" probably included those declaring that Christ's "flesh and bones" were resurrected. Also, he must have found it difficult to make sense out of their predestination affirmation that God chose those whom he would "deliver from curse and damnation" before the world was created. Moreover, he may have thought, like his Unitarian mother, that the Trinity doctrine affirms that three equals one, a mathematical absurdity.

Darwin learned that a former vice-chancellor of his university, Dr. John Lightfoot, had discovered by means of his expert knowledge of Hebrew that the world was created by the Trinity on September 21, 3928 B.C.[26] Lightfoot supplied more precision than that used by seventeenth-century Archbishop James Ussher to establish the 4004 B.C. date, which had long been printed as an editorial note at the beginning of the King James Version of the Bible. Indeed, Darwin fancied that Ussher's "date was somehow in the Bible."[27] Dating the beginning of the universe at about six thousand years ago was done by biblical literalists who started with established dates in the Greco-Roman culture that have biblical references, and then worked backward using genealogies given in the Hebrew Bible. The fifth chapter of Genesis, then presumed to be the world's oldest and most authoritative book, contains a large portion of the biblical chronology. Methuselah's nearly one thousand years was combined with other antediluvian life spans of hundreds of years each.

Also at this time Darwin carefully read *An Exposition of the [Apostles']* *Creed*, a standard text for divinity students by the seventeenth-century scholar John Pearson.[28] Darwin "fully accepted" the doctrine that the Son of God "was conceived by the Holy Ghost" and "born of the Virgin Mary." Then, after his death, "he descended into hell" before arising and ascending into the three-storied universe's heaven, where he awaits to reenter the earth's atmosphere to judge the living and the dead. Among other things, the creed also affirms "the resurrection of the body and the life everlasting." Thomas Huxley commented that Darwin's study of standard theological works "assured him that his religious opinions left nothing to be desired on the score of orthodoxy."[29]

PALEY'S SWAY OVER THE PROSPECTIVE PRIEST

The backbone of the university curriculum consisted of mastering concise and lucidly written texts by William Paley, the late archdeacon of Carlisle Cathedral. Darwin was more aware than the other students of the eminent Paley, because he lived in his hallowed old room at Christ's College. In order to pass the bachelor of arts examination, Darwin had to show competence in classical languages and in Euclid's geometry as well demonstrate a thorough knowledge of Paley's *Principles of Moral and Political Philosophy* and his *Evidences of Christianity*. Darwin recalled half a century later:

> I am convinced that I could have written out the whole of the *Evidences* with perfect correctness, but not of course in the clear language of Paley. The logic of this book and as I may add of his *Natural Theology* gave me as much delight as did Euclid. The careful study of these works, without attempting to learn any part by rote, was the only part of the Academic Course which, as I then felt and as I still believe, was of the least use to me in the education of my mind. I did not at that time trouble myself about Paley's premises; and taking these on trust I was charmed and convinced by the long line of argumentation.[30]

In the *Evidences*, Paley indirectly responded to the most influential skeptical essay ever written on miracles, in which Hume had shown that claims made pertaining to supernatural happenings have never been firm enough to support belief in violation of natural law. Paley attempted to reinstate the traditional argument from Gospel miracles to prove the truth of the Christian religion. Of primary importance, he contended, was Jesus' reanimation of Lazarus, which displayed Jesus' divinity to his disciples.[31] The corpse of Jesus' friend had been buried for a couple of days, and "stinketh," according to the Gospel of John, but Jesus proved that he was the unique Son of God by causing it to breathe again. Paley believed that it was Jesus' dazzling miracles rather than his sublime message that moved his disciples to die for him. Moreover, Paley claimed that Christianity's superiority over Islam is because of Muhammad's inability, according to the Quran, to perform supernatural works.[32]

The notes that Darwin made on his copy of the *Evidences* show that he did not completely share Paley's uncritical interpretation of the Gospels as a student. Pertaining to Jesus, he wrote, "There must have been a certain degree of imposture in his miracles and prophecies."[33] Evidently he was then already in doubt over biblical stories of supernatural feats.

After earning his degree at Cambridge, Darwin studied on his own initiative the last of Paley's trilogy, *Natural Theology or Evidences of the Existence and Attributes of the Deity Collected from the Appearances of Nature*. In contrast to the theme of the *Evidences*, Paley argued here for God's existence to explain the regularities rather than the irregularities of nature.

Darwin found persuasive Paley's restatement of one of the classic theological arguments. In earlier centuries, the church had established belief in God's existence primarily on the authority of biblical affirmations, but Paley attempted to base that belief also on design in nature. He posited that the minutest organisms and the largest phenomena of the heavens, as seen by microscope or telescope, verify the personal craftsmanship of the Creator. Paley was especially concerned to illustrate the exquisite way organisms were fitted for the places they occupied. In *Natural Theology* an entire chapter is devoted to an empirical examination of eye structure, comparing its complexity with that of the telescope.[34] Paley believed that a reasonable person is compelled to conclude that neither the intricate mechanical instrument nor the anatomical part could exist without an originating intelligent Designer. As a cure for atheism, he encouraged those with that malady to examine the eye. Darwin agreed with Paley that truth should be based more on fact than on feeling.

Paley's diagrams, showing the particulars of intricate organic structures, made a lasting impression on Darwin. He said, "I do not think I hardly ever admired a book more than Paley's 'Natural Theology.' I could almost formerly have said it by heart."[35] Paley had made careful observations and marshaled large amounts of data to support theological generalizations. Darwin learned that the best method for establishing a theory on any subject is to gather empirical evidence and to compose a monograph from what can be induced that is "one long argument from the beginning to the end."[36] He would develop a logical method similar to Paley's, supporting propositions that cannot be directly proven by huge quantities of relevant data.

The natural theology of Paley continued a theme that had begun with the ancient Greek philosophers. Subsequently the apostle Paul displayed some interest in it when he wrote, "God's eternal power and divine nature, invisible though they are, have been understood and seen through the things he has made."[37] In the Middle Ages, Aquinas was the main Christian theologian to continue the tradition with his famous five proofs for God's existence. The necessity for a First Cause to set the celestial spheres moving and the need for a Designer to explain the universe's prevailing order were the proofs that fascinated Paley.

Whereas mathematics had been appealed to in the seventeenth century to demonstrate God's orderliness in nature, in the following centuries the physical and biological sciences were examined for evidences of Divine Providence. Loren Eiseley explains the popularity of natural theology:

> There was a general conception of God as a kind of master workman who had personally supervised the creation of even the tiniest organisms of the living world. . . . A feeling that religious insight could be obtained from the observation of God's works in the things about us led to a great proliferation of works upon natural theology. . . . The search for design in nature soon became a mania and everything was made to appear as though created specifically to serve man. There were Bronto-(thunder) theologies, Insecto-theologies, Astro-theologies. . . . Man stood at the center of all things and the entire universe had been created for his edification and instruction: . . . animals run on four feet because it made them better beasts of burden, and flowers grew for his enjoyment.[38]

Charles Darwin accepted Paley's criticism of the evolutionary ideas of Erasmus Darwin and French naturalist Jean Lamarck. Paley denounced both Dr. Darwin and Lamarck's similar subsequent ideas in this way:

> They would persuade us to believe that . . . every plant, indeed every organized body which we see, are only so many out of the possible varieties and combinations of being, which the lapse of infinite ages has brought into existence; that the present world is the relic of that variety; millions of other bodily forms and other species having perished, being by the defect of their constitution incapable of preservation, or of continuance by generation. Now there is no foundation whatever for this conjecture in any thing which we observe in the works of nature; no such experiments are going on at present; no such energy operates, as that which is here supposed, and which should be constantly pushing into existence new varieties of beings.[39]

CLERICAL MENTORS AND FRIENDS

At Cambridge, science was an extracurricular activity that some students engaged in apart from their regular studies. Darwin studied informally with John Henslow, who was devoted to observing nature for evidence of the divine handiwork. Darwin met with him almost daily: "I became very intimate with Professor Henslow, and his kindness was unbounded; he continually asked me to his house, and allowed me to accompany him in his long walks. He talked on all subjects, including his deep sense of religion, and was entirely open."[40] Darwin was mainly interested in learning biology from him, but he agreed with the opinion that Henslow was "a man who knew every branch of science. . . . His knowledge was great in botany, entomology, chemistry, mineralogy, and geology."[41] Henslow was self-taught, for there were no prior instructors at Cambridge in those disciplines.

Darwin admired Henslow's priestly qualities, and he wrote at length about them many years later:

> He was deeply religious, and so orthodox, that he told me one day, he should be grieved if a single word of the Thirty-nine Articles were altered. . . . He was free from every tinge of vanity or other petty feeling; and I never saw a man who thought so little about himself or his own concerns. His temper was imperturbably good, with the most winning and courteous manners; yet, as I have seen, he could be roused by any bad action to the warmest indignation

and prompt action. . . . Henslow's benevolence was unbounded, as
he proved by his many excellent schemes for his poor parishioners.[42]

Henslow had become the rector of a large rural Anglican parish after
Darwin graduated from Cambridge. Darwin gave him this high tribute:
"I fully believe a better man never walked this earth."[43]
Henslow saw potential in Darwin that his authoritarian father had
overlooked, and he sought to draw out that talent. To his "most kind old
master," Darwin recalled, "Those old days when I used as an undergraduate to be so much at your house were certainly amongst the most
happy and best days which I have ever spent."[44] Darwin ended up in the
top 6 percent of those who earned the regular liberal arts degree. In
order to become ordained in the Anglican Church, that preparation
needed to be supplemented by "reading divinity" with a tutor for an
additional year, so Darwin anticipated doing that study with Henslow.[45]
Due largely to Henslow's influence, Darwin saw no conflict between
being a clergyman and a natural philosopher ("scientist" was not then
a designation). Studying about God and nature were presumed to be
totally compatible; consequently, students and faculty believed that
increasing scientific knowledge would strengthen one's theological
certitude. Darwin assumed that he would become a country parson
and would have leisure to pursue his scientific hobbies amid his religious duties.
It was not uncommon for Protestant clergy in England to have a serious interest in the natural world. Because of their puritanical view that
a waste of time was sinful, a number of Anglican divines cultivated serious avocations. For example, Rev. William Buckland was professor of
geology at Oxford before being appointed dean of Westminster Abbey.
After finding cave remains of creatures not extant in Britain, he claimed
that he had found evidence for the last catastrophe at the time of
Noah.[46] At Cambridge, Darwin became acquainted with the writings of
Rev. John Herschel, who was the most famous English scientist at that
time as well as a serious Christian. Darwin valued everything Herschel
said, and especially admired his *Preliminary Discourse on the Study of
Natural Philosophy*, a treatise that had just been published showing the
unity of authentic science and religion. Along with a travel journal by
Baron Humboldt, it was the book that most influenced Darwin during
his last year at Cambridge. He testified that the books stirred up in him
"a burning zeal to add even the most humble contribution to the noble
structure of Natural Science."[47] Believing that "truth is single," Herschel
stated, "every advance toward generality has . . . been a step toward

simplification" that brings humans "nearer to their Creator."[48] He called Galileo's persecutors bigots, who "would make all nature bend to their narrow interpretations of obscure and difficult passages in the sacred writings."[49] Herschel said, "The Divine Author of the universe cannot be supposed to have laid down particular laws, enumerating all individual contingencies, which his materials have understood and obey."[50] In addition to being an astronomer, he published essays in mathematics, geology, geography, and botany.

Charles Whitley, who became a vicar in Northumberland and an instructor in natural philosophy at Durham University, was a friend of Darwin at Cambridge. He attributed to Whitley's influence the taste that he acquired for fine art. Pertaining to his university years, he said, "Many of the pictures in the National Gallery in London gave me much pleasure; that of Sebastian del Piombo exciting in me a sense of sublimity."[51] Darwin specialist Janet Browne comments:

> *Raising of Lazarus* . . . was Sebastiano's greatest work, casting Christ in the role of healer, the divine physician, to raise Lazarus from the dead. The outstretched arm calling up life, the vivid colour, and Lazarus's animal energy as he pushes away from his tomb suggest that Darwin's feelings were not cramped by scientific aridity; on the contrary, he leaned towards grandiose emotional experiences that swept him away on a tide of powerful sentiment. Furthermore, the religious theme did not impede his enjoyment. Sebastiano's text from St. John's Gospel went straight to the heart of Christianity, encompassing creation, resurrection, faith, and disbelief: "I am the resurrection, and the life." For the impressionable young Darwin, the sense of intense wonder was as readily inspired in an artistic and theological context as in exploring nature.[52]

Darwin also attributed to Cambridge camaraderie his learning to appreciate religious music:

> From associating with these men and hearing them play, I acquired a strong taste for music, and used very often to time my walks so as to hear on week days the anthem in King's College Chapel. This gave me intense pleasure, so that my backbone would sometimes shiver. I am sure that there was no affectation or mere imitation in this taste, for I used generally to go by myself to King's College, and I sometimes hired the chorister boys to sing in my rooms.[53]

Darwin's most influential friends at Cambridge were either students planning to enter the Anglican priesthood or faculty priests. The last of these was Rev. Adam Sedgwick, a prominent geologist and champion of orthodoxy, who interpreted all sciences as aids to religion. The human species, he claimed, "was called into being within a few thousand years of the days in which we live—not by a transmutation of species (a theory no better than a phrensied dream) but by a provident contriving power."[54] In 1830, Henslow arranged for Darwin to accompany Sedgwick on an excursion to the mountains of North Wales in search of the earliest strata containing fossils. There Darwin was able to learn firsthand Sedgwick's excellent field techniques.[55]

At this time Henslow was asked by Rev. George Peacock, a member of the Cambridge University Senate, for the name of someone to sail on H.M.S. *Beagle* as a companion of Captain Robert FitzRoy, who would be returning to the southern coast of South America to complete his hydrography mission. Great Britain, now an imperial superpower, was augmenting rule by conquest with rule by commerce. The brisk trade from Britain to the region had made reliable naval charts of coastlines and ports a necessity. Since captains did not fraternize with their crews, FitzRoy was hopeful of finding a "gentleman" to dine with and to relieve his loneliness on his second long voyage. There was already a naturalist in the crew, but his social class was not high enough to be accepted as a peer by the aristocratic captain. Also, FitzRoy had learned from his previous voyage that the expedition needed someone with geological knowledge to record information about minerals of commercial value near the shore.[56] Henslow nominated Darwin, who was several years younger than the captain, and informed Darwin that he was "the best qualified person" for the position. His mentor urged him to dismiss "any modest doubts or fears" about his suitability for the voyage.[57] Actually, Darwin's only training in geology had been the several-week trip with Sedgwick. Henslow influenced Darwin's career more than any other person, first by being his Cambridge guru, and second by nominating him for an adventure of a lifetime to faraway places.

When the opportunity arose for pursuing what was emerging as his true calling, Darwin unhesitatingly wanted to shelve the idea of immediately becoming an Anglican priest. But his father, wondering again if his son was a good-for-nothing, thought it would be unfitting for the divinity student to take the *Beagle* post. Charles could not have gone without his approval, because the father had to pay for the son's food and other personal expenses on the voyage. However, to do so would be no burden for a man of his wealth.

Henshaw Ward, a friend of the Darwin family, tells of the upheaval that FitzRoy's solicitation caused:

Dr. Darwin strongly objected to having his clerical son set off on a madcap expedition around the world in a little brig, studying sea-weeds and consorting with rough young naval officers. Charles had always shown a fondness for gallivanting away from duties. Was it not time that he began to care for his career? "How could any man of common-sense advise you to go? If you can find one such man, I will give my consent."[58]

Dr. Darwin's brother-in-law, the younger Josiah Wedgwood, came to his nephew's defense. Charles's future father-in-law wrote, "I should not think that it would be in any degree disreputable to his character as a Clergyman. I should on the contrary think the offer honourable to him, and the pursuit of Natural History though certainly not professional, is very suitable to a Clergyman." Wedgwood concluded, "Looking upon Charles as a man of enlarged curiosity, it affords him such an opportunity of seeing men and things as happens to few."[59]

Freed for the first time from his father's domination, Darwin rushed back to Cambridge to learn more from Henslow about the *Beagle* opportunity. Recognizing his inexperience, he was apprehensive about whether or not FitzRoy would find him a fit companion. If he passed muster, the southern hemisphere experience would be much grander than the excursion he had planned following the completion of his college degree. Naturalist Alexander von Humboldt's description of Tenerife in the Canary Islands had made him eager to visit there and study the flora and geology of that distant place. Darwin was excited by the thought of years rather than weeks on a voyage to learn about the "glories" of creation.

Notes

1. Joseph Priestley, *A History of the Corruptions of Christianity* (Keene, N.H.: Prentiss, 1838), 16, 144, 148, 289–90.

2. *Correspondence*, 9:407.

3. Charles Darwin's introduction to Ernst Krause, *Erasmus Darwin* (London: Murray, 1879), 45.

4. *Autobiography*, 22, 26.

5. Ibid., 25.

6. Ibid., 28.

7. Samuel Butler, *The Life and Letters of Dr. Samuel Butler* (London: Murray, 1896), 1:196–97.

8. *Autobiography*, 28, 44.

9. Ibid., 44–45.

10. William Shakespeare, *As You Like It* 2.1.12.

11. *Autobiography*, 45.

12. Ibid., 48.

13. *Correspondence*, 1:19.

14. Ibid., 1:36.

15. Ibid., 1:39, 41.

16. LLD, 2:357.

17. Adrian Desmond and James Moore, *Darwin* (New York: Warner, 1992), 48.

18. David Kohn, ed., *The Darwinian Heritage* (Princeton: Princeton University Press, 1985), 442.

19. Karl Marx, *Capital, Great Books of the Western World*, ed. Robert Hutchins (Chicago: Encyclopaedia Britannica, 1952), 50:320.

20. *Autobiography*, 58.

21. Ibid., 60.

22. *Correspondence* 1:84.

23. Ibid., 1:48.

24. Ibid., 1:104.

25. *Autobiography*, 57.

26. John Lightfoot, *The Whole Works* (London: Dove, 1822), 2:71; 4:112.

27. *Correspondence*, 9:62.

28. *Autobiography*, 56–57.

29. Thomas Huxley, *Darwiniana* (New York: Appleton, 1896), 264.

30. *Autobiography*, 59.

31. William Paley, *Works* (Philadelphia: Crissy, 1857), 322; John 11:11–46.

32. Paley, *Works*, 286–87, 364.

33. Quoted in John Durant, ed., *Darwinism and Divinity* (New York: Blackwell, 1985), 65.

34. Paley, *Works* 391.

35. *Correspondence*, 7:388.

36. *Autobiography*, 140.

37. Romans 1:20.

38. Loren Eiseley, *Darwin's Century* (Garden City, N.Y.: Anchor, 1961), 176–77.

39. Paley, *Works*, 399.

40. Paul Barrett, ed., *The Collected Papers of Charles Darwin* (Chicago: Chicago University Press, 1977), 2:73.

41. *Autobiography*, 64.

42. Ibid., 65.

43. *Correspondence* 9:133.

44. Ibid., 7:11.

45. Ibid., 1:104.

46. William Buckland, *Reliquiae Diluvianae* (London: Murray, 1823).

47. *Autobiography*, 67–68, 107.

48. John Herschel, *A Preliminary Discourse on the Study of Natural Philosophy* (Philadelphia: Carey, 1831), 11, 13, 270.

49. Ibid., 7.

50. Ibid., 28.

51. *Autobiography*, 61.

52. Janet Browne, *Charles Darwin* (New York: Knopf, 1995), 1:105–6.

53. *Autobiography*, 61.

54. Adam Sedgwick, *A Discourse on the Studies of the University* (London: Parker, 1833), 26.

55. *Autobiography*, 69.

56. *Diary*, xii.

57. *Correspondence*, 1:128.

58. Henshaw Ward, *Charles Darwin* (New York: Home Library, 1943), 56.

59. *Correspondence*, 1:134.

CHAPTER TWO
The Christian Voyager

Darwin began a letter to Professor Henslow with "Gloria in excelsis!" He borrowed that angelic exclamation from Luke's Christmas story to express his jubilation over a successful interview with Captain FitzRoy in London. The letter ended with "There is indeed a tide in the affairs of men."[1] That line from Shakespeare continues with an ominous forecast for those who do not cast off at full tide: "Omitted, all the voyage of their life / Is bound in shallows and in miseries."[2]

Had FitzRoy, an ardent member of Britain's conservative Tory party, realized that Darwin was just as ardently a Whig, that might have been a basis for rejecting him as one of the men aboard the *Beagle*. Also, the captain later informed Darwin that he had almost been excluded because of his pug nose. According to Darwin, the phrenologist skipper, who had a prominent beak, "doubted whether anyone with my nose could possess sufficient energy and determination for the voyage."[3] But, as it turned out, "FitzRoy generously offered to give up half his cabin to any one who would volunteer to go as naturalist."[4] Free accommodations but no salary were to be provided for this special appointment on a voyage that was intended to last several years.

The influence of Darwin's religious training at Cambridge became evident in his discussions and practices while on the sailing expedition. He wrote, "Whilst on board the *Beagle* I was quite orthodox, and I remember being heartily laughed at by several of the officers (though themselves orthodox) for quoting the Bible as unanswerable authority on some point of morality."[5] John Campbell has perceptively described Darwin's concept of God at that time: "The 'orthodoxy' of Darwin's *Beagle* years is singularly one dimensional. In keeping with the awesome, remote and sublime character of the Deity in whom he believes, Darwin does not love God, he is merely overwhelmed by his power."[6]

On Sundays, Darwin limited his readings to the Greek New Testament. He noted that the six dozen members of the ship's crew gave remarkable attention to the Sunday religious services performed on board.[7] The *Beagle* artist, Augustus Earle, painted a detailed scene of the ship company participating in a typical service. The painting, now in the British National Maritime Museum, depicts FitzRoy reading from either the Bible or from the Anglican Book of Common Prayer while seated below decks in a chair on which the British flag is draped. Darwin and others are shown following the reading in their own books with various degrees of intentness.[8]

Darwin indicated later that Milton's *Paradise Lost* was his favorite book by an English author and that he always took it with him when he could choose only one literary volume on his excursions away from the *Beagle*.[9] Since Milton had also studied at Christ's College in Cambridge, Darwin had been tutored by those who gave his works special attention. He apparently accepted Milton's depiction of God as an artisan with a magician's flair.

During his voyaging, Darwin became thoroughly familiar with *Principles of Geology*, which had recently been published by Charles Lyell, professor of geology at King's College in London. He advocated uniformitarianism, the radically new position that the earth's present geological condition came about as the result of continual seismic action from earliest times, in accord with natural law. Lyell had studied under William Buckland at Oxford but disagreed with his view of severe discontinuities in the geological process. Darwin became convinced of the truth of Lyell's theory and rejected the conventional wisdom, called catastrophism, which was championed by the leading naturalists. Georges Cuvier, a French Protestant classifier, was certain that the Almighty restocked plants and animals after spasmodic cataclysms, the last being the Noachian deluge. Lyell gave geological evidence that the earth is not thousands, but millions of years old, and that there is a steady state of continental development. Accordingly, he reasoned, terrestrial changes have not been precipitated by divine judgment but by such processes as the erosion of mountains and the silting of rivers.

Lyell, a Unitarian, was convinced that God operated without miraculous intervention in the nonhuman sphere. At the conclusion of his magnum opus he wrote, "In whatever direction we pursue our researches, whether in time or space, we discover everywhere the clear proofs of a Creative Intelligence, and of his foresight, wisdom, and power."[10] Biographer Janet Browne thinks that Lyell's "clearly expressed faith in the Creator" had an impact that "can hardly be overestimated in assessing the state of Darwin's mind on religious matters."[11] Darwin referred to Lyell as a religious "liberal" and "a strong theist."[12]

From Brazil, Darwin wrote kinsman William Fox, who had continued his pursuit of entomology as rector in a Cheshire parish: "I hope
my wanderings will not unfit me for a quiet life, and that in some future
day, I may be fortunate enough to be qualified to become, like you a
country Clergyman. And then we will work together at Natural
History."[13]

Browne provides insight into the characters of Darwin and Fox
through this comparison:

> It was Fox—himself the most good-natured of men—who brought
> out the best in Darwin. . . . The two of them were very alike in their
> ideals and aspirations, mutually supportive in their intention to
> take Holy Orders, each comfortable with the idea of becoming a
> country parson, vastly amused by their largely imaginary search
> for prospective parsonage wives. . . . In many ways the similarities
> continued through to the end of their lives. Fox, in effect, became
> the man that Darwin never was, for if Darwin, instead of seizing
> the chance of joining the *Beagle* expedition, had stuck to his
> father's new plan of entering the church, he would have become
> just like his cousin, both in his future responsibilities as a country-
> loving gentleman-parson and in the same open-hearted, inquiring
> personality that found fulfillment in hosts of children, relatives,
> and animals, keeping abreast with scientific journals, making a few
> experiments in the garden and poultry yard.[14]

Brother Erasmus, who had no liking for either rural or religious life,
wrote Charles disdainfully in 1832: "I am sorry to see in your last letter
that you still look forward to the horrid little parsonage in the desert. I
was beginning to hope I should have you set up in London in lodgings
somewhere near the British Museum or some other learned place. My
only chance is the Established Church being abolished."[15] "Eras" had
become an aesthete, living in London on his father's money; he had
already abandoned medicine as a career, without anything to replace it.

RELIGIOUS PERSPECTIVES IN SOUTH AMERICA

Gertrude Himmelfarb rightly notes that some fellow biographers overlook Darwin's religious expressions during his voyage. "Carried away by
the zeal of hindsight," she said, they tend to hasten the change of both
Darwin's religious views and his evolutionary views, even though there
is no evidence to support such.[16] While in South America, Darwin probably recalled appreciatively what Paley had written in the conclusion of

Natural Theology about the sanctuary of nature: "The world thence-forth becomes a temple, and life itself one continued act of adoration. . . . Every organized natural body, in the provisions which it contains for its sustentation and propagation, testifies a care on the part of the Creator. . . . We see no signs of diminution of care by multiplicity of objects, or of distraction of thought by variety."

With religious awe, and by appropriating a metaphor from a text of Paley and from his grandfather Erasmus's "Temple of Nature" poem, Darwin told of his experiences in South America:

> Among the scenes which are deeply impressed on my mind, none exceed in sublimity the primeval forests, undefaced by the hand of man, whether those of Brazil, where the powers of life are predomi-nant, or those of Tierra del Fuego, where death and decay prevail. Both are temples filled with the varied productions of the God of Nature:—No one can stand unmoved in these solitudes, without feeling that there is more in man than the mere breath of his body.[17]

After a long climb up the Andes mountains, Darwin had another experience of the sublime that late in life he recalled as being almost as momentous as the reverence that overcame him in the pristine forests of Brazil. While standing on a lofty summit and surveying the magnifi-cence all around, he felt "as if his nerves had become fiddle-strings and had all taken to rapidly vibrating."[18] He compared his ecstasy to the thrill of listening to Handel's finest oratorio: "It was like watching a thunderstorm, or hearing in full orchestra a chorus of the Messiah."[19]

◆ ◆ ◆

Darwin had predominantly negative impressions of the Roman Catholics he encountered in South America. He described the "cun-ning, sensuality and pride" of some monks in Rio de Janeiro and noted that one of them reminded him of Martin Schoen's engraving of Judas Iscariot.[20] Darwin recorded a comment directed toward the Araucanian Indians that lived on the most fertile land of Chile: "My friend the Padre at Cudico bitterly regretted that it should be so wasted and wished with *Christian* humanity, that all the provinces would unite and make a complete end of the Indian race."[21] Darwin found it unconscionable that Argentine General Juan Rosas had led soldiers professing to be Christians on an extermination campaign against native Americans. After reporting the massacre of women and the selling of children as slaves, Darwin asserted: "Everyone here is fully convinced that this is the justest war, because it is against barbarians. Who would believe in this age in a Christian, civilized country that such atrocities were committed?"[22] But in Buenos Aires, Darwin appreciated the great enthusiasm at Catholic services, in comparison to what he associated with Anglicans, and by the equality evidenced among Catholic worshipers. "The Spanish lady with her brilliant shawl kneels by the side of her black servant," he observed.[23]

Shipmate Robert Hamond and Darwin requested a chaplain at Buenos Aires to administer the sacrament of Holy Communion to them before they set out for dangerous Tierra del Fuego, located at the tail of the continent, south of the Straits of Magellan. Hamond later remembered, "We were both then young and looked on that [Eucharist] ordinance . . . as a sort of vow to lead a better life."[24] After encountering a severe Cape Horn storm, Darwin conventionally expressed the hope that "Providence" would spare the *Beagle* from more bad weather.

Darwin was of the opinion that the Fuegians were cannibals. He learned of a Fuegian boy's explanation of why people of his tribe ate old women rather than dogs: "Dog catch otter,—woman good for nothing,—man very hungry."[25] Darwin perceived that philosopher Jean Rousseau's romantic treatment of the pre-civilization "noble savage" displayed his lack of travel to remote places on the globe. Regarding the Fuegian "savages," he asked, "Have they remained in the same state since the creation of the world?"[26] In that intensely cold region Darwin was amazed that "the Fuegians survive without the protection of clothes, or of any building worthy to be called a hovel."[27] He became convinced that he had encountered the most primitive people on Earth, and living among them briefly was for him like an amazing adventure into human prehistory.

Aboard the *Beagle* was Richard Matthews from the Church Missionary Society, whom FitzRoy had brought along to set up a mission in Tierra del Fuego. The crew built Matthews a place to live, but when the brig returned, they had to rescue him: the Indians had tortured him and destroyed his property. Darwin was unable to interpret any of their behavior as expressing religious worship. He became aware of the effect of environment on the habits of three Fuegians, two boys and one girl, who were being returned to their homeland after having been taken to England for Anglicization by FitzRoy on his earlier *Beagle* voyage. The veneer of Christian culture they had acquired soon peeled off after they were returned to their native land.

As a Protestant, Darwin attracted attention in one Spanish coastal town. A resident there noticed that he engaged in the unusual practice of washing his face in the morning: "He eyed me with much suspicion; perhaps he had heard of ablutions in the Mahomedan religion; knowing me to be a Heretic, probably he came to the conclusion that all Heretics are Turks."[28] Also, in Chile "several very pretty Signoritas" accused Darwin of not being a Christian because his religion permitted priests to engage in matrimony, which they presumed was defiling for holy men. "I assured them I was a sort of Christian," Darwin said, but "they would not hear of it."[29] "He could only be 'a sort of Christian' in South America because Europeans habitually used the word to designate slave-owning Spanish Catholics," comments James Moore.[30] In Peru, he encountered another prejudice against Protestants that contributed to his low esteem for the religion imported from Spain. After a Catholic Church was broken into and the communion bread and plate were stolen, the enraged townspeople decided that only heretics would "eat God Almighty." Consequently, some Englishmen who happened to be living in the community were suspected and tortured.[31] In Spanish colonies, Darwin found it unacceptable that Christian forgiveness was mainly applied to the rich who had committed enormous crimes.[32]

INDIGNATION OVER SLAVERY

As one who was raised a liberal Christian, Darwin related his faith not only to natural grandeur and denominational distinctions but also to expressions of social justice. He was proud that some religiously motivated citizens of England had successfully campaigned to eliminate slavery in British colonies. Both his grandfathers had strong antislavery convictions and had helped to make the emancipation movement a social force in the 1780s. In introducing a biography of Dr. Erasmus Darwin, Charles inserted a couplet that his grandfather had composed when the antislavery debate was sputtering in Parliament: "Hear him, ye Senates! hear this truth sublime. / He who allows oppression shares the crime." Dr. Darwin also wrote this poignant poem:

> The slave, in chains, on supplicating knee,
> Spreads his wide arms, and lifts his eye to Thee;
> With hunger pale, with wounds and toil opress'd,
> "Are we not brethren?" Sorrow chokes the rest.[33]

Maternal grandfather Josiah Wedgwood coined what would serve as the seal of the Society for the Abolition of the Slave Trade by reversing

the question of Cain, the prototype murderer in the Bible. He contributed to the society by manufacturing at his pottery factory hundreds of medallions bearing the image of a chained African asking, "Am
I not a man and a brother?" As Browne points out: "These stirring
words and pictures were an integral part of Darwin's upbringing; the
milestones that marked the progress of emancipation were to him family events, telescoped and romanticised in Wedgwood and Darwin
household legend to make it seem as if the poet and the potter have
forced abolition just the day before yesterday."[34]

Darwin realized that the British nation, which had been heavily
involved in the Atlantic slave-trading enterprise, was now in the fore-
front of the abolition movement.[35] Parliamentarian William Wilberforce
and Rev. John Newton, devout Anglicans, had inspired many in the
Church of England to regard slave liberation as integral to the expression of their religion.[36] Darwin knew that Paley had condemned slavery
as "brutal" and "wicked" in his *Moral and Political Philosophy*, which
was written at the time Wilberforce introduced abolitionist legislation
in Parliament.[37] While Darwin was in Brazil, Parliament had moved
beyond banning the shipping of slaves out of Africa to passing a law in
1833 to abolish slavery in the British Empire.

Darwin had earlier learned to respect blacks for their abilities. While
studying in Edinburgh, taxidermist John Edmonstone, a freed slave
from South America, taught him to stuff animals. "I used often to sit
with him," Darwin said, "for he was a very pleasant and intelligent
man."[38] Using him as an example, Darwin was struck by the similarity
between the mind of "a full-blooded negro" and the mind of a white person.[39] He recognized that "Negroes have become excellent musicians,"
even though Europeans did not usually appreciate their syncopated
music when they heard it in Africa.[40] Darwin's racial viewpoint stood in
bold relief to that of Cuvier, who had asserted that Negroes constituted
"the most degraded race among men, whose forms approach nearest to
those of inferior animals, and whose intellect has not yet arrived at the
establishment of any regular form of government."[41]

Before leaving England, Darwin was smugly told that his antislavery
fervor would subside after living in slave countries. But he wrote to his
family from his ship: "The only alteration I am aware of is forming a
much higher estimate of the Negros character. It is impossible to see a
negro and not feel kindly towards him; such cheerful, open honest expression and such fine muscular bodies."[42] He stated that he admired the
strong family loyalty of blacks "who are ranked by the polished savages in

England as hardly their brethren, even in God's eyes."[43] Darwin was less impressed with the intellects and the physiques of the Portuguese in Brazil than with the African workers they had imported, and he ventured the thought that families of the current slaves would eventually rule the country.[44] His sympathies were always with the oppressed rather than with the oppressors, and he even entertained the radical idea that a Haitian-type revolution of Brazilian slaves might be a good thing. Darwin was impressed that runaway slaves would risk their lives to avoid recapture. He told of a woman who jumped from a mountain ledge to evade being returned to her master: "In a Roman matron this would have been called the noble love of freedom: in a poor negress it is mere brutal obstinancy."[45]

The slave brutality that Darwin witnessed in Brazil prompted an outcry, exposing the heart of his religion that would palpitate throughout his life:

> I thank God, I shall never again visit a slave-country. . . . I have stayed in a house where a young household mulatto, daily and hourly, was reviled, beaten, and persecuted enough to break the spirit of the lowest animal. I have seen a little boy, six or seven years old, struck thrice with a horse-whip (before I could interfere) on his naked head, for having handed me a glass of water not quite clean. . . . Picture to yourself the chance, ever hanging over you, of your wife and your little children—those objects which nature urges even the slave to call his own—being torn from you and sold like beasts to the first bidder! And these deeds are done and palliated by men, who profess to love their neighbours as themselves, who believe in God, and pray that his Will be done on earth! It makes one's blood boil, yet heart tremble, to think that we Englishmen and our American descendants, with their boastful cry of liberty, have been and are so guilty.[46]

Like Jesus, Darwin was indignant over the hypocrisy of those who claimed to live by the Torah's love command but did not actually extend to others the affection they had for themselves. We see that Darwin was primarily interested in religion as a source of practical conduct. This is also reflected in a comment he sent in 1835 to Fox: "You are a true Christian and return good for evil."[47]

FitzRoy claimed that black slaves were generally well treated and better off under the rule of white masters. He defended a Brazilian slaveholder by telling of visiting his plantation where many slaves answered in the negative when asked if they were unhappy and wished to be free. Darwin greatly angered his captain by pointing out that the slaves' responses in that situation were obviously worthless, because they knew what punishment awaited those who did not say what their master wanted to hear.[48] FitzRoy later showed that he accepted the justification used by Europeans for enslaving Africans when he defended an eisegesis of the story of Noah that was widely accepted. He claimed that the curse upon the descendants of Ham, Noah's son, pertained to the black race.[49]

A decade later, Darwin commented on "the sin of Brazilian slavery." Disgusted to read that Lyell had condoned slavery and had disapproved of abolitionists on his lecture tour of America, Darwin asked him, "How could you relate so placidly that atrocious sentiment about [slave auctioneers] separating children from their parents?"[50] For years Darwin was haunted by the memory of seeing slaves tortured in Brazil when he felt that he could not intervene.[51]

CHALLENGES TO THEOLOGICAL DOCTRINES

Some journal notations of Darwin while on the *Beagle* show that he was beginning to deviate from a general assumption of biblical interpreters. In contrast to their view that the garden of Eden was in western Asia, he wrote, "The Tropics appear the natural birthplace of the human race."[52] On the South American coast, Darwin found spectacular fossils of "the great ante-diluvial animal the Megatherium,"[53] along with other extinct mammal fossils. After pondering the problem of reconciling accepted religious beliefs with his discovery of bones of creatures that had vanished from the earth before recorded time, he questioned the conventional wisdom that the universe has been in existence for only about six thousand years.

Darwin happened to be in a field in Chile during a severe earthquake, and the movements of the ground made him dizzy. Farther up the coast, he visited the city of Concepción and described its cathedral as "the grandest pile of ruins" he had ever seen. He also witnessed islands being formed by lava surging upward through cracks in the earth's surface. The geological experiences soon caused him to reject the biblical notion that earthquakes were disturbances caused by God to punish wickedness, and to view them as the result of the earth's unstable crust floating on a lake of molten rock, proving what Lyell had written.[54]

On the *Beagle*'s return home by way of the Pacific Ocean, the volcanic Galápagos Islands gave Darwin more puzzles for his religious as well as for his scientific cogitations. "The natural history of these islands is eminently curious," he wrote. "Most of the organic productions are aboriginal creations, found nowhere else. . . . We seem to be brought somewhat near to that great fact—that mystery of mysteries—the first appearance of new beings on this earth."[55] The presence of immense tortoises on the Galápagos, along with other amazing inhabitants, caused him to wonder if he was at a "centre of creation."[56] As he compared birds of the South American mainland with the Galápagos birds, he found that some of the species varied little from one another. He wondered why God would bother to create bird species unique to the islands to perform similar functions. An alternative explanation to the divine-fiat, specific-creation doctrine might make more sense, he thought. FitzRoy did not hesitate to explain the characteristics of some Galápagos birds so as to support special creation: "All the small birds that live on these lava-covered islands have short beaks, very thick at the base, like that of a bull-finch. This appears to be one of those admirable provisions of Infinite Wisdom by which each created thing is adapted to the place for which it was intended."[57]

Another challenge to Darwin's biblical ideas occurred in Australia, where he reflected on the minute differences between some of its native species and those found elsewhere on Earth. He raised and then dismissed this thought: "An unbeliever in everything beyond his own reason, might exclaim 'Surely two distinct Creators must have been [at] work.'"[58]

VISITING PROTESTANT MISSIONARY AREAS

Finding the Tahitians as noble as he found the Fuegians ignoble, Darwin told of the religious, educational, and moral impact of missionaries in Tahiti. He commended the progress that had resulted from two generations of missionary work: "The march of improvement, consequent on the introduction of Christianity through the South Sea, probably stands by itself on the records of the world."[59] Several missionaries he praised by name, including a Mr. Nott, who translated the whole Bible into the Tahitian language during his forty years on the island. While that immense undertaking was being accomplished in a previously unwritten language, some of the natives became literate so they could learn from books on their own.

Missionary work in Tahiti had been harshly criticized in Otto von Kotzebue's published journal. The Russian explorer's antipathy toward English missionaries, Darwin surmised, may have arisen from his disappointment that Tahitian women, because they had become Christians, were not as promiscuous as his men had been expecting.

Darwin faulted Kotzebue for not recognizing that the London Missionary Society, which had been working in Tahiti since 1795, had ended the previous profligate priesthood, human sacrifices, and tribal wars. Moreover, "dishonesty, intemperance and licentiousness had been greatly reduced by the introduction of Christianity."[60] Darwin was especially impressed with the elimination of widespread female infanticide on the Pacific isles after the missionaries settled there.[61]

Darwin was also impressed that the Tahitians with whom he came in contact "fall on their knees and utter with apparent sincerity a prayer in their native tongue" before going to bed.[62] He noticed that his guide would eat only after saying a blessing: "He prayed as a Christian should do, with fitting reverence, and without fear of ridicule or ostentation."[63] One of the queen's officials wrote a letter to FitzRoy, which in translation reads: "I feel very much gratified by your great kindness in giving me a trunk, and several other things. . . . Dear friends may the peace of the Messiah, who is the King of Peace, be with you."[64]

After visiting a Tahitian church, Darwin reported: "The Chapel is a large airy framework of wood; it was filled to excess by tidy clean people of all ages and sexes. . . . The appearance was quite equal to that in a country Church in England. The singing of the hymns was decidedly very pretty."[65] He admired the way Christianity had promoted a merry and peaceful life.

Although Darwin occasionally mentioned attractive women he saw in different places, there is nothing to suggest that he followed the general tendency of sailors and satisfied his lust in visited ports. He even thought it unbecoming that the only thing a Tahitian woman wore was a flower in her hair.[66] As the *Beagle* visited tropical islands on its return home, Darwin wrote to Fox expressing a longing for a partner with whom he could share such romantic scenes: "Imagine what a fine opportunity for writing love letters,—oh that I had a sweet Virginia to send an inspired epistle to.—A person not in love will have no right to wander amongst the glowing bewitching scenes."[67] He felt somewhat forlorn because Fanny Owen, the girlfriend he had while at Cambridge, had married during his absence.

In New Zealand, Darwin found many worthless English residents and sympathized with the missionaries who said that "the only protection which they need and on which they rely is from the native Chiefs against Englishmen!"[68] He noted that cannibalism had been almost eliminated there as a result of mission work. Darwin was convinced that the converts' civilized morality was a byproduct of their new theology. "So excellent is the Christian faith," he asserted, "that the outward conduct of the believers is said most decidedly to have been improved by its doctrines."[69] Missionary Matthews, whose intention to initiate work in Tierra del Fuego had been aborted, disembarked to remain in New Zealand where the conditions were more favorable. Darwin contributed to the large fund that *Beagle* officers raised for constructing a church in New Zealand.

In Australia, Darwin admired the skills of the aborigines he encountered, finding them "good-humoured and pleasant" and "far from such utterly degraded beings as usually represented."[70] While on that continent he shared with Henslow his impression of missionaries: "It is . . . admirable to behold what the Missionaries both here and at New Zealand have effected.—I firmly believe they are good men working for the sake of a good cause. I much suspect that those who have abused or sneered at the Missionaries have generally been such as were not very anxious to find the Natives moral and intelligent beings."[71]

As the *Beagle* sailed toward England, FitzRoy and Darwin co-authored an article on "The Moral State of Tahiti." Their first writing intended for publication was an appeal to support missionaries, and it appeared in an 1836 issue of the *South African Christian Recorder*.[72] Browne finds this significance in what they wrote:

> Their interest in mission activity . . . brought to a focus important issues concerning human origins, questions about the relationship of mankind with the natural environment, and moral themes of progress and improvement. By wishing to give credit to missionaries for taking the first and hardest steps in spreading European values throughout the world, they were openly subscribing to a particular view of human nature, a view based on the concepts of racial unity and a capacity for progress through education and the alleviation of external circumstances.[73]

◆ ◆ ◆

The high point of Darwin's brief stay in South Africa was his opportunity to have several visits with John Herschel,[74] who was in Cape Town to make astronomical observations in the Southern Hemisphere. He probably shared with Darwin some of the theological notions he had recently mailed to Lyell. Herschel had expressed several provocative ideas, one of which Darwin would later cite: "The Creator . . . operates through a series of intermediate causes and in consequence, the origination of fresh species, could it ever come under our cognizance, would be found to be a natural in contradistinction to a miraculous process." He also stated: "We must interpret it [Scripture] in accord with *whatever* shall appear on fair enquiry to be the *truth* for there cannot be two truths.... The days of Creation [may reasonably be extended] to many thousand millions of years." Herschel's letter contained a further bit of biblical criticism: If alleged miracles are not limited, then "the earth revolved backward on its axis 15° in the time of Hezekiah and more in that of Joshua."[75]

After nearly five years at sea, Darwin returned to his native land, never to travel again beyond Britain. Before arriving home he learned that Professor Henslow had published excerpts from his letters and that his findings had impressed some English naturalists. On receiving that approval, Darwin acknowledged that his intention to become a priest had died a "natural death."[76] The full approval of his father for a vocational change in the returning Odyssean had been prepared by a letter that Dr. Butler shared with him. After becoming aware of both the quality and quantity of the specimen cases that had been shipped to Cambridge during the *Beagle*'s voyage, Professor Sedgwick had written Darwin's former headmaster:

> [Darwin] is doing admirable work in South America, and has already sent home a collection above all price. It was the best thing in the world for him that he went out on the voyage of discovery. There was some risk of his turning out an idle man, but his character will now be fixed, and if God spares his life, he will have a great name among the naturalists of Europe.[77]

Notes

1. *Correspondence*, 1:140–42.
2. William Shakespeare, *Julius Caesar* 4.3.219.
3. *Autobiography*, 72.
4. MLD, 1:247.
5. *Autobiography*, 85.
6. John Campbell, "Nature, Religion and Emotional Response: A Reconsideration of Darwin's Affective Decline," *Victorian Studies* (December 1974): 167.
7. *Diary*, 13, 31.
8. Alan Moorehead, *Darwin and the Beagle* (New York: Harper, 1969), 242–43.
9. *Autobiography*, 85.
10. Charles Lyell, *Principles of Geology* (London: Murray, 1833), 3:384.
11. Janet Browne, *Charles Darwin* (New York: Knopf, 1995), 1:324.

12. *Autobiography*, 100.
13. *Correspondence*, 1:286.
14. Browne, *Darwin*, 1:96.
15. *Correspondence*, 1:259.
16. Gertrude Himmelfarb, *Darwin and the Darwinian Revolution* (London: Chatto, 1959), 380.
17. *Diary*, 444.
18. LLD, 2:238.
19. *Voyage*, 331.
20. *Diary*, 79.
21. Ibid., 293.
22. Ibid.,180.
23. Ibid., 114.
24. Quoted in Browne, *Darwin*, 1:326.
25. *Correspondence*, 1:303.
26. *Diary*, 223.
27. *Descent*, 350.
28. *Diary*, 155.
29. Ibid., 257.
30. David Kohn, ed., *The Darwinian Heritage* (Princeton: Princeton University Press, 1985), 446.
31. *Diary*, 345.
32. Ibid., 287.
33. Erasmus Darwin, *The Botanic Garden* (London, 1791), 2:425–28.
34. Browne, *Darwin*, 1:197.
35. *Voyage*, 512.
36. William Phipps, *Amazing Grace in John Newton* (Macon, Ga.: Mercer, 2001), 173–204.
37. William Paley, *Works* (Philadelphia: Crissy, 1857), 67.
38. Quoted in Benjamin Farrington, *What Darwin Really Said* (New York: Schocken, 1966), 14.
39. *Descent*, 348.
40. Ibid., 569–70.
41. Georges Cuvier, *Essay on the Theory of the Earth* (New York: Kirk, 1818), 160.
42. *Correspondence*, 1:312–13.
43. *Diary*, 134.
44. Ibid., 80.
45. *Voyage*, 19.
46. Ibid., 511–12.
47. *Correspondence*, 1:459.
48. *Autobiography*, 74.
49. Robert FitzRoy, *Narrative of the Surveying Voyages* (London: Colburn, 1839), 2:644.

50. *Correspondence*, 2:242.

51. LLD, 2:377.

52. *Diary*, 68.

53. Ibid., 109.

54. Isaiah 29:6; *Diary*, 300.

55. *Diary*, 360.

56. Ibid., 356.

57. Ibid., 402.

58. *Voyage*, 387.

59. *Diary*, 445.

60. Ibid., 377.

61. *Descent*, 392.

62. *Correspondence*, 1:471.

63. Diary, 372–73.

64. FitzRoy, *Narrative*, 2:547.

65. *Diary*, 377.

66. Ibid., 375.

67. *Correspondence*, 1:493.

68. *Diary*, 384.

69. Ibid., 393.

70. Ibid., 398.

71. *Correspondence*, 1:485.

72. Paul Barrett, ed., *The Collected Papers of Charles Darwin* (Chicago: Chicago University Press, 1977), 1:19–38.

73. Browne, *Darwin*, 1:331.

74. *Diary*, 427.

75. Walter Cannon, ed., "Two Letters from John Herschel to Charles Lyell, 1836–37," *Proceedings of the American Philosophical Society* 105 (1961): 305, 308; see Isaiah 38:8 and Joshua 10:13.

76. *Autobiography*, 57.

77. Samuel Butler, *The Life and Letters of Dr. Samuel Butler* (London: Murray, 1896), 2:116.

CHAPTER THREE

The Unorthodox Theorist

By the time Darwin returned from his forty-thousand-mile voyage in 1836, he had laid aside his earlier intention to become a priest. The last openness he had expressed toward becoming a parson was just before leaving South America: "To a person fit to take the office the life of a Clergyman is a type of all that is respectable and happy. I do not know what to say."[1] His outlook on religion was changing even as his view of biology was being transformed by his reflection on the massive evidence he had accumulated.

THE BIBLE REVISITED

Darwin recalled that he was "led to think much about religion" between 1836 and 1839, and a lengthy section on that topic in his *Autobiography* records those thoughts.[2] Recognizing the incompatibility between the traditional scriptural inerrancy doctrine and his discoveries about nature was a necessary step toward opening his mind to other possibilities. According to George Dorsey, "Darwin at the age of thirty was himself entirely convinced that whatever species are or were, the answer to their origin was not to be found in the Book of Genesis but by looking at species themselves—in other words, in the Book of Nature."[3] At the time, Darwin was analyzing his voyage findings and synthesizing ideas that they supported. His reexamination of the doctrines he had accepted in both theology and science occurred during the same period; transitional thoughts and hesitant opinions came to his mind in both areas.

Typical of conventional religionists, Darwin viewed the rejection of his previous belief in the literal truth of every biblical verse as a diminution of his faith, not as an enlargement of it. The Christian Scriptures precipitated doubts in his mind; about the earlier part, he recalled: "I had gradually come, by this time, to see that the Old Testament from its manifestly false history of the world, with the Tower of Babel, the rainbow as a sign, etc., etc., and from its attributing to God the feelings of a revengeful tyrant, was no more to be trusted than the sacred books of the Hindoos, or the beliefs of any barbarian."[4]

Darwin informed his sister Caroline that the traditional date for human creation was inaccurate:

> You tell me you do not see what is new in Sir J. Herschel's idea about the chronology of the Old Testament being wrong— . . . it is not to the days of creation which he refers, but to the lapse of years since the first man made his wonderful appearance on this world— As far as I know everyone has yet thought that the six thousand odd years had been the right period but Sir J. thinks that a far greater number must have passed since the Chinese [and] the Caucasian languages separated from one stock.[5]

Especially problematic to Darwin were the special creationists who believed that God had stamped each type of organism with an indelible character as distinctive now as when it was created. They maintained that each species has an unchanging and unique essence, even though environmental factors might cause variations in appearance. In 1837, in his first notebook on transmutation (subsequently called evolution), he reflected on the creationists' inconsistency: "We can allow planets, suns, universe, nay whole systems of [the] universe to be governed by laws, but the smallest insect, we wish to be created at once by special act."[6] Darwin conceived of evolutionary law in biology as parallel to gravitational law in astrophysics. Both Isaac Newton and Darwin believed that a rational God who established a law-abiding cosmos was more worthy of devotion than a capricious one. In that notebook, Darwin recorded his earliest theologizing on natural selection: "Astronomers might formerly have said that God ordered each planet to move in its particular destiny. In the same manner God orders each animal created with certain forms in certain countries, but how much more simple and sublime [a] power . . . [to] let animals be created . . . by the fixed laws of generation."[7]

Eighteenth-century Swedish taxonomist Carolus Linnaeus was the principal contributor to the fixity of species doctrine. His work, as he conceived it, was to discover the "species" and "genera" organization revealed in the divine plan. Linnaeus believed that the multitude of organisms he named and compartmentalized, including the genus *Homo* for humans and *simia* for nonhuman primates, had been unchanged since the time of the garden of Eden, and that "of all the species originally formed by the Deity, not one is destroyed."[8] By contrast, Darwin did not think of "species" and "variations" as innately natural concepts but as categories that classifiers had invented to designate degrees of permanence in organisms. He reflected theologically in 1835 on the need for a continual birth of species to compensate for extinct species he had observed in South American fossil finds. The supposition of an absolute loss of species, he reasoned, would be "in contradiction to the fitness which the Author of Nature has now established."[9]

The Genesis flood story almost rivaled the creation story in the difficulties it presented to nineteenth-century naturalists. Responding to this problem for conservatives, the Earl of Bridgewater left a large legacy to the Royal Society to support the production of scholarly monographs reinforcing Paleyan apologetics, especially on geological matters. This resulted in the publication in the 1830s of a series of books entitled *The Bridgewater Treatises on the Power, Wisdom, and Goodness of God as Manifested in Creation*. One essay was contributed by William Kirby, who used the new knowledge of the earth's geography to declare that Mount Ararat, referred to in Genesis as where the ark rested after the worldwide flood, was in the Himalayas, and that Noah's menagerie dispersed from there to repopulate all parts of the globe.[10] Darwin wondered how beasts could have moved from their alleged originating place in Asia to continents separated by oceans, and how some marsupials, such as those found only in Australia, could have left no trace of offspring along their migrating path.[11]

FitzRoy, in the last chapter of the narrative he wrote about his adventures after his *Beagle* voyage, attempted to rescue the Genesis story of a deluge from the scorn of some geologists. The story tells about six-hundred-year-old Noah and his family building an ark measuring about 75 x 450 x 45 feet and filling it with at least one representative of each male and female terrestrial creature. Then the Lord submerged even the mountains by releasing water from subterranean cavities and by opening sluice gates—called "windows"—over the earth's solid dome—called the "firmament"—to release the water above. All humans and land animals that were not aboard the ark allegedly drowned. It carried food sufficient to keep all voyagers alive until the waters subsided, when they were able to disembark after a year passed to repopulate the earth.[12] FitzRoy admitted that when he was on the *Beagle* he had expressed doubts about this Genesis story.[13] But his wife, whom FitzRoy married after the voyage, convinced him that the account was verbally inspired by God and must be accepted as literally true. He claimed that the fossil seashells Darwin found thousands of feet above sea level provided "indubitable proofs" that the Noachian flood covered the earth's high mountains. But, FitzRoy surmised, Noah was selective of those admitted to the ark, and some creatures who were too young and small, or too old and large, were excluded.[14]

Darwin had interpreted that fossil find in the Andes as evidence of land having been pushed upward by volcanic eruptions from beneath the ocean, similar to what happened when the *Beagle* was in the region.[15] Geologist Lyell thought that FitzRoy's treatment of the biblical flood "beats all the other nonsense he has ever read on the subject," and Darwin in an 1838 letter expressed his agreement.[16] With some amusement, Lyell's protege presumed that FitzRoy would explain the extinction of large animals, whose fossilized bones were found in Argentina and elsewhere, by claiming that Noah made the door of his ark too small to take any of those species on board.[17]

The difficulties that Darwin had with the Hebrew Scriptures were only slightly greater than those pertaining to the New Testament. He was splashed by waves of the international storm caused by literary criticism of the Gospels that originated among German scholars. Darwin commented, "[T]he Gospels cannot be proved to have been written simultaneously with the events. . . . [T]hey differ in many important details, far too important as it seemed to me to be admitted as the usual inaccuracies of eyewitnesses." Darwin had especially in mind the alleged resurrection of Jesus, the central event of the Gospels, which each of the four evangelists report in a sharply different manner. While acknowledging that he found aspects of his religion dubious, Darwin was reluctant to jettison doctrines he had earlier accepted. As an empiricist and a Christian, Darwin longed for historical support of the New Testament from sources apart from Christian writers. He often daydreamed that the letters of ancient Romans then being discovered or the excavations at Pompeii had "confirmed in the most striking manner all that was written in the Gospels."[18]

Whereas Paley had appealed to the Gospel miracles as bedrock support for the truth of Christianity, Darwin could no longer accept the supernaturalism therein as giving any evidence of its authenticity. Darwin judged the culture of Jesus' time to be "credulous to a degree almost incomprehensible by us."[19] In earlier years Darwin had naïvely accepted such miracles as Jesus' curse causing a fig tree to die immediately because it was not bearing fruit out of season to satisfy his hunger.[20] Now he wondered how "any sane man" could find those stories believable.

Direct divine intervention into the established natural order was now viewed by Darwin as neither necessary nor admissible: "The more we know of the fixed laws of nature the more incredible do miracles become. . . . I gradually came to disbelieve in Christianity as a divine revelation."[21] "Revelation" is here used in accord with the meaning given by Paley, who asked in *Evidences of Christianity*: "In what way can a revelation be made, but by miracles? In none which we are able to conceive."[22] For Paley, "revelation" referred to the alleged biblical violations of the ordinary order of nature, rather than to the disclosure of God in history through human lives. Darwin's faith had mainly rested on two supports at Cambridge, Paley's works and Pearson's commentary on the Creed. From now on, Darwin had no use for "revealed" theology but he retained a respect for natural theology, that is, reasoning about God that was based on the facts of experience rather than on the alleged miracles of Scripture.

Darwin gradually began to see that the most important truth proclaimed in the Gospels did not depend on the reader accepting their supernatural aspects. Sound injunctions pertaining to duties could be retained. For example, the literal fig tree episode could be treated figuratively as an injunction to bear moral fruit. Or, the metaphor attributed to Jesus, "I am the bread of life," could be interpreted to mean that those with his spirit give attention to supplying "daily bread" to all who are in need. As an old man, Darwin looked back on his religious evolution in this manner.

> Beautiful as is the morality of the New Testament, it can hardly be denied that its perfection depends in part on the interpretation which we now put on metaphors and allegories. But I was very unwilling to give up my belief. . . . But I found it more and more difficult, with free scope given to my imagination, to invent evidence which would suffice to convince me. Thus disbelief crept over me at a slow rate, but was at last complete.[23]

Pertaining to the Bible, Darwin observed: "[L]ittle is there said of intellectual cultivation, main source of the intense happiness."[24] He also took issue with what he thought it affirmed as the motivator for good conduct. The Old Testament motivator is the desire to avoid punishment in this life by a fearsome God, and the New Testament incentive is the hope of being rewarded with a blissful heavenly life. Historian Josef Altholz describes Darwin as being among those Victorians who were becoming "too moral to be orthodox":

> The conflict between humane ethics and rigorous dogma was responsible for some of the more spectacular losses of faith in the

1840s. How could a benevolent and sensitive conscience accept the morality of a Jehovah who behaved, as the young Darwin put it, like a "revengeful tyrant" and who condemned the majority of his human creatures to an eternity of torment disproportionate to their wickedness or based on no personal fault at all.[25]

OTHER RELIGIOUS REFLECTIONS

The year 1837 saw the coronation of Queen Victoria, who would reign for the rest of the century. It also marked the beginning of Darwin's musings on species that would shake to the core some assumptions of Victorian religion and science. Darwin jotted down this radical insight at the time: "Animals, our fellow brethren in pain, disease, and suffering; our slaves in the most laborious works, our companions in our amusements, they may partake of our origin in one common ancestor; we may be all netted together."[26] A year later Darwin added another unorthodox note: "Man in his arrogance thinks himself a great work worthy [of] the interposition of the deity. More humble and I believe truer to consider him created from animals."[27]

Visits with humans in Tierra del Fuego and with simians in the London zoo enabled Darwin to narrow the gulf between the species to which they belonged: "Let man visit Ourang-outang in domestication, hear expressive whine, see its intelligence, . . . see its affections. . . . Let him look at savage, roasting his parents, naked, artless, not improving yet improvable and then let him dare boast of his proud preeminence."[28] Darwin resolved, "I will never allow that because there is a chasm between man . . . and animals that man has different origin."[29]

In 1838 Darwin started notebooks that he labeled "Metaphysics," which Silvan Schweber calls, with some exaggeration, "an account of Darwin's search for God."[30] Included were notes in response to a review of *Positive Philosophy*, a new book by French philosopher Auguste Comte, who had argued that primitive, childlike humans explain nature theologically. In that fictional stage of knowledge, numerous independent godlings are presumed to have direct control over certain spheres of nature, causing phenomena such as floods and earthquakes. Comte then contended that those uncoordinated powers of imaginary beings are then consolidated under the supposed providential control of a single being.[31] As human understanding progresses, in Comte's scheme, depersonalized natural laws are substituted for an intervening deity.

Observing that "zoology itself is now purely theological," Darwin commended the "grand *idea* of Comte," which properly labeled the low state of factual knowledge.[32] Darwin related an incident from his South American experience to illustrate how the primitive, lower-stage religion is a barrier to scientific development. When he was trying to understand how the massive Andes range was formed, he was told by people living there that such an effort was useless because the simple answer is that God did it.[33]

Darwin suspected that humans, aware that their actions, often irrational, express their own desires, extrapolate that erratic acts in nature are caused by the whim of God.[34] He puzzled over the general "unwillingness to consider Creator as governing by law." The probable reason for preferring an intervening special providence, he thought, is that "as long as we consider each object an act of separate creation, we admire it more, because we can compare it to the standard of our own minds."[35] Darwin wrote, "I dare say when thunder and lightning were first proved to be due to secondary [scientific] causes, some regretted to give up the idea that each flash was caused by the direct hand of God."[36] He criticized those who fail to recognize God's "most magnificent laws, of which we profane in thinking not capable to produce every effect of every kind which surrounds us."[37] Darwin thought that the dignity of God was enhanced when weather, health, and other spheres were governed by rational law and not by the unpredictable anger of a deity or the touch of an angel.

In an 1838 notebook, Darwin amusingly tried on "materialist" as a self-designation, prompting him to exclaim, "Oh you materialist!" This mirror exercise has caused some interpreters to assume that he was privately affirming that ultimate reality was matter.[38] But he provided this clarification in another note: "By materialism, I mean, merely the intimate connection of kind of thought with form of brain." The term pertained to his reflection on how psychological traits originate and was unrelated to atheistic metaphysical materialism.[39]

Darwin jotted marginalia in 1838 on pages of John Macculloch's *Proofs and Illustrations of the Attributes of God*, which Paul Barrett has published under the title *Essay on Theology and Natural Selection*. Darwin affirmed that Macculloch's views were "the very same as mine about our origin of a notion of a Deity."[40] Macculloch had argued that humans find it necessary to conclude that God exists when they probe the cause of their own existence. Recognizing that they do not produce themselves, they look for prior causes: "We trace, or conjecture these, as far as we can; but there is still a preceding one; and the ultimate one must be the primary power, a Deity; The Deity."[41] His reasoning was similar to that of René Descartes, the seventeenth-century French rationalist, who inferred the existence of God based on the certainty of himself.

Darwin took issue with Macculloch's Paleyan belief that God created plants to prevent erosion of valuable soil. He thought that the august Creator works more indirectly:

> If we were to presume that God created plants to arrest earth (like a Dutchman plants them to stop the moving sand) we lower the creator to the standard of one of his weak creations. . . . The plants were no more created to arrest the earth, than the earth revolves to form rain to wash down earth from the mountains upheaved by volcanic forces, for these marsh plants. All flow from some grand and simple laws.[42]

No longer did Darwin accept the cogency of Paley's argument for the existence of God from design in nature: "We can no longer argue that, for instance, the beautiful hinge of a bivalve shell must have been made by an intelligent being, like the hinge of a door by man. There seems to be no more design in the variability of organic beings and in the action of natural selection, than in the course which the wind blows. Everything in nature is the result of fixed laws."[43] The fixed law that Darwin especially had in mind pertains to nature evolving through a regular process of trial and error.

In September of the same year, Darwin stated that his wide range of reading led him to think deeply about religion. During that month he read Rev. Thomas Malthus's seminal essay, *The Principle of Population (1798)*, written while he was serving a parish in Surrey. Darwin must have had sophisticated tastes for pastimes, for he said he read this academic monograph "for amusement"! Malthus's thesis was that humans, along with other organisms, generally multiply exponentially while the food supply increases only arithmetically, causing overpopulation and a struggle for existence. The insight Darwin found in Malthus's work supplied him with an essential element for completing his biological theory.[44]

As might be expected for someone studying theology at Cambridge when Paley was teaching there, Malthus identified Providence with natural law: "It accords with the most liberal spirit of philosophy to believe that no stone can fall, or plant rise, without the immediate agency of divine power. But we know from experience, that these operations of what we call nature have been conducted almost invariably according to fixed laws."[45]

But the operations of nature, Malthus thought, in no way guarantee that populations will be provided with even their basic needs for survival. Since population increases disproportionately to food supply, the parson alleged that poverty, famine, disease, war, and death are the result of God's laws. Belief in a benevolent as well as just Deity did not cause Malthus to overlook bleak sociological data. He expressed hope that human restraints on propagation, by late marriages and continence—rather than by immoral contraception—would decrease suffering in the present world, and that the deserving would be rewarded with a better life after death.

William Wordsworth was another Englishman whose writings Darwin found intriguing, and a copy of his poems is filled with Darwin's marks. In the late 1830s, he read "The Excursion" twice,[46] perhaps because his feeling of awe in the Brazilian forests had been similar to those of the main character, the Wanderer. In that epic, the Wanderer told of his quest for life's meaning in nature, supplementing his biblically based faith with religious and moral understanding derived from nature:

> Early had he learned
> To reverence the [biblical] volume that displays
> The mystery, the life which cannot die;
> But in the mountains did he *feel* his faith.
> All things, responsive to the writing, there
> Breathed immortality, revolving life,
> And greatness still revolving. . . .
> Oft as he called those ecstasies to mind,
> And whence they flowed; and from them he acquired
> Wisdom, which works thro' patience; thence he learned
> In oft-recurring hours of sober thought
> To look on Nature with a humble heart.

Darwin's spirit probably resonated on reading that the Wanderer found more good than evil in nature:

> The vast Frame
> Of social nature changes evermore
> Her organs and her members, with decay
> Restless, and restless generation, powers
> And functions dying and produced at need,—
> And by this law the mighty whole subsists;
> With an ascent and progress in the main.[47]

HIS EVENTFUL THIRTIES

Realizing that he would soon be entering the fourth decade of life—middle age according to that era's life expectancy—Darwin began to think seriously about matrimony. The pros and cons on the subject that he jotted down contain humorous and religious sentiments. Heading the "Marry" column was "Children—(if it please God)—constant companion. . . . Picture to yourself a nice soft wife on a sofa with good fire, and books and music perhaps." Under "Not Marry" he listed, among other things, the loss of the freedom to go to America or "up in a Balloon." His internal soliloquy concluded with the resolve that he should find some "angel" who would keep him active and he should learn to tolerate marital-bond constrictions, facetiously commenting: "there is many a happy slave."[48]

Darwin turned to the Wedgwood family in his search, for it had been a repeated source of spouses for the Darwin family. Caroline had already joined her father in marrying a Wedgwood, Josiah III. Also, the Josiah who founded the ceramics industry married a Wedgwood relation. Moreover, Charles's brother Erasmus was long in love with Fanny Wedgwood, his first cousin, even though she had already married. At that time few feared a bad genetic outcome from close relatives intermarrying and reproducing. Indeed, Queen Victoria would soon marry Albert, her German first cousin.

Charles had long taken special interest in Emma, an attractive Wedgwood of his own age and affluent middle class, whom he had known since childhood. She was the youngest of eight children of Josiah Wedgwood, who continued his father's name and china manufacturing. Emma had the best education then available for women, having been tutored in French, Italian, and German. She was instructed in dancing on her first trip to Paris at age ten. Several years later she attended a school in London for a year, and at eighteen she studied for several months in Geneva. The lessons she received from Frederic Chopin helped her become accomplished on the piano. She developed "a many-sided interest in the world, in books, and in politics" and was noted for her ability to "read aloud clearly and well."[49]

In 1827, Charles made his first and only trip across the English Channel, accompanying a family group to escort Emma home. Her affection for him may have been a factor in her turning down several marriage proposals. When the *Beagle* returned to England she expressed her eagerness to see Darwin, and to prepare for conversing with him she read Francis Head's account of his Argentina journey.[50]

When later describing characteristics of appealing women, Darwin probably had especially in mind the most influential person of his life: "In civilised life man is largely, but by no means exclusively, influenced in the choice of his wife by external appearance. . . . Civilised men are largely attracted by the mental charms of women, by their wealth, and especially by their social position." To show the biological significance of marital matches, years later Darwin quoted an insight of German philosopher Arthur Schopenhauer: "The final aim of all love intrigues, be they comic or tragic, is really of more importance than all other ends in human life. What it all turns upon is nothing less than the composition of the next generation. . . . It is not the weal or woe of any one individual, but that of the human race to come, which is here at stake."[51]

In May 1838 Charles Whitley inquired about whether his former Cambridge friend was thinking connubially. Darwin responded by describing his preoccupation with several writing projects, but he flippantly added: "As for a wife, that most interesting specimen in the whole series of vertebrate animals, Providence only knows whether I shall ever capture one or be able to feed her if caught. All such considerations are hidden far in futurity, but at the end of a distant view, I sometimes see a cottage and some white object like a petticoat."[52]

In the latter half of 1838, Darwin was romantically transformed. He visited with Emma in July and suddenly fell in love. His scientific notebook during the year contained some perceptions that would not be expected of a Victorian gentleman. He became aware of the lust that humans and horses had in common: "Stallion licking udders of mare strictly analogous to men's affect for women's breasts."[53] The description of kissing he made during the months he was courting Emma may likewise have had a personal reference: "Ones tendency to kiss, and almost bite, that which one sexually loves is probably connected with flow of saliva and hence with action of mouth and jaws."[54] Some of this exuberance may have contributed to Emma describing her "Charley" as "the most affectionate person possible."[55]

Psychologist Robert Wright comments on Darwin's excitement at this time:

So far as anyone knows, Darwin went through his bachelor years without ever having sexual intercourse. How little does it take to arouse a man who has been so long deprived? When the *Beagle* docked in Peru, Darwin saw elegant ladies shrouded in veils that exposed only one eye. "But then," he wrote, "that one eye is so black and brilliant and has such powers of motion and expression that its effect is very powerful." It is not surprising that when Emma Wedgwood was placed within reach—her whole face visible, and her body soon to be his—Darwin began to salivate. (Literally, it would seem.)[56]

Darwin proposed to Emma in November 1838; two months later— the week of their wedding—he wrote her: "I think you will humanize me, and soon teach me there is greater happiness than building theories and accumulating facts in silence and solitude. My own dearest Emma, I earnestly pray, you may never regret the great, and I will add very good, deed, you are to perform on the Tuesday: my own dear future wife, God bless you."[57]

Emma's religious orientation was an important factor in her life, as James Moore indicates: "She was a sincere Christian like all Wedgwoods of her generation: Unitarian by conviction, Anglican in practice."[58] She shared the Wedgwood commitment to liberal religion along with con-firmation in the Church of England. Having a critical approach to the Bible, Emma rejected the commonplace assumption of its verbal inspira-tion.[59] She was regular in praying, attending church, and in taking Communion. Not only did she teach Sunday school, she wrote lessons for her pupils. When the sister nearest her age died in 1832, she wrote this prayer:

> Oh, Lord, help me to become more like her, and grant that I may join her with Thee never to part again. I trust that my Fanny's sweet image will never pass from my mind. Let me always keep it in my mind as a motive for holiness. What exquisite happiness it will be to be with her again, to tell her how I loved her who has been joined with me in almost every enjoyment of my life.[60]

Robert Darwin advised his son to avoid disclosing his religious doubts to his fiancée, because some women agonize, especially when ill, over their spouse's salvation.[61] He was probably speaking out of per-sonal experience, for he had earlier married Emma's Wedgwood aunt. When Susannah was in poor health, her suffering may have been increased, he thought, by his revealing to her his religious apathy. But Charles was too transparent to conceal from Emma his true state of mind. Prior to marriage he shared with her his ideas on religion and she expressed gratitude for his being frank about some "honest and conscientious doubts."[62] Emma appreciated his candor and observed that he was "not like the rest of the Darwins, who will not say how they really are."[63]

Recognizing that Charles's religious orientation was not as unwaver-
ing as hers, Emma expressed her wish that they not neglect spiritual
matters while they indulged in marital happiness. "There is only one
subject in the world that ever gives me a moment's uneasiness," she said,
"and I do hope that though our opinions may not agree upon all points
of religion we may sympathize a good deal in our *feelings* on the subject."[64] In pursuing this concern, she wrote him: "Will you do me a
favour? yes I am sure you will, it is to read our Saviour's farewell discourse to his disciples which begins at the end of the 13th chap. of St.
John. It is so full of love to them and devotion and every beautiful feeling. It is the part of the New Testament I love best."[65] That Gospel passage also tells about Jesus' acceptance of the disciple Thomas, who
wanted empirical evidence to overcome his doubts. Since the Gospel of
John was one that Darwin had earlier acknowledged to be his favorite,
he readily complied with her request and assured her that his religious
concerns were in "earnest."[66]

An Anglican church wedding for Emma and Charles was conducted
in Shropshire by their mutual cousin, John Wedgwood. The newlyweds
then boarded a train, the new mode of travel, and chugged to London
where they lived in a rented house. Soon after marriage, in part to clar-
ify her own thinking, Emma wrote a letter to her husband—even
though he was not away from home—pertaining to matters she deemed
vital. While commending his commitment to religious duty, she was
apprehensive over his theological skepticism. In particular, she perceived
that he had no doubt about how one ought to act with loving-kindness
toward others even though his faith foundation was eroding. Also, in an
articulate and profound manner, Emma expressed misgivings about his
disposition: "May not the habit in scientific pursuits of believing nothing till it is proved, influence your mind too much in other things
which cannot be proved in the same way, and which if true are likely
to be above our comprehension?" She testified to the value of prayer
and wondered if he was cutting himself off from receiving religious
communication and knowledge, which she viewed as neither unreasonable nor superstitious. Being anxious over his lack of conviction
about eternal life, she said, "I should be most unhappy if I thought we
did not belong to each other for ever." Charles did not lightly dismiss
the issues she raised, and years later he added a message to the end of
his wife's letter: "When I am dead, know that many times, I have kissed
and cryed over this."[67]

Regarding life after death, Darwin was increasingly aware of ways in
which all creatures share the same origin and destiny. Humans may

delude themselves, he thought, if they think they are unique vis-à-vis immortality. Although Emma assumed that belief in personal immortality was the sine qua non of religion, nearly all the writers of the Hebrew Bible did not accept the doctrine. Charles's view paralleled that of one of those writers: "That which befalleth the sons of men befalleth beasts; . . . as the one dieth, so dieth the other; yea, they have all one breath; so that a man hath no preeminence above a beast. . . . All go unto one place; all are of the dust, and all turn to dust again. Who knoweth the spirit of man that goeth upward, and the spirit of the beast that goeth downward to the earth?"[68]

For Darwin, the directing hand of a personal God had become far removed. He viewed the Creator as staying within the confines of the law of nature, causing no meddling disruptions. Emma understood that stance, for it was vintage Unitarian theology. To conclude a sketch of his theory, in 1842 Darwin wrote:

> It is derogatory that the Creator of countless systems of worlds should have created each of the myriads of creeping parasites and slimy worms which have swarmed each day of life on land and water on this one globe. . . . From death, famine, rapine, and the concealed war of nature we can see that the highest good, which we can conceive, the creation of the higher animals has directly come. . . . The existence of such [evolutionary] laws should exalt our notion of the power of the omniscient Creator.[69]

According to Darwin, God does not personally fashion every species of insect, or other varieties of animals and plants, but relies for their production on the reaction of complex chemical compounds with their environment in the context of natural law. In rejecting special creation, Darwin aimed at exalting rather than debasing the notion of an omniscient Creator. Laws imply a lawgiver, so Darwin thought he had conceived of the wisdom of God in a more sublime way. Continual intervention in order to tinker with the established law of nature was out of character for the God he revered. Darwin viewed God as having responsibility for the cosmic order and as leaving much of the suffering to the impersonal operation of natural selection. Since the overall outcome of the Creator's law is good, Darwin thought of this theology as an improvement over Judeo-Christian orthodoxy.

During the several years that the Darwins resided in London, they attended King's College Church. Emma thought that one of Charles's illnesses was the result of his being chilled in its unheated sanctuary.[70]

In 1841 he expressed his reluctance to be the "Godpapa" for Fox's first son, who later became a priest. He and Emma disliked becoming proxies and vowing to believe anything for someone else.[71] Living in the metropolis enabled the Darwins to have frequent contact with his brother and to enjoy the stimulus of nonfamily companionship. Although Charles could interact frequently with writers such as Thomas Carlyle and Charles Lyell, whom he had previously known only through their books and correspondence, he disliked the urban environment. London was pockmarked with the ugly results of the industrial revolution: the great wealth disparity of the residents bred wretched slums, and disease-spreading rats, well water, and toilet facilities accompanied rapid population growth. England was then suffering from the worst economic depression of the century, which added to the squalor. Finding the smoke of the world's largest city unhealthy and its fast tempo of life unappealing, the Darwins, including now their babies William and Anne, withdrew in 1842 to the village of Downe. The only means of public transportation to reach it was a wearisome two-hour stagecoach ride over the eighteen miles from London. Darwin was able to purchase a former parsonage, Down House, along with the extensive fields to which it was attached, near the parish church. He fulfilled his previously expressed interest in living in a quiet parsonage, but without the responsibility of being the parson. Surrounded by the chalk hills of Kent, Darwin settled like a country squire and served his community in such roles as vestryman and magistrate for the next forty years.

A month after their move, the Darwins were in the graveyard of the Church of St. Mary in Downe to bury their third child, a daughter who had been born and baptized in the village. Over the next fourteen years, one other child did not survive infancy, but six more children did. Emma read the Bible to them and taught them a simple Unitarian creed that stressed God's oneness and Jesus' ethical teachings. Following their parents' example, to enhance family respectability the Darwins had their children confirmed in the Church of England.[72]

"Wives are young men's mistresses, companions for middle age, and old men's nurses."[73] For Darwin's spouse, those roles overlapped. Emma was thirty at marriage and was pregnant during most of her years before menopause. Also, since Charles took few opportunities to leave his village to visit with peers living elsewhere, and was ill for a large portion of his years in Down House, her roles as companion and nurse began when she married and continued throughout their wedded life. Emma had some awareness of what was ahead when she wrote before marriage, "Don't be ill any more my dear Charley till I can be with you to nurse you."[74] She later said, "[N]othing marries one so completely as sickness,"[75] and by that measure she was inextricably bound to her spouse.

While living in Downe, as John Bowlby observes, Darwin's "social values continued to be close to those of his parson-naturalist friends and had nothing in common with either revolutionary politics or militant atheism."[76] Rev. Brodie Innes, the curate of Downe from 1846 onward, became Darwin's comrade for the rest of his life. Innes recalled, "In all parish matters he was an active assistant; in matters connected with the schools, charities, and other business, his liberal contribution was ever ready."[77] At Innes's request, Darwin served as treasurer of the Coal and Clothing Club that provided welfare for the needy in their village. In this regard he proposed to Innes an investment scheme that would provide the village with funds to assist the poor who were confronted with emergencies. When the Downe Friendly Society was established for that purpose, Darwin administered the funds.[78] In addition, he regularly contributed substantial support to the Sunday school in Downe and was a member of the parish council.[79] This "pillar of the parish" is described by Moore: "His infants had been christened in Downe church, where the family attended regularly [and sat in their own rented pew]. He himself seldom went, but he gave generously toward church repairs and sent his boys—William, George, Francis, Leonard, and Horace—to be tutored by nearby clergymen."[80] They studied at a school run by Rev. Charles Pritchard, later astronomy professor at Oxford.

Darwin and Innes got along amicably because they both recognized that biblical and scientific inquiries were independent. Innes said, "The study of natural history, geology, and science in general, should be pursued without reference to the Bible. . . . The Book of Nature and Scripture came from the same Divine source, ran in parallel lines, and when properly understood would never cross." In much the same way, according to Innes, Darwin said after many years of friendship, "You are a theologian, I am a naturalist, the lines are separate. I endeavour to discover facts without considering what is said in the Book of Genesis. I do not attack Moses, and I think Moses can take care of himself. . . . I cannot remember that I ever published a word directly against religion or the clergy."[81]

After Innes left the Downe parish, Rev. George Pfinden became the vicar from 1871 to 1911. He preached an anti-evolution sermon when Darwin was present that was, in part, the cause of his ceasing to attend church.[82] But he kept in contact with the former parson, and said,

"Innes and I have been fast friends for thirty years, and we never thoroughly agreed on any subject but once, and then we stared hard at each other, and thought one of us must be very ill."[83] Their disagreements were probably less about religious matters than about politics, Innes's Tory conservatism clashing with Darwin's Whig liberalism.

Darwin continued to have high respect for priests, especially if they had a naturalist bent. For many years he was a companion of Rev. Leonard Jenyns, who published papers on zoology while a vicar in Cambridgeshire, of Rev. Frederick Hope, a prominent entomologist, and of Rev. Charles Whitley, a natural philosopher.[84] Also, Rev. Algernon Wells wrote an essay on animal instinct that Darwin evaluated critically.[85] He acknowledged being stimulated by the "great horticultural knowledge" of Rev. William Herbert, who established that "botanical species are only a higher and more permanent class of varieties,"[86] and by Dorset parson Pickard Cambridge, who taught him about the sexual habits of spiders.[87] In addition, Rev. S. Lockwood, an American naturalist, informed Darwin about the musical powers of mice.[88] A mutual respect is evident in the relationships Darwin had with many clergymen, and his correspondence with them exceeded that of any other professional group. Unfortunately, Darwin was unaware of the work of Rev. Gregor Mendel, an Austrian contemporary, whose foundational gene research would have augmented Darwin's theory with a much needed mechanism for inheritance.

◆ ◆ ◆

In 1844, *Vestiges of the Natural History of Creation* was published anonymously and became a bestseller on both sides of the Atlantic. Some guessed that it was written by Darwin, but the author was actually Robert Chambers, a Scottish editor. He and his brother later published *Chambers's Encyclopaedia*, which for more than a century has been issued in updated editions. Recognizing that his views would be highly controversial and damaging to his reputation, Chambers prudently did not identify himself with his book during his lifetime. Darwin found in *Vestiges* "a grand piece of argument against mutability of species."[89] His copy of the book displays that he read it closely and was much stimulated by its content. Chambers deviated from Paley in viewing the earth as evolving over millions of years, and he rejected the biblical assertion that it had at one time been completely submerged under water. He thought that the uniformity of natural law should be applied to biological as well as to geological history. According to Chambers, organisms gradually increase in complexity as they adapt to environmental circumstances. He viewed God as the Creator of general laws governing natural development, but not as the micromanager of applications:

> The ordinary notion ... [is] that the Almighty Author produced the progenitors of all existing species by some sort of personal or immediate exertion. But ... can we suppose that the august Being who brought all these countless worlds into form by the simple establishment of a natural principle flowing from his mind, was to interfere personally and specially on every occasion when a new shell-fish or reptile was to be ushered into existence on *one* of these worlds? Surely, this idea is too ridiculous to be for a moment entertained. ... To a reasonable mind the Divine attributes must appear not diminished or reduced in any way by supposing a creation by law, but infinitely exalted.[90]

Chambers did not shirk from drawing on embryonic data in speculating about human beginnings:

> It has pleased Providence to arrange that one species should give birth to another, until the second highest gave birth to man. ... Every individual amongst us actually passes through the characters of the insect, the fish, and reptile ... before he is permitted to breathe the breath of life! ... If He, as appears, has chosen to employ inferior organisms as a generative medium for the production of the higher ones, even including ourselves, what right have we, His humble creatures, to find fault? There is, also, in this prejudice, an element of unkindliness towards the lower animals, which is utterly out of place. These creatures are all of them part products of the Almighty Conception, as well as ourselves. All of them display wondrous evidences of His wisdom and benevolence.[91]

Referring to evolution as "development," Chambers integrates it with the rest of divine law in his summary:

> It is most interesting to observe into how small a field the whole of the mysteries of nature thus ultimately resolve themselves. The inorganic has one final comprehensive law, GRAVITATION. The organic, the other great department of mundane things, rests in like manner on one law, and that is DEVELOPMENT. Nor may even these be after all twain, but only branches of one still more comprehensive

law, the expression of that unity which man's wit can scarcely separate from Deity itself.[92]

Although Darwin could agree with much that was in *Vestiges*, he was irritated by its assumption of progress in nature toward a goal, which had previously been championed by his grandfather and by the French naturalist Lamarck. On a slip of paper inserted in his copy of *Vestiges*, he wrote: "Never use the word higher and lower."[93] Darwin wrote Joseph Hooker, director of the Royal Botanic Gardens, "Heaven defend me from Lamarck['s] nonsense of a 'tendency to progression.'"[94] Darwin also remarked to him, "An unavoidable wish to compare all animals with men, as supreme, causes some confusion."[95] Later, Darwin may have chosen the title *The Descent of Man* rather than *The Ascent of Man* to avoid suggesting that the rise of humans to supremacy in nature is a motif of evolution. But Darwin was frequently to cause confusion in his writings by forgetting that the look-alike words *process* and *progress* refer to categorically different concepts.

Darwin viewed *Vestiges* "as a valuable lightning rod in channeling off the initial thunders of orthodoxy."[96] For example, Adam Sedgwick, the highly reputed geologist, wrote a hysterical attack of several hundred pages on the "inner deformity and foulness" of *Vestiges*: "If the book be true, the labours of sober induction are in vain; religion is a lie; human law is a mass of folly, and a base injustice; morality is moonshine; our labours for the black people of Africa were works of madmen; and man and woman are only better beasts!"[97] Darwin recognized that the harsh criticism that *Vestiges* was receiving was no doubt a precursor of what he would encounter if his somewhat similar ideas were disclosed.

In the same year that *Vestiges* was published, Darwin composed a fifty-thousand-word "essay" on new species arising from older species. Were he to publish his theory of transmutation, Darwin fantasized that it would be "like confessing a murder," because it would bear witness that he was a principal killer of the Deity who created changeless species.[98] His imagining the public trial and punishment that his British culture could inflict on one who had committed deicide, with his pen being the murder weapon, caused him to keep his essay hidden from the public. In addition, Darwin's body was in no shape for combat; it had long lost its robustness of the *Beagle* years and his psychosomatic ailments increased along with his personal anxieties. Moreover, he imagined that he could overwhelm the doubtful after gathering more evidence and by including illustrations that were more convincing. By publishing a compelling scientific case for his theory in some future year, he hoped that reputable naturalists would spare him from ridicule. Consequently, he was apprehensive to let even his colleagues know about his theory, and many years would pass before the closet evolutionist would come out with his "one long argument" for evolution.

Lyell strongly recommended that Darwin avoid becoming entangled in controversy. Lyell continued to write about special creation: "Species may have been created in succession at such times and in such places as to enable them to multiply and endure for an appointed period, and occupy an appointed space on the globe." That position was for Darwin "a believing in what the human mind cannot grasp" and belonged to the category of believing in the Trinity.[99] Whereas Darwin had eagerly accepted Lyell's geological insights and acknowledged in 1844, "I always feel as if my books came half out of Lyell's brains,"[100] there was no eagerness on Lyell's part to encourage his protégé as he developed his theory.

While Darwin was hatching out and hiding revolutionary ideas in biology, Rev. Baden Powell (not to be confused with his namesake son who founded the Boy Scouts) was both thinking and publishing his radical views on the Bible. He did not find William Buckland's attempt to reconcile Genesis and geology plausible. Buckland, Powell's Oxford colleague, speculated that a long historical period transpired between the declaration "In the beginning God created the heaven and the earth" and the week of specific creations described in the rest of the opening chapter of the Bible.[101] Nor did Powell think that harmony could be achieved by converting those six days into periods of millions of years— which still would confront the reasonable person with the preposterous notion that there were several days and nights, as well as the creation of vegetation and photosynthesis, before the sun's creation.[102] He believed that the distinctive biblical message was not damaged by the new scientific theories on the development of the earth and life. In 1845 he reviewed fossil and other scientific findings to show that they imposed no barrier to the Bible's religious message. Pertaining to the creation narrative, Powell affirmed "that it *cannot* be *history*—it *may* be *poetry.*" He contended that the literary form of the ancient writers was inadequate for explaining natural events, but that the Bible did convey some revelation of God's nature. Powell felt that the undeveloped moral and intellectual capacity of the Hebrew people must be taken into account in interpreting their Scriptures, and that historical advancement and spiritual receptivity can effect a fuller comprehension of true religion.[103]

Darwin spent much of 1848 in mental depression and physical illness. In an effort to recover, he gave much attention to spiritual literature. He read Samuel Coleridge's religious writings and gave a good evaluation to *Evidences of the Genuineness of the Gospels* by Harvard professor Andrews Norton.[104] Norton had written three volumes in 1846 on how the Gospels are related to eyewitness accounts of Jesus. Also, Darwin found a biography of Rev. John Sterling engaging because both had had similar doubts and illnesses. "Christianity is a great comfort and blessing to me," Sterling testified, "although I am quite unable to believe all its original documents."[105] Adrian Desmond and James Moore comment on Emma's role in this situation: "She now drew from her inner source of strength, binding Charles to herself with cords of love, ministering to his daily needs and praying for him. They failed to see eye-to-eye on the question of eternal life. . . . But she could bear Christian witness in this stressful time and help him rest."[106] When he visited his dying father in Shrewsbury, he wrote her, "I do long to be with you and under your protection for then I feel safe. God bless you."[107]

AN AGONIZING DECADE

Darwin's great distress over the long period of bodily degeneration of his aged father, who weighed more than three hundred pounds, reveals his hypersensitivity to the suffering of all fellow creatures. This characteristic, which affected his religious outlook, can also be illustrated by his boyhood practice of killing worms in a salt solution rather than impaling them alive on his fishing hook.[108] Likewise, while a student, he gave up his passionate love of shooting for sport on seeing a bird he had shot that was not quite dead a day later.[109] Darwin's horror of witnessing patients' suffering during surgical operations contributed to his dropping out of medical school. Also, he was highly indignant over the torture of slaves in Brazil. His writings show that he was repelled by the enormous wasting of life that he witnessed as a naturalist. He found shocking "the dreadful but quiet war of organic beings" transpiring in what appeared to be "peaceful woods and smiling fields."[110]

Beginning in 1850, during his beloved eldest daughter Anne's prolonged illness, Darwin scrutinized religion in depth by reading three recent books by Francis Newman: *History of the Hebrew Monarchy*, *The Soul*, and *Phases of Faith*. The latter book, Newman's account of his mutations from orthodoxy to "moral theism," was one of the few rated "excellent" of the hundreds of books on his reading list.[111] Unlike his more famous brother, Cardinal John Henry Newman, Francis did not find the prevailing Christian orthodoxy appealing and rejected his earlier plan to become a clergyman. *Phases of Faith*, his spiritual autobiography, struck a responsive note among many Britons and went through six editions in ten years. Darwin no doubt appreciated Newman's candid rejection of the historicity of the creation and Noah's ark stories, which had conventionally been dated as happening about three to four thousand years B.C.E. Finding science trustworthy, especially Herschel's astronomy, Newman rejected his early belief in the Bible's infallibility.[112] He had been influenced by the article "Creation" by Powell, his friend and former Oxford teacher.[113]

Newman was offended by the Hebrews' presumption that God sanctioned the atrocities they committed against their enemies. Also, he was "aghast" over the doctrine of an eternal hell, because "infinite retaliation for finite offences" contains "intolerable moral difficulties." More positively, Newman stated that "religion is the handmaid to Morals: we must be spiritual in order that we may be in the highest and truest sense moral." He associated relevant religion with expressions of social justice, such as had been displayed by the abolitionists. Darwin no doubt identified with Newman's conclusion, "The age is ripe for . . . a religion which shall combine the tenderness, humility, and disinterestedness, that are the glory of the purest Christianity, with that activity of intellect, untiring pursuit of truth, and strict adherence to impartial principle, which the schools of modern science embody." Such will bring "peace on earth and goodwill towards men."[114] In a parallel manner, Darwin had earlier cited the good news of the Christmas messengers as "the most perfect description of happiness that words can give."[115] Peace loving and philanthropic, Darwin patterned his moral life after that Gospel hope.

From the Malvern spa where Darwin and his daughter had gone for therapy, he wrote Emma of Anne's death. His uses of the divine name appear to be more than perfunctory: "I pray God Fanny's note may have prepared you. . . . Our poor dear dear child has had a very short life but I trust happy, and God only knows what miseries might have been in store for her. . . . God bless her."[116] James Moore, a thorough researcher of some episodes in Darwin's religious life, describes the pathetic situation:

> Nothing before or after would so expose the sacred interiors of Darwin's and Emma's relationship. . . . Emma, in her ninth pregnancy at the age of forty-three, helpless now except to save the life within her, paralysed at the coming of each post, breathing prayers along with medical advice in daily letters. . . . The unborn infant, the beloved daughter, Darwin himself on the Malvern hillside—all

suspended between life and death, earth and heaven, in Easter-week. . . . Darwin meanwhile informed his cousin Fox, . . . "Thank God she suffered hardly at all and expired as tranquilly as a little angel." . . . All through the anguished week's letters to Emma, the most frank and uncontrived religious expressions of gratitude, hope and blessing had jostled uncomfortably against the bleakest utterances of grief and despair. "Oh my own it is very bitter indeed," he had written on Good Friday, after a night in which Annie had been expected to die; "God preserve and cherish you."[117]

Darwin struggled then with his residual belief in a Providence that rewards the good with health and longevity. He wrote Fox at that time, "She was my favourite child; her cordiality, openness, buoyant joyousness and strong affections made her most lovable."[118] His disenchantment with Christianity reached a crisis with Anne's death at the age of ten. It provided him with the final evidence of the falsity of the pietism, summarized by this biblical proverb: "There shall no evil happen to the just."[119] A dozen years later he recalled his "unutterable bitterness" over Anne's death.[120] Toward the end of his life, Darwin called this the "one very severe grief" his family had suffered and he acknowledged that he still shed tears over her.[121] To an interviewer at that time, Edward Aveling, he acknowledged, "I never gave up Christianity until I was forty years of age."[122] If "forty" is taken as a round number to cover several years, Darwin dated the time when he could no longer find comfort in his traditional religion to the period of Anne's terminal illness.

An omnipotent and benevolent God, Darwin reasoned, would have had compassion on the sufferings of innocent Anne and would have restored her to health. Since such special Providence did not happen, Darwin came to understand existentially what he had earlier discerned theoretically: that God does not intervene in natural processes regardless of the injustice of the situation. He rejected divine omnipotence, one of God's principal attributes according to Judaism, Christianity, and Islam. This move, however, should not be equated with his complete loss of faith and his becoming a religious unbeliever.

Apart from the consideration of divine involvement in Anne's tragic death, her bouts with disease may have provoked mixed feelings in Darwin that his own choice of a mate may have been a contributing cause. Pertaining to his many children, he acknowledged, "They are not very robust; some of them seem to have inherited my detestable constitution."[123] In 1858 he also wrote, "How strange and unhappy it is that now we have had five children all failing in *precisely* the same way."[124] His last child and namesake was retarded and died that year. After Darwin became more aware of hereditary problems that could result from marrying a close relative, he wrote of infirmities caused by generations of inbreeding.[125] The weaknesses displayed by several of his children was probably due, at least partially, to the combination of his own and his parents' consanguineous marriages. The match was genetically unwise, but splendid if measured by a blending of temperaments. The veneration he gave Emma in 1858 was befitting what one might give a divinity: "Ah Mammy, I wish you knew how I value you; and what an inexpressible blessing it is to have one whom one can always trust—one always the same, always ready to give comfort, sympathy and the best advice.—God bless you my dear, you are too good for me."[126]

In spite of his traumatic experience with Anne, Darwin occasionally expressed the then current view of all evolutionists—that nature was headed toward perfection. In an 1857 letter, Darwin wrote, "I think it can be shown that there is such an unerring power at work in *Natural Selection* (the title of my book), which selects exclusively for the good of each organic being."[127] In that manuscript, which he was then writing, he commented on how "nature's productions bear the stamp of a far higher perfection than man's product by artificial selection." He asserted:

> See how differently Nature acts! By nature I mean the laws ordained by God to govern the Universe. She cares not for mere external appearance. . . . There will be here no caprice, no favouring: the good will be preserved and the bad rigidly destroyed, for good and bad are all exposed during some period of growth or during some generation, to a severe struggle for life. Each being will live its full term and procreate its kind, according to its capacity to obtain food and escape danger.[128]

While writing his book on natural selection in 1856, Darwin exclaimed to Hooker, "What a book a devil's chaplain might write on the clumsy, wasteful, blundering low and horribly cruel works of nature!"[129] Darwin was fully aware of the pain that accompanies the evolutionary selective process. Increase in complexity necessitates mutations, many of which cause suffering and death. Even so, Darwin argued that some people are so impressed with the suffering in the world that they overlook "the endless beautiful adaptations which we everywhere meet with." He suggested that the world has a "generally beneficent arrangement" and that there is an excess of happiness over misery.[130]

Notes

1. *Correspondence*, 1:460.
2. *Autobiography*, 85–96.
3. George Dorsey, *The Evolution of Charles Darwin* (New York: Doubleday, 1927), 161.
4. *Autobiography*, 85.
5. *Correspondence*, 2:8.
6. *Notebooks*, 573.
7. Ibid., 195.
8. Carolus Linnaeus, *Reflections on the Study of Nature* (Dublin, 1786), 11.
9. Quoted in Sandra Herbert, "The Place of Man in the Development of Darwin's Theory of Transmutation," *Journal of the History of Biology* (fall 1974): 233.
10. Genesis 8:4; William Kirby, *On the Power, Wisdom and Goodness of God, as Manifested in the Creation of Animals* (London: Bohn, 1853), 1:87.
11. *Notebooks*, 196.
12. Genesis 6–7.
13. Robert FitzRoy, *Narrative of the Surveying Voyages* (London: Colburn, 1839), 2:658.
14. Ibid., 2:667–68, 671.
15. *Voyage*, 328–29.
16. *Correspondence*, 2:236.
17. Ibid., 7:413.
18. *Autobiography*, 86.
19. Ibid., 86.
20. Mark 11:12–14, 20.
21. *Autobiography*, 86.
22. William Paley, *Works* (Philadelphia: Crissy, 1857), 272.
23. *Autobiography*, 86–87.
24. *Notebooks*, 549.
25. Gerald Parsons, ed., *Religion in Victorian Britain* (Manchester: Manchester University Press, 1988), 4:157.
26. *Notebooks*, 228–29.
27. Ibid., 300.
28. Ibid., 264.
29. Ibid., 310.
30. Silvan Schweber, "The Origin of the *Origin* Revisited," *Journal of the History of Biology* (fall 1977): 233.
31. Auguste Comte, *The Positive Philosophy* (New York: Blanchard, 1855), 26.
32. *Notebooks*, 566.
33. *Correspondence*, 9:226.
34. *Notebooks*, 535.
35. Ibid., 559.

36. *Correspondence*, 7:381.

37. *Notebooks*, 553.

38. Ibid., 291; for further discussion, see Frank Brown, *The Evolution of Darwin's Religious Views* (Macon, Ga.: Mercer, 1986), 17.

39. Neal Gillespie, *Charles Darwin and the Problem of Creation* (Chicago: University of Chicago Press, 1979), 139.

40. *Notebooks*, 572.

41. John Macculloch, *Proofs and Illustrations of the Attributes of God* (London: Duncan, 1837), 1:94.

42. *Notebooks*, 633.

43. *Autobiography*, 87.

44. *Autobiography*, 120.

45. Thomas Malthus, *Essay on the Principle of Population* (London: Johnson, 1798), 362.

46. *Autobiography*, 85.

47. William Wordsworth, "The Excursion," 1.214–41; 7.999–1005.

48. *Autobiography*, 232–34.

49. Henrietta Litchfield, ed., *Emma Darwin* (New York: Appleton, 1915), 1:62, 117, 141, 185; 2:46, 48.

50. Ibid., 1:255, 272.

51. *Descent*, 571, 578.

52. *Correspondence*, 7:469.

53. *Notebooks*, 536.

54. Ibid., 574.

55. Litchfield, *Emma*, 2:51.

56. Robert Wright, *The Moral Animal* (New York: Pantheon, 1994), 120–21.

57. *Correspondence*, 2:166.

58. James Moore, *The Darwin Legend* (Grand Rapids: Baker, 1994), 36.

59. *Autobiography*, 87.

60. Litchfield, *Emma*, 1:142, 250.

61. *Autobiography*, 95.

62. *Correspondence*, 2:123.

63. Litchfield, *Emma*, 1:51.

64. *Correspondence*, 2:169.

65. Ibid., 2:123.

66. Ibid., 2:126.

67. *Autobiography*, 236–37.

68. Ecclesiastes 3:19–21.

69. Francis Darwin, ed., *The Foundations of the Origin of Species: Two Essays Written in 1842 and 1844* (Cambridge: Cambridge University Press, 1909), 51–52.

70. Litchfield, *Emma*, 2:38.

71. *Correspondence*, 2:303; 10:819.

72. Litchfield, *Emma*, 2:173.

73. Francis Bacon, "Of Marriage and Single Life," *Essays* (1625).

74. *Correspondence*, 2:150.

75. Gertrude Himmelfarb, *Darwin and the Darwinian Revolution* (London: Chatto, 1959), 133.

76. John Bowlby, *Charles Darwin* (New York: Norton, 1991), 248.

77. LLD, 1:120.

78. *Correspondence,* 7:5, 433.

79. *Correspondence,* 4:138.

80. Moore, *The Darwin Legend*, 39–40.

81. LLD, 2:82–83.

82. David Kohn, ed., *The Darwinian Heritage* (Princeton: Princeton University Press, 1985), 481.

83. Quoted in Gavin de Beer, *Charles Darwin* (London: Nelson, 1963), 269.

84. *Autobiography,* 61, 66.

85. *Notebooks,* 582.

86. *Origin,* 2, 32, 137.

87. *Descent,* 391, 402.

88. *Descent,* 568.

89. *Correspondence*, 3:258.

90. Robert Chambers, *Vestiges of the Natural History of Creation* (New York: Wiley, 1845), 116–19.

91. Ibid., 177.

92. Ibid., 268–69.

93. *Correspondence,* 7:229.

94. Ibid., 3:2.

95. Ibid., 5:197.

96. Charles Gillispie, *Genesis and Geology* (Cambridge: Harvard University Press, 1951), 217.

97. J. W. Clarke and T. M. Hughes, *The Life and Letters of the Reverend Adam Sedgwick* (Cambridge: Cambridge University Press, 1890), 2:84.

98. *Correspondence,* 3:2.

99. *Autobiography,* 126; *Correspondence,* 3:345–46.

100. *Correspondence,* 3:55.

101. William Buckland, *Geology and Mineralology* (Philadelphia: Carey, 1837), 1:25.

102. Baden Powell, *The Connexion of Natural and Divine Truth* (London: Parker, 1838), 250–55.

103. Baden Powell, "Creation," *A Cyclopaedia of Biblical Literature* (New York: Ivison, 1860).

104. *Correspondence,* 4:476.

105. Quoted in Adrian Desmond and James Moore, *Darwin* (New York: Warner, 1992), 359.

106. Ibid., 362.

107. *Correspondence,* 4:147.

108. *Autobiography,* 27.

109. LLD, 1:142.

110. *Notebooks*, 429.

111. *Correspondence*, 4:479.

112. Francis Newman, *Phases of Faith* (London: Manwaring, 1860), 67–69, 74.

113. Pietro Corsi, *Science and Religion: Baden Powell and the Anglican Debate, 1800–1860* (New York: Cambridge University Press, 1988), 213, 270, 273–74.

114. Newman, *Faith* 44, 47, 111, 175.

115. Dorsey, *Darwin*, 42.

116. *Correspondence*, 5:24.

117. James Moore, ed., *History, Humanity and Evolution* (Cambridge: Cambridge University Press, 1989), 198, 217–18, 220.

118. *Correspondence*, 5:32.

119. Proverbs 12:21.

120. LLD, 2:224.

121. *Autobiography*, 97–98.

122. Edward Aveling, *The Religious Views of Charles Darwin* (London: Freethought, 1883), 5.

123. *Correspondence*, 7:50.

124. *Correspondence*, 7:158.

125. *Origin*, 145.

126. *Correspondence*, 7:80.

127. Charles Darwin and Alfred Wallace, *Evolution by Natural Selection* (London: Cambridge University Press, 1958), 265.

128. R. C. Stauffer, ed., *Charles Darwin's Natural Selection* (London: Cambridge University Press, 1975), 224.

129. *Correspondence*, 6:178.

130. *Autobiography*, 88.

CHAPTER FOUR

The Evolutionary Tree of Life

ENTER GRAY AND WALLACE

In 1839, Joseph Hooker introduced Darwin to Asa Gray, the first professor employed by the new University of Michigan, and soon they began to correspond about taxonomy questions. Gray was soon recognized as America's foremost botanist and in 1842 was appointed professor of natural history at Harvard. During the several decades the brilliant scientist was director of the Harvard Botanical Gardens, he served as president of the American Association for the Advancement of Science and as regent of the Smithsonian Museum.

Gray, whose background was in "New School" Presbyterianism, belonged to one of the more progressive branches of the Calvinism that had been the predominant theology of northeastern America for more than two centuries. He later described himself in broader terms as "one who is scientifically, and in his own fashion, a Darwinian, philosophically a convinced theist, and religiously an acceptor of the 'creed commonly called the Nicene,' as the exponent of the Christian faith."[1] Two years younger than Darwin, Gray became his first and only close friend in the United States. The Englishman was pleased to find someone in another nation with whom he could confidentially share his ideas and from whom he could learn his errors.

The differing theological positions of Gray and Darwin would result in much correspondence between them. The first theological issue they discussed pertained to one way Gray differentiated between the formation of biological varieties and species. He accounted for the former by natural selection and for the latter by God's direct creation. But Darwin, who believed that varieties and species have a like origin, wrote him in 1857: "What a jump it is from a well marked variety, produced by natural cause, to a species produced by the separate act of the Hand of God!"[2] Impressed by Gray's openness to new ideas, Darwin sent him a letter that same year which admitted, "As an honest man I must tell you that I have come to the heterodox conclusion that there are no such things as independently created species—that species are only strongly defined varieties."[3] He then sent Gray an abstract of his natural selection theory, a mailing which was soon to provide proof that he had formulated his theory prior to learning that Alfred Wallace had independently come to the same conclusion. Wallace, who was then an English explorer in the East Indies, had sent Darwin a paper in 1858 containing essentially the evolutionary theory that Darwin had privately written out many years earlier.

After the natural selection theory of Wallace and Darwin was unveiled at a meeting of the Linnean Society of London and subsequently published, they must have been delighted to find their theory applied by Rev. Henry Tristram to North African ornithology. In his article on the topic, Tristram stated that he felt "convinced of the truth of the views set forth by Messrs. Darwin and Wallace," and went on to comment: "Knowing that God ordinarily works by natural means, it might be the presumption of an unnecessary miracle to assume a distinct and separate origin for many of those which we term species. . . . Every peculiarity of difference in the living inhabitants of each country is admirably adapted by the wisdom of their beneficent Creator for the support and preservation of the species."[4]

But the ideas contained in the co-authored natural selection paper generally attracted little attention. Darwin could only remember one published review, which concluded "that all that was new in them was false, and what was true was old." This convinced him how necessary it was "that any new view should be explained at considerable length in order to arouse public attention."[5]

THE *ORIGIN OF SPECIES*

After many years of gestation, the *Origin of Species by Means of Natural Selection* finally emerged in November 1859. More than a dozen years earlier Darwin had his wife pledge that she would publish his natural selection manuscript, which he considered to be his most important scientific contribution, in case he died suddenly before it was accomplished. Now, fifty years old, Darwin felt fulfilled—"Like a good Catholic who has received extreme unction, I can sing nunc dimittis."[6] Likewise, Darwin was contented to see, exposed for public scrutiny, the newborn theory that would give his life completion. Actually, Darwin lived more than twenty years longer, and in 1881 wrote similarly about his anticipation over the publication of a subsequent work: "My strength will then probably be exhausted, and I shall be ready to exclaim 'Nunc dimittis."[7]

Darwin's exposition of natural selection in the *Origin* will now be examined with a focus upon its theological content. According to biologist John Durant, "[T]he *Origin of Species* is the last great work of Victorian natural theology," and it was addressed to an audience that was made up mainly of natural theologians.[8] Viewing the *Origin* as a stealth response to Paley's highly influential *Natural Theology* is a help in understanding its purpose. But before tracing Darwin's sequencing of significant ideas, a summary of his field theory is necessary, because the logic of his argument is often buried in the overwhelming supportive facts marshaled in his ponderous text. On the basis of his meticulous and sometimes brilliant observations, he discussed these main tenets: 1) organisms reproduce organisms of the same species, but their members (excepting twins) are never genetically identical; 2) the reproductive potential of populations far exceeds what available resources can sustain; 3) organisms and species that have, by chance, small genetic variations more compatible with the environment are more likely to avoid extinction; and 4) those organisms best adapted will survive and breed offspring with even more variations, which gradually will form new species over a long period of time. Darwin had the synoptic vision to fit these simple ideas into a comprehensive understanding of the mechanism of evolution.

To set the tone for examining the argument of the *Origin*, Darwin placed three epigraphs from eminent Christian philosophers at its beginning. By using them, he attempted to head off polarized thinking that truth was arrived at by either a totally theological approach or by a totally scientific approach. The first quotation was by Rev. William Whewell, a philosopher of science, from his essay that had been included among the popular Bridgewater Treatises. He was the Cambridge professor with whom Darwin had conversed on "grave subjects" while a student.[9] When Darwin resided in London, Whewell persuaded him to serve as secretary of the Geological Society while Whewell was president. Subsequently, when Darwin was developing his theory, he frequently cited Whewell's *History of the Inductive Sciences*.[10] The term "scientist" became accepted as a result of its use in that acclaimed book, published in 1833.

For placement in the frontispiece of the *Origin*, Darwin found this significant sentence by Whewell: "But with regard to the material world, . . . events are brought about not by insulated interpositions of

Divine power, exerted in each particular case, but by the establishment of general laws." The words echo Isaac Newton's widely accepted theology that God does not directly intervene in the natural order. As will be shown, Darwin's last words in the *Origin* reaffirm Whewell's viewpoint on "Divine power."

Other parts of Whewell's treatise were no doubt unappealing to Darwin. For example, Whewell argued that divine design is manifested in God's coordination of the length of the solar year with the twelve-month cycle needed for plants to survive.[11] Darwin was irritated by Whewell's arrogance in thinking that the length of night was designed to conform to the amount of sleep time needed for humans.[12] Because of his respect for Whewell's prestige, Darwin was aghast to learn later that this Master of Trinity College attempted to curtail freedom of inquiry by refusing to permit a copy of the *Origin* to be placed in his college's library.

The second introductory quotation in Darwin's magnum opus affirms that the natural order presupposes the continuity of a rational agent. It comes from Joseph Butler, the outstanding eighteenth-century bishop of Durham. That defender of rational Christian orthodoxy saw reason and revelation as companions, not as combatants. Darwin took from Butler's *Analogy of Revealed Religion* a somewhat opaque sentence conveying the need for divine creativity working without interruption from the beginning of the world onward. Butler said, "The only distinct meaning of the word 'natural' is *stated, fixed*, or *settled*; since what is natural as much requires and presupposes an intelligent agent to render it so, *i.e.*, to effect it continually or at stated times, as what is supernatural or miraculous does to effect it for once."

The last quotation launching the *Origin* is Francis Bacon's famous plea for an endless investigation into two complementary areas. Bacon had attended Cambridge University in the sixteenth century, when it was the center of England's Protestant Reformation, and his view on the relationship between religion and science exercised a powerful influence for centuries on students attending the institution. In the opening chapter of his *Advancement of Learning*, he commended a persistent search into both the Bible and empirical science. Bacon recognized the temptation to neglect "the highest cause" by those who rivet their attention on the immediate scientific cause. Comprehension of Bacon's outlook is best served by placing Darwin's quotation, italicized below, in its fuller context:

The Apostle [Paul] . . . saith, "Knowledge bloweth up, but charity [*agape*, loving-kindness] buildeth up." . . . Divers great learned men have been heretical whilst they have sought to fly up to the secrets of the Deity by the waxen wings of the senses. . . . A little or superficial knowledge of philosophy may incline the mind of man in atheism, but a further proceeding therein doth bring the mind back again to religion. For in the entrance of philosophy, when the second causes, which are next unto the senses, do offer themselves in the mind of man, if it dwell and stay there it may induce some oblivion of the highest cause; but when a man passeth on further, and seeth the dependence of causes, and the works of Providence, then, according to the allegory of the poets, he will easily believe that the highest link of nature's chain must needs be tied to the foot of Jupiter's chair. *To conclude, therefore, let no man upon a weak conceit of sobriety, or an ill-applied moderation, think or maintain that a man can search too far, or be too well studied in the book of God's word, or in the book of God's works, divinity or philosophy; but rather let men endeavor an endless progress of proficience in both*; only let men beware that they apply both to charity, and not to swelling; to use, and not to ostentation; and again, that they do not unwisely mingle or confound these learnings together.

Darwin learned from Bacon that science explains happenings by secondary causes, and that attention to both "the highest cause" and "the second causes" are needed for full comprehension. The two essential parts of knowledge, which should not be confused, consist of God's testament in nature and in the Bible. Bacon also urged that naturalists concentrate on observation and move away from baseless speculation. Accordingly, pertaining to his early post-*Beagle* period, Darwin wrote: "I worked on true Baconian principles, and without any theory collected facts on a wholesale scale."[13]

James Moore comments on Darwin's three introductory quotations: "He might almost have said the *Origin* was "like a Bridgewater Treatise," which was the way he described to his publisher his next book, *Orchids*.[14] Moore suggests that Darwin, like the Bridgewater authors, tended to use "Nature" as a locution for God.[15] One of those writers, Peter Roget, explained:

In order to avoid the too frequent, and consequently irreverent, introduction of the Great Name of the SUPREME BEING into familiar discourse on the operations of his power, I have, throughout this Treatise, followed the common usage of employing the term

Nature as a synonym, expressive of the same power, but veiling from our feeble sight the too dazzling splendour of its glory.[16]

♦ ♦ ♦

The chapter entitled "An Historical Sketch" at the beginning of the *Origin* credits Erasmus Darwin as being the first to postulate the transformation of species in his book *Zoonomia, Or the Laws of Organic Life*. Dr. Darwin criticized the notion that the world had suddenly appeared by divine fiat, exclaiming: "What a magnificent idea of the infinite power of THE GREAT ARCHITECT! . . . It would seem to require a greater infinity of power to cause the causes of effects, rather than to cause the effects themselves."[17] He joined earlier theologians who had thought it more appropriate to conceive of God as operating in the biological realm more through gradual, natural processes rather than through instantaneous decrees.

Darwin acknowledged that seven years after *Zoonomia* was published in 1794, Jean Lamarck made this contribution to science and theology: "He upholds the doctrine that all species, including man, are descended from other species. He first did the eminent service of arousing attention to the probability of all change in the organic, as well as in the inorganic world, being the result of law, and not of miraculous interposition."[18] Darwin became aware of Lamarck through his contacts with zoologist Robert Grant, the one professor he appreciated while studying in Edinburgh. About him, Darwin recalled in his *Autobiography*:

> He one day, when we were walking together burst forth in high admiration of Lamarck and his views on evolution. I listened in silent astonishment, and as far as I can judge, without any effect on my mind. I had previously read the *Zoonomia* of my grandfather, in which similar views are maintained, but without producing any effect on me. Nevertheless it is probable that the hearing rather early in life such views maintained and praised may have favoured my upholding them under a different form in my *Origin of Species*.[19]

Credit was also given to *Vestiges* in the *Origin*'s historical chapter by the citation of a key sentence from it: "Animated beings, from the simplest and oldest up to the highest and most recent, are, under the providence of God . . . tending, in the course of generations, to modify organic structures in accordance with external circumstances, . . . these being the 'adaptations' of the natural theologian."[20] Although Lamarck and the author of *Vestiges* were accused of atheism, they both acknowledged a Creator who guaranteed that evolution was moving toward perfection.[21] Darwin may have said little about Lamarck out of concern that the Frenchman's doctrine of the inheritance of acquired characteristics might be confused with his rejection of such.

Darwin opened his introductory chapter by announcing his detective-like determination "to throw some light on the origin of species—that mystery of mysteries, as it has been called by one of our greatest philosophers." He was alluding to John Herschel's expression of wonder in a letter to Charles Lyell, "That mystery of mysteries, the replacement of extinct species by others".[22] Reflecting on data he had gathered while on his *Beagle* odyssey, Darwin appropriated Herschel's mysteries phrase to refer to his puzzlement before inducing how species developed. At the end of the Introduction, Darwin confessed his "profound ignorance" regarding the nature of many organisms, while boldly declaring that he was "fully convinced that species are not immutable" and that the common judgment that "each species has been independently created is erroneous."[23]

In his "Struggle for Existence" chapter, Darwin dealt with the intricacies of nature. Understanding the earth, he perceived, involves becoming aware of "the mutual relations of all organisms," including both their competition and dependence on one another:

> What a struggle must have gone on during long centuries between the several kinds of trees each annually scattering its seeds by the thousand; what war between insect and insect—between insects, snails, and other animals with birds and beasts of prey—all striving to increase, all feeding on each other, or on the trees, their seeds and seedlings, or on the other plants which first clothed the ground and thus checked the growth of the trees! . . . When we reflect on this struggle, we may console ourselves with the full belief, that the war of nature is not incessant, that no fear is felt, that death is generally prompt, and that the vigorous, the healthy, and the happy survive and multiply.[24]

The "struggle for existence" phrase—perhaps better called striving to reproduce—was not intended to emphasize combative activity within a species. When parents procreate in an environment characterized by debilitating disease, intolerable temperature, and food scarcity, most of their offspring will probably languish passively without clashing among one another, and die before reproducing. In effect, the first command of the Bible, "Be fruitful and multiply," is modified in the *Origin* to read, "Multiply, vary, let the strongest live and the weakest die."[25]

Rejecting the view that species have a pre-established fixed design, Darwin argued that struggle and chance have determined the life of organisms. Their survival is due less to individual efforts than to their having, by accident, been born with slight mutations that prove more useful in the perpetual competition for food. The fortuitous variations are unregulated by Providence. Through trial and error, organisms survive if they can adapt to the often inhospitable environment. Those fortunate survivors reproduce their kind, minutely altered, while the rest gradually become extinct. Darwin appealed to the law of nature to explain the phenomena, but it differs from Newton's idea of natural law. In evolution there is a statistical law that has a random element.

John Greene clarifies the significance of chance for Darwin, and what he meant by the term:

> In the static view of nature, chance and change had been the opposites of design and permanence. The forms of the species were products of intelligent design and possessed an immutability appropriate to their divine origin. Varieties, on the other hand, were products of time and circumstance, of *chance*, not in the sense that they were uncaused or independent of natural law, but rather in the sense that they were not part of the original plan of creation.[26]

In the next chapter, "Natural Selection," Darwin compared the natural selector with the human selector, pointing out that although the former takes much longer than the breeder who makes an artificial selection, nature acts efficiently. Durant points out the way in which Darwin and Paley shared the same methodology: "A form of *analogical* argument was at the core of the respective theses. In Paley's *Natural Theology* the analogy was between human artifact and divine artifact. In Darwin's *Origin of Species* it was between human selection (as practised on plants and animals under domestication) and natural selection."[27] Darwin *inferred* natural selection, which he was unable to observe in operation, from what he knew about the way plant and animal breeders made selections.

To some extent, Darwin substituted natural selection for Providence. This is especially apparent in his 1842 treatment of his theory:

> If a being infinitely more sagacious than man (not an omniscient creator) during thousands and thousands of years were to select all

the variations which tended towards certain ends . . . for instance, if he foresaw a canine animal would be better off, owing to the country producing more hares, if he were longer legged and [had] keener sight—[then a] greyhound [would be] produced.[28]

After publishing the *Origin*, Darwin realized that his basic terminology, "natural *selection*," misleadingly suggests that Mother Nature picks out what she hopes will be an improvement. He reflected that "natural preservation" might have been a better way of expressing his concept and that he would use it if he were starting over on the *Origin*.[29] He intended to say that individuals within a population are preserved if they can cope with their environment long enough to produce offspring that can fend for themselves.

Darwin's uses of "Nature" in the *Origin* sometime have overtones of theological affirmations and might be interpreted as circumlocutions for a personal God. Darwin acknowledged that some claimed that he wrote "of natural selection as an active power or Deity."[30] Consider these anthropomorphisms: "The hand of Nature," and "We behold the face of nature bright with gladness." Also, "natural selection" suggests that nature, like human breeders of livestock, makes a conscious choice to preserve promising offspring in order to improve the species. For example, Darwin wrote: "Natural selection is daily and hourly scrutinising, throughout the world, the slightest variations; rejecting those that are bad, preserving and adding up all that are good; silently and insensibly working . . . at the improvement of each organic being."[31] Darwin's metaphor here is similar to the notion of a deity selecting desired variations.

The only diagram in the *Origin* provides a superb way of plotting trajectories of natural selection over the course of time. Darwin called it the "Tree of Life," a widely known metaphor with positive Judeo-Christian associations. That was the name given to one of the two symbolic trees in the garden of Eden. The "tree of life" there represents life without death, and in the paradisaical visions of the Christian Bible's final book it represents everlasting life of "saints" who have physically died.[32] Darwin explained his terrestrial figure in this way:

The limbs divided into great branches, and these into lesser and lesser branches, . . . may well represent the classification of all extinct and living species. . . . From the first growth of the tree, many a limb and branch has decayed and dropped off; and these . . . are known to us only in a fossil state. . . . As buds give rise by growth to fresh buds, and these, if vigorous, branch out and overtop all sides many a feebler branch, so by generation I believe it has been with the great Tree of Life, which fills with its dead and broken branches the crust of the earth, and covers the surface with the everbranching and beautiful ramifications.[33]

The trunkless plant that Darwin sketched was like a large bush with numerous branches attaining the same height, and was not like a pyramidal tree with Homo sapiens at the apex. Progressive development is not apparent, and no main branch stands out as the predetermined goal of evolution. The unlabeled branches include humans along with cousins they find embarrassing: for example, crabgrass, insects, reptiles, and apes. The diagram depicts more dead than live foliage, a reminder that each shoot is precarious. Elsewhere Darwin suggested: "The tree of life should perhaps be called the coral of life, base of branches dead; so that passages [that is, connecting links] cannot be seen.... The bottom of the tree of life is utterly rotten and obliterated in the course of ages."[34]

Darwin boldly theorized that every form, present and primordial, is the offspring of a common progenitor:

All animals and plants are descended from some one prototype....
All living things have much in common, in their chemical composition, their cellular structure, their laws of growth, and their liability to injurious influences.... Certain low forms are so far intermediate in character that naturalists have disputed to which kingdom they should be referred.[35]

Darwin dealt with the question of "whether species have been created at one or more points of the earth's surface" by "the agency of a miracle." He argued that land animals of the same species are not found naturally in places isolated by a wide sea and where migration is unlikely. He concluded: "[T]he view of each species having been produced in one area alone, and having subsequently migrated from that area ... is the most probable.... Land may at a former period have connected islands or possibly even continents together, and thus have allowed terrestrial productions to pass from one to the other."[36]

Species that resemble one another on different islands are descended from the same ancestor, Darwin argued, and after migration they became modified to enhance survival in the varied environments. To him, this was more plausible than the theory that each species was independently created. Whewell, typical of naturalists then, believed God created species in the garden of Eden that were essentially different from one another.[37] The species could never be basically changed, but could be subject to extinction by divine decree. But Darwin, a nominalist, contended that taxonomists deceive themselves in claiming that species have changeless classifications, because those categories are, to some extent, in the minds of the classifiers.

Taxonomists also erred, according to Darwin, in assigning the formation of species to a direct action of the Creator while attributing to natural law the formation of varieties. In support of this position, they claimed that varieties can be intercrossed but species are invariably sterile when mating is attempted. Relying in part on the research of William Herbert and others, Darwin showed that plant hybrids are sometimes fertile,[38] indicating that there is no God-given rigid distinction between species and varieties and that it is reasonable to think that all are indirectly created. Darwin held that species first emerged as varieties and should be thought of as "only well-marked varieties." Thus, neither species nor varieties are special creations that appeared when physical elements were "commanded suddenly to flash into living tissue."[39]

Contrary to the then-popular opinion, Darwin hypothesized that species have indeterminate boundaries and are not absolutely distinct. The hypothesis is based on the fact that no offspring is exactly like its parent and that the variations are inherited. In time, the accumulated incremental variations favorable to the environment cause increasing divergence; eventually, the degree of difference is large enough to be labeled a new species. Thus, Darwin removed the rigid differentiation between species and variations, treating the former as long-continued variations.

Darwin viewed the embryo as a microcosm of an individual's evolutionary history. He could also, by his theory, sensibly explain vestigial body parts that are no longer useful:

> On the view of each organism with all its separate parts having been specially created, how utterly inexplicable is it that organs bearing the plain stamp of inutility, such as the teeth in the embryonic calf [that will never cut through the gums] or the shrivelled wings under the soldered wing-covers of many [non-flying] beetles, should so frequently occur. Nature may be said to have taken pains to reveal her scheme . . . but we are too blind to understand her meaning."[40]

In the *Origin*'s chapter on variations, Darwin discussed the zebra-like strips on mule hybrids:

He who believes that each equine species was independently created, will, I presume, assert that each species has been created with
a tendency to vary, both under nature and under domestication, in
this particular manner, so as often to become striped like the other
species of the genus; and that each has been created with a strong
tendency, when crossed with species inhabiting distant quarters of
the world, to produce hybrids resembling in their stripes, not their
own parents, but other species of the genus. To admit this view is,
as it seems to me, to reject a real for an unreal, or at least for an
unknown, cause. It makes the works of God a mere mockery and
deception; I would almost as soon believe, with the old and ignorant cosmogonists, that fossil shells had never lived, but had been
created in stone so as to mock the shells living on the seashore.[41]

Here Darwin expressed his disgust with those who start with theological presuppositions and fabricate an explanation for observations that
will reinforce their doctrine, rather than start with the empirical facts
and hypothesize a reason that can be experimentally tested. Moreover,
he thought it was disingenuous to assume that God, by sleight of hand,
created a world that only appeared to have evolved. Darwin could not
believe that God misleads those engaged in honest scientific pursuits.

Demonstrating that the earth rotates on its axis and around the sun,
Copernicus had shown that a psalmist was not speaking literally when
s/he stated: "[T]he earth can never be moved."[42] Darwin recognized that
there had been a virtual universal rejection of the heliocentric theory
because it violated both biblical and commonsense assumptions. But
even though it was more satisfying to ordinary people's intellect and
pride to presume that the sun circles around the land where they live,
eventually it was painfully recognized that God did not create a geo-
centric or androcentric universe. As earthlings gain more understanding and modesty, they learn that the Creator made a mobile earth—no
matter what the Bible states. Scientists have learned, Darwin asserted,
that the dictum "vox populi, vox Dei" cannot be trusted.[43]

Turning to current views on natural theology in his own culture,
Darwin dealt with the person "who believes that each being has been
created as we now see it . . . in separate and innumerable acts of . . . the
Creator." One alleged act was carefully examined, the special creation of
the eye, because Paley had used that organ to show the defect of evolutionary theory. Paley asserted:

There is another [wrong] answer, which has the same effect as the
resolving of things into chance; which answer would persuade us to

believe that the eye, the animal to which it belongs, . . . are only so many out of the possible varieties and combinations of being, which the lapse of infinite ages has brought into existence; that the present world is the relic of that variety; millions of other bodily forms and other species having perished, being by the defect of their constitution incapable of preservation, or of continuance by generation.[44]

The eye structure was Paley's exhibit A for proving special Providence. He had described the incredible intricacy of its parts: the iris, cornea, rods, cones, retina, and optic nerve. Then he argued that just as the presence of a telescope impels rational persons to be convinced that it could not exist without the involvement of an intelligent designer, so the structure of the natural eye, by the same logic, impels them to accept the existence of a designer of nature. Darwin questioned: "May not this inference be presumptuous? Have we any right to assume that the Creator works by intellectual powers like those of man? . . . May we not believe that a living optical instrument might thus be formed as superior to one of glass, as the works of the Creator are to those of man?"[45]

Darwin suggested that God's method is too sophisticated for comparison with the relatively simplistic way a human works in a short period of time to make a final product. He criticized the naïve identification of current theology with the order established by the Creator, and the assumption that God lacks the ability to construct the eye in a more complex manner than a telescope engineer might operate. Responding to those who found unbelievable the notion that there had been a series of transitional forms of the eye, he theorized that the eye has slowly developed over "millions of years," beginning with a spot of light-sensitive tissue that proved to have survival advantage. Modifications of that nerve continued through environmental interactions until an animal eye was formed that provides a distinct image.

Darwin observed: "[T]he belief that species were immutable productions was almost unavoidable as long as the history of the world was thought to be of short duration."[46] He realized that his theory was dependent on the multiplication by a large factor of the traditional date for the earth's origin. Darwin even found overly restricting to his theory the calculation by Lord Kelvin (William Thomson) that the sun was not old enough to have a planet more than a 100 million years in age.[47] That leading physicist of the Victorian era dismissed Darwin's theory because he believed the earth's history was not long enough to allow for the evolutionary process. Based on geological erosion, Darwin extrapolated that the earth was several times older than Kelvin's figure, but another century was to pass before scientists discovered through radioactive decay that the age of the earth was ten times older than even Darwin had estimated.

According to Darwin, some naturalists believe "that many structures have been created for the sake of beauty, to delight man or the Creator (but this latter point is beyond the scope of scientific discussion), or for the sake of mere variety." By contrast, he shows that flowers are conspicuous in order to attract insects and effect fertilization. Also, "a ripe strawberry or cherry is as pleasing to the [human] eye as to the palate . . . but this beauty serves merely as a guide to birds and beasts, in order that the fruit may be devoured and the matured seeds disseminated."[48]

Darwin found that seeking pleasure is a greater motivating force for animals than fleeing pain, resulting in more happiness than suffering among organisms.[49] His sanguine outlook that nature, on balance, has a smiley face in spite of the cruelties of evolution is in accord with Paley's view that ultimately ours is "a happy world." The works of both men contain overtones of a power working to improve the general good of creation. The sentiment accounts for the only explicit reference to Paley in the *Origin*: "Natural selection will never produce in a being any structure more injurious than beneficial to that being, for natural selection acts solely by and for the good of each. No organ will be formed, as Paley has remarked, for the purpose of causing pain or for doing an injury to its possessor."[50]

The similarity between the natural theology of Bacon and that of Darwin can be detected in the penultimate paragraph of the *Origin*. Since God, the primary cause, does not interfere with nature but works through secondary causes, there should be no conflict between science and religion. Natural selection can be integrated with the doctrine that the existence and preservation of all organisms is ultimately due to the will of God. Darwin harmonizes God, the final goal as well as the primary cause, with evolutionary causation:

> To my mind it accords better with what we know of the laws impressed on matter by the Creator, that the production and extinction of the past and present inhabitants of the world should have been due to secondary causes, like those determining the birth and death of the individual. When I view all beings not as special creations, but as the lineal descendants of some few beings which lived long before the first bed of the Cambrian system was deposited [several hundred million years ago], they seem to me to

become ennobled. . . . We may feel certain that the ordinary succession by generation has never once been broken, and that no cataclysm has desolated the whole world. Hence we may look with some confidence to a secure future of great length. And as natural selection works solely by and for the good of each being, all corporeal and mental endowments will tend to progress towards perfection.[51]

"Progress towards perfection" does not follow from Darwin's theory; it appears to be a residue of his religious hope. In the New Testament, Christians are encouraged to "go on unto perfection."[52] A vestige of Paley's *Natural Theology* is displayed here; Paley stated that "perfection" was the Creator's intention in making structures such as the eye.[53] The epoch-making *Origin* ends with an affirmation that evolutionary law was impressed by God upon nature to cause the production and extinction of species. Darwin's perspective on that operation does not single out humans as "the most exalted" of creatures:

It is interesting . . . to reflect that these elaborately constructed forms, so different from each other, and dependent upon each other in so complex a manner, have all been produced by laws acting around us. These laws, taken in the largest sense, are Growth and Reproduction; Inheritance which is almost implied by reproduction; Variability from the indirect and direct action of the conditions of life and from use and disuse; a Ratio of Increase so high as to lead to a Struggle for Life, and as a consequence to Natural Selection, entailing Divergence of Character and the Extinction of less-improved forms. Thus, from the war of nature, from famine and death, the most exalted object which we are capable of conceiving, namely, the production of the higher animals, directly follows. There is grandeur in this view of life, with its several powers, having been originally breathed by the Creator into a few forms or into one; and that, whilst this planet has gone cycling on according to the fixed law of gravity, from so simple a beginning endless forms most beautiful and most wonderful have been, and are being evolved.

That concluding sentence of the *Origin* comes virtually unchanged from Darwin's 1842 sketch of his theory. Especially noticeable in it is the breath metaphor that his readers would associate with the Eden creation story of God breathing life into Adam's nostrils. Thus, Darwin attempted to square his conclusion with the mythic account of divine inspiration. Reference here to "the Creator" is in accord with the rest of the *Origin*, where "Creator" and its cognates are used dozens of times.

Although Darwin did not make explicit that the human species must also be included among the organisms descended from a few primordial forms, the implication was obvious for anyone using unclouded logic.

When Darwin wrote about "creation" in the *Origin*, he was adopting the commonplace term of naturalists at that time. In 1855, Baden Powell stated: "The term 'creation' indeed, especially as respects new species, seems now, by common consent, to be adopted among geologists as a mere *term of convenience*, to signify simply the fact of origination of a particular form of animal or vegetable life, without implying anything as to the *precise mode* of such origination."[54] Darwin explained in 1859 that the *Origin* "is not more *un*-orthodox than the subject makes inevitable. . . . I do not discuss the origin of man. . . . I do not bring in any discussion about Genesis, etc."[55] Probing the origin of *life* was not germane because he was investigating the common ancestor of species. He was not trying to write a new genesis book; rather, he was accounting for changes that had occurred among observable organisms during the course of history. He insisted that scientific explanation should not use theology to explain natural processes. His concern was with the ongoing organic world, leaving open the question of ultimate origins. Just as one can function as a physicist while recognizing that the origin of energy is inscrutable, so one can be a biologist without understanding the origin of life.

In the conclusion of the *Origin*, beginning with the third edition, Darwin tried to impress on readers that there is "no good reason why the views given in this volume should shock the religious feelings of any one." In comparing reactions to his law of evolution with Newton's law of gravity, "the greatest discovery ever made by man," Darwin pointed out that Gottfried Leibnitz, the famous German philosopher, had attacked the gravitational law "as subversive of natural, and inferentially of revealed, religion."[56] Darwin contrasted Leibnitz's reactionary judgment with the wisdom of "a celebrated author and divine." That person had written Darwin that he had "gradually learned to see that it is just as noble a conception of Deity to believe that he created primal forms capable of self-development into all forms needful pro-tempore and pro-loco, as to believe that He required a fresh act of intervention to supply the lacunas which he himself had made. I question whether the former be not the loftier thought."[57] With some editing—substituting "creation" for "intervention," and "voids" for "lacunas"—this quotation was included in all later editions of the *Origin*.[58]

Darwin privately disclosed that Rev. Charles Kingsley, to whom he had sent a complimentary copy of the *Origin*, was the first person to endorse his theory with enthusiasm, and that he was the "divine" who had been quoted.[59] Kingsley had studied at Cambridge a few years after Darwin and, like so many other ministers then, had integrated a study of nature with his vocation as parson. Darwin quoted his findings on the habits of a certain fish in one of his writings.[60] Kingsley's 1863 acclaimed novel, *The Water Babies*, depicts Mother Nature sitting placidly while creation is evolving on its own. He asserted: "We knew of old that God was so wise that He could make all things: but, behold, He is so much wiser than even that, that He can make all things make themselves."[61] Kingsley not only accepted new scientific ideas but also was receptive to the new literary criticism of the Bible.

Kingsley had written Darwin that the *Origin* "would improve instead of injuring natural theology," to which Darwin replied that "he certainly had not meant to do any harm."[62] Darwin wrote anatomist Thomas Huxley that he found "sound sense" in Kingsley's natural theology. Although Huxley was generally anticlerical, he got to know Kingsley personally and praised him as "an excellent Darwinian."[63]

Darwin was pleased to find support at this crucial time for the theological view he had expressed two decades earlier: "How far grander than idea from cramped imagination that God created [by direct intervention] . . . a long succession of vile molluscous animals. How beneath the dignity of him who is supposed to have said let there be light and there was light."[64] Darwin was of the opinion that those who accepted a doctrine of special creation and the immutability of species did not recognize the greatness of God. In the *Origin* he faulted the way they hide their ignorance under such phrases as "plan of creation," and then he went on to suggest what truly might be described as such.[65] Rather than serving as the "Devil's Chaplain," Darwin now viewed himself as increasing the grandeur of Earth's Creator.

THEISM AFFIRMED

Many years after the *Origin* was published, Darwin described his theological stance when he was writing the treatise:

Another source of conviction in the existence of God, connected with the reason and not with the feelings, . . . follows from the extreme difficulty or rather impossibility of conceiving this immense and wonderful universe, including man with his capacity for looking far backwards and far into futurity, as the result of blind chance or necessity. When thus reflecting I feel compelled to look to a First Cause having an intelligent mind in some degree analogous to that of man; and I deserve to be called a Theist. This conclusion was strong in my mind about the time, as far as I can remember, when I wrote the *Origin of Species*; and it is since that time that it has very gradually with many fluctuations become weaker.[66]

In 1878 Darwin recalled that when he was gathering data for the *Origin* his faith in "a personal God" was "firm." He also commented that he had never troubled himself with the insoluble question of the eternity of matter.[67]

According to the *Oxford English Dictionary*, "theism" was first used in the seventeenth century to refer to belief in a god while recognizing the existence of other gods (henotheism) or to belief in the only God (monotheism), in contrast to atheism or polytheism. In the eighteenth century, theism was used interchangeably with deism, the belief in a supreme Being while rejecting supernatural miracles. For its nineteenth-century meaning, the *Dictionary* quotes from an 1877 monograph: "Theism is the doctrine that the universe owes its existence and continuance . . . to the reason and will of a self-existent Being."[68]

In contrast to a deist who accepts God as a remote creator, someone who was called a theist in Darwin's day believed that God also continually sustains the world in a non-miraculous manner. In Thomas Carlyle's words, a deist believes in "an absentee God, sitting idle, ever since the first Sabbath, at the outside of His Universe and *see*ing it go." Darwin appreciated the emphasis of his friend Carlyle on the spirit of God pervading nature, inspiring an awareness that "through every star, through every grass-blade, and most, through every Living Soul, the glory of a present God still beams."[69] That quotation is from *Sartor Resartus*, a book that Darwin evaluated as "excellent."[70] Carlyle treated the whole of nature as sacred, and he looked askance at alleged miraculous interventions as a verification of revelation.

Further clarification can be given to Darwin's theological outlook when he wrote the *Origin* by examining an essay by John Stuart Mill entitled "Theism." Mill, a London acquaintance, was then the most outstanding English philosopher, and Darwin respected his viewpoints.[71] Continuing in the natural theology tradition, Mill singled out the argument from design for God's existence as the only plausible one; he thought it gave a high probability, although it falls short of providing strict proof. Mill argued that the universe operates with invariable laws, and he found Darwin's theory of natural selection "in no way whatever inconsistent with Creation." Mill's deity has immense but not infinite power, and desires good for the creation.[72] Since Mill stressed individual liberty, he thought it would be unreal if a God of unlimited power were in control of the world. If Darwin had joined Mill in thinking of God as steadfast love at the expense of curtailing omnipotence, he would probably have remained a firm theist.

When he writes about the *Origin*, Peter Bowler, an eminent Darwin interpreter, adds details about Darwin's religious outlook:

> Everything worked in accordance with natural law, but the laws themselves had been instituted for a purpose by a wise God who chose to achieve His ends indirectly rather than by the exercise of supernatural power. Natural selection explained the existence of suffering in the world: it was necessary because only by this means could species adapt to an ever-changing environment. Darwin also hoped that, in the long run, natural selection would tend to improve species by making them more adaptable and more intelligent. There might be no "main line" of evolution aimed at a single goal, but there was a general pressure tending to improve the level of organization in most branches of the tree of life. The conclusion of the *Origin of Species* stressed the view that there might be a long-range purpose built into evolution, and thus encouraged the book's readers to see the theory as an extension of traditional religious values.[73]

Notes

1. Asa Gray, *Darwiniana* (Cambridge: Harvard University Press, 1965), 5.
2. *Correspondence*, 6:493.
3. Ibid., 6:432.
4. Henry Tristram, untitled article in *The Ibis* (1859), 1:429, 433.
5. *Autobiography*, 122.
6. *Correspondence*, 7:398. His reference was to the opening words of a Latin hymn that was based on Luke's nativity story of Jesus. Aged Simeon, satisfied to see the Christ on whom he rested his hopes for Israel's fulfillment, said, "Lord, now lettest thou thy servant depart in peace" (Luke 2:29).
7. *Autobiography*, 133.
8. John Durant, ed., *Darwinism and Divinity* (New York: Blackwell, 1985), 16.
9. *Autobiography*, 66.
10. Edward Manier, *The Young Darwin and His Cultural Circle* (Dordrecht: Reidel, 1978), 20, 51–55.
11. William Whewell, *Astronomy and General Physics* (London: Pickering, 1833), 28.

12. *Notebooks*, 347.

13. *Autobiography*, 119.

14. *Correspondence*, 9:273.

15. David Kohn, ed., *The Darwinian Heritage* (Princeton: Princeton University Press, 1985), 474–75.

16. Peter Roget, *Animal and Vegetable Physiology* (London: Pickering, 1840), 1:11.

17. Erasmus Darwin, *Zoonomia, Or the Laws of Organic Life* (Philadelphia: Earle, 1818), 1:437.

18. *Origin*, 1.

19. *Autobiography*, 49.

20. *Origin*, 3.

21. Loren Eisley, *Darwin's Century* (New York; Doubleday, 1961), 236, 193.

22. Walter Cannon, ed., "Two Letters from John Herschel to Charles Lyell, 1836–37," *Proceedings of the American Philosophical Society* 105 (1961): 305.

23. *Origin*, 6–7.

24. Ibid., 37, 39.

25. Genesis 1:28; *Origin*, 135.

26. John Greene, *The Death of Adam* (Ames: Iowa State University Press, 1959), 304.

27. Durant, *Darwinism*, 50.

28. Charles Darwin and Alfred Wallace, *Evolution by Natural Selection* (Cambridge: Cambridge University Press, 1958), 45.

29. *Correspondence*, 8:397.

30. *Origin*, 40.

31. Ibid., 32, 42.

32. Genesis 3:22; Revelation 2:7; 22:14.

33. *Origin*, 64.

34. *Notebooks*, 177, 285.

35. *Origin*, 241.

36. Ibid., 183, 165.

37. William Whewell, *The Philosophy of the Inductive Sciences* (London: Parker, 1840), 1:476.

38. *Origin*, 137–39.

39. Ibid., 236, 240.

40. Ibid., 239.

41. Ibid., 78.

42. Psalm 104:5.

43. *Origin*, 85.

44. William Paley, *Works* (Philadelphia: Crissy, 1857), 399.

45. *Origin*, 87.

46. Ibid., 239.

47. Ibid., 164.

48. Ibid., 94–95.

49. *Autobiography*, 89–90.

50. *Origin*, 96; Paley, *Works*, 471.

51. *Origin*, 243.

52. Hebrews 6:1.

53. Paley, *Works*, 398.

54. Baden Powell, *Essays on the Spirit of the Inductive Philosophy, the Unity of Worlds, and the Philosophy of Creation* (London: Longsman, 1855), 399.

55. *Correspondence*, 7:270.

56. *Origin*, 239.

57. *Correspondence*, 7:380.

58. *Origin*, 239.

59. *Correspondence*, 8:444. Kingsley had been selected as a chaplain to Queen Victoria because his orthodoxy as an Anglican priest was sound (Colin Russell, *Cross-Currents* [Grand Rapids: Eerdmans, 1985], 166–67). Professing to live by the theme of Jesus' teaching in Luke 4:18, he recognized that "the business for which God sends a Christian priest to a Christian nation is to preach liberty, equality, and brotherhood" (Quoted in Una Pope-Hennessy, *Canon Charles Kingsley* [New York: Macmillan, 1949], 106).

60. *Descent*, 444.

61. *Correspondence*, 10:633–35.

62. Quoted in Hunter DuPree, *Asa Gray* (Cambridge: Harvard University Press, 1959), 359.

63. Quoted in Adrian Desmond, *Huxley* (Reading: Addison-Wesley, 1997), 488.

64. *Notebooks*, 343.

65. *Origin*, 240–43.

66. *Autobiography*, 92–93.

67. LLD, 2:412.

68. Robert Flint, *Theism* (Edinburgh: Blackwood, 1877), 18.

69. Thomas Carlyle, *Sartor Resartus* (1834): 2:7; 3:8.

70. *Correspondence*, 4:462.

71. *Descent*, 304, 316, 566.

72. John Stuart Mill, *Theism* (New York: Liberal Arts Press, 1957), 27–38, 77.

73. Peter Bowler, *Darwinism* (New York: Twayne, 1993), 41.

CHAPTER FIVE

Religious Controversies over Natural Selection

IN BRITAIN

In the month that the *Origin* was published, Darwin braced himself for the wrath to come. Worried about being fired upon by the "heavy guns" of prominent naturalists, he stayed in his Downe trench while his book was publicly debated. In concluding a letter to Thomas Huxley, he anticipated the usual public reaction, "Farewell, my good and admirable agent for the promulgation of damnable heresies!"[1] Huxley was soon to exclaim, "My reflection, when I first made myself master of the central idea of the *Origin*, was, 'How extremely stupid not to have thought of that!'"[2] But he reported that others received the book quite differently: "Bigots denounce it with ignorant invective; old ladies of both sexes consider it a decidedly dangerous book."[3]

Darwin was distraught by the many nonanalytic reactions to the *Origin* in scientific as well as in theological journals. Although he had gained favorable attention as a scientist to this point, a reviewer in the conservative *Quarterly Review* now scorned him as a person who sought "to prop up his utterly rotten fabric of guess and speculation" with a theory that was "utterly dishonourable to science." George Dorsey comments on the British reaction to the *Origin*: "Darwin's immediate fate, like that of every apostle of light from Christ onward, was to be pilloried for blasphemy." In 1860, "not a scientific academy or society, not a college or university in the world, came forward to greet him."[4] Leo Henkin observes: "*The Origin of Species* came into the theological world like a plough into an ant-hill. Everywhere those rudely awakened from their old comfort and repose swarmed forth angry and confused."[5]

Harriet Martineau, a prolific writer who knew Darwin personally, responded to the *Origin* in an unusual manner. In 1860, she wrote to philosophically oriented Fanny Wedgwood that the monograph would have been improved if theological comments had been omitted:

I rather regret that C. D. went out of his way two or three times to speak of "the Creator" in the popular sense of the First Cause; and also *once* of the "final cause" of certain cuckoo affairs. . . . Those who would otherwise agree with him turn away because his view is "derived from," or "based on," "theology." . . . It seems to me that having carried us up to the earliest group of forms, or to the single primitive one, he and we have nothing to do with how those few forms, or that one, came there.[6]

The denouncer of natural selection who most annoyed Darwin was Richard Owen, England's leading comparative anatomist and the superintendent of natural history at the British Museum. Darwin found "extremely malignant" his review of the *Origin* that appeared in the prestigious *Edinburgh Review* in April 1860. Thinking that Darwin "restricts the Divine power," Owen attacked him on theological and other grounds.[7] Darwin claimed that he was not disturbed by the abuse he was receiving from churchmen, but was hurt by the harsh criticism of naturalists such as Owen who predicted that the *Origin* would be forgotten in ten years.[8] In the 1840s Darwin had admired Owen and had consulted with him on zoological matters, but after his attacks on the *Origin*, Darwin acknowledged that he had become a "bitter enemy," probably "out of jealousy at its success."[9]

Geologist Adam Sedgwick, who had been young Darwin's role model, wrote him shortly after the *Origin* was published:

I have read your book with more pain than pleasure. Parts of it I admired greatly; parts I laughed at till my sides were almost sore; other parts I read with absolute sorrow; because I think them utterly false and grievously mischievous. . . . I humbly accept God's revelation of himself both in His works and in His word; and do my best to act in conformity with that knowledge which He only can give me. . . . If you and I do all this we shall meet in heaven.[10]

At a meeting of the Cambridge Philosophical Society in May 1860, Sedgwick leveled this broadside against natural selection: "It is a system embracing all living nature, vegetable and animal; yet contradicting— point blank—the vast treasure of facts that the Author of Nature has, during the past two or three thousand years, revealed to our senses." Perverting the argument in the *Origin* for the evolution of whales from land animals, he wrote in a review: "Darwin seems to believe that a white bear, by being confined to the slops floating in the Polar basin, might be turned into a whale." Sedgwick categorically dismissed

Darwin's theory because he thought Darwin failed to attain the main purpose of science, which was to "teach us to see the finger of God in all things animate and inanimate."[11] Sedgwick had a good reason to reject Darwin's theory—if it triumphed, his own literalistic interpretation of the Genesis creation story would no longer be plausible and his prestige would be threatened.

Finding Sedgwick's savage criticism at the society meeting morally "revolting," John Henslow stepped in where Darwin feared to tread. His old advisor told of his defense after Sedgwick "cast a slur" on Darwin's hypothesis:

> I got up, as Sedgwick had alluded to me, and stuck up for Darwin as well as I could, refusing to allow that he was guided by any but truthful motives, and declaring that he himself believed he was exalting and not debasing our views of a Creator, in attributing to him a power of imposing laws on the Organic World by which to do his work, as effectually as his laws imposed on the inorganic had done it in the Mineral Kingdom.

Sedgwick retreated by lamely claiming that his main attack was upon "an Oxford Divine," Baden Powell, who had recently published that he "accepted all Darwin had suggested, and applied these suggestions . . . to his own views."[12]

Darwin most wanted to impress favorably Sir John Herschel, the elder statesman of physical science whom Darwin appealed to with high praise in the *Origin*'s introduction. But after sending him a copy, Darwin indirectly learned that he called the natural selection theory "the law of higgledy-pigglety." Darwin wrote Charles Lyell: "What this exactly means I do not know, but it is evidently very contemptuous. If true this is a great blow and discouragement."[13] Although Herschel had called for a natural law pertaining to the origin of species as early as 1836, he nevertheless posited divine intervention for directing the course of evolution. He asserted, "An intelligence, guided by a purpose, must be continually in action to bias the direction of the steps of change—to regulate their amount—to limit their divergence—and to continue them in a definite course."[14] Responding to that position, Darwin wrote:

> One cannot look at this Universe with all living productions and man without believing that all has been intelligently designed; yet when I look to each individual organism, I can see no evidence of this. For, I am not prepared to admit that God designed the feathers

in the tail of the rock-pigeon to vary in a highly peculiar manner in order that man might select such variations and make a Fan-tail. . . . I cannot see design in the variations of structure in animals in a state of nature,—those which were useful to the animal being preserved and those useless or injurious being destroyed.[15]

In 1860, Lyell published a note entitled "Natural Selection Deified" in which he referred to "Brahma," the Hindu name for the divine Creator. In response, Darwin expressed his continual concern about presuming God's direct role in natural selection. To make his point, he again used pigeons as his example, because he had performed experiments on his estate with those rapidly propagating fowls. One variety had a puffed-out crop, or craw, the result of breeding by fanciers, including himself, who selected features they deemed attractive for generation after generation. Darwin argued that since it was recognized that such artificial variations are not preordained by God, neither are variations pre-designed in natural species:

> I must say one more word about our quasi-theological controversy about natural Selection. . . . Do you consider that the successive variations in size of the crop of the Pouter Pigeon, which man has accumulated to please his caprice, have been due to "the creative and sustaining powers of Brahma"? In the sense that an omnipotent and omniscient Deity must order and know everything, this must be admitted; yet in honest truth I can hardly admit it. It seems preposterous that a maker of Universes should care about the crop of a Pigeon solely to please men's silly fancies. But if you agree with me in thinking such an interposition of the Deity uncalled for, I can see no reason whatever for believing in such interpositions in the case of natural beings, in which strange and admirable peculiarities have been naturally selected for the creature's own benefit. . . . For the life of me I cannot see any difficulty in Natural selection producing the most exquisite structure, *if such structure can be arrived at by gradation.*[16]

Later that year Darwin used a different approach for presenting to Lyell the same issue of species formation:

> No astronomer in showing how the movements of Planets are due to gravity, thinks it necessary to say that the law of gravity was designed that the planets should pursue the courses which they pursue. I cannot believe that there is a bit more interference by the

Creator in the construction of each species, than in the course of the planets. It is only owing to Paley and Co, as I believe, that this more special interference is thought necessary with living bodies.[17]

In writing Lyell in 1861, Darwin used the same analogy to make his case more strongly: "Astronomers do not state that God directs the course of each comet and planet. The view that each variation has been providentially arranged seems to me to make Natural Selection entirely superfluous, and indeed takes the whole case of the appearance of new species out of the range of science." Darwin was willing to accommodate Lyell's theology to this extent: "I do not wish to say that God did not foresee everything which would ensue. . . . It may be said that God foresaw how they [physical objects] would be made."[18]

In another letter to Lyell in 1861, Darwin commented on those who believe that each organic variation is ordained by God: "Of course it may be said that when you kick a stone, or when a leaf falls from a tree, that it was ordained before the foundations of the world were laid, exactly where that stone or leaf should lie. In this sense the subject has no interest for me."[19] Darwin resorted to making fun of Lyell's special Providence claim by asking:

> Honestly tell me . . . whether you believe that the [pug] shape of my nose (eheu) was "ordained and guided by an intelligent cause." . . . If you say that God *ordained* that at some time and place a dozen slight variations should arise, and that one of them alone should be preserved in the struggle for life and the other eleven should perish in the first, or few first, generations. . . . It comes to merely saying that everything that is, is ordained. . . . Why should you or I speak of variation as having been ordained and guided more than does an astronomer in discussing the fall of a meteoric stone. He would simply say that it was drawn to our earth by the attraction of gravity. . . . Would you have him say that its fall at some particular place and time was "ordained and guided without doubt by an intelligent cause on a preconceived and definite plan"? Would you not call this theological pedantry or display? I believe it is not pedantry [for most people] in the case of species, simply because their formation has hitherto been viewed as beyond law,—in fact this branch of science is still with most people under its theological phase of development.[20]

Darwin's patient but persistent discussions with Lyell eventually paid off. At a Royal Society dinner in 1864, he jettisoned his reluctance to apply evolution to humankind and testified to his natural selection conversion. Darwin regarded Lyell as the "Lord Chancellor" of science, whose judgment would carry much weigh in overcoming resistance to natural selection, so his verdict after several years of deliberation was highly satisfying. That same year the Copley Medal of the Royal Society, Britain's highest scientific honor, was bestowed on Darwin.

Surprisingly, the objections to Darwin's theory among scientists were mainly religious in nature. They thought it limited the role of God, and hence undermined both personal faith and the welfare of the church. Many of the scientists on the frontiers of discovery in nineteenth-century England were also priests in the Church of England, or at least had had theological training. They had spent their lives integrating the nature they observed with the theology they studied. But the idea that God attends separately to the creation of species loomed so large in their minds that they were unable to imagine the place of God in a much older and larger universe. From a psychological perspective, accepting a more modest place for humans in such a world was a conceptual leap too humiliating to take when first confronting the theory. Some of these scientists were also unable to accept the diminished personal status that refutation of their own published works would bring.

Darwin was pleased to find a few positive reviews of the *Origin*. He sent a letter of thanks to Frederick Hutton for his review in an 1861 issue of *The Geologist*.[21] Hutton had responded to Sedgwick's condemnation of Darwin's theory as "atheistical" by asking, "Why should it be thought irreligious to believe the Maker of all things in His *first* designs should have foreseen the necessity of future modifications to future altered conditions, and have provided accordingly in His *first type-plans* for their future illimitable adaptations to the . . . earth's ever-altering conditions?"[22]

Cambridge philosopher Henry Fawcett showed that the *Origin* posed no threat to religion. Fawcett's 1860 review of the book suggested that Darwin was performing a theological service in biology similar to what Isaac Newton rendered in astronomy when he enunciated his gravitational laws:

Newton's discovery is now found in numerous religious works as a favourite illustration of the wisdom of the Creator; and it is now considered that a hymn of praise is sung to God when we expound the simplicity of the Newtonian laws. The day will doubtless come when he who shall unfold, in all their full simplicity, the laws which regulate the organic world, will be held, as Newton is now, in grateful remembrance for the service he has done not only to science, but also to religion. . . . Those who, like Mr. Darwin, endeavour to explain the laws which regulate the succession of life, do not seek to detract one iota from the attributes of a Supreme Intelligence."[23]

Fawcett also reported to Darwin that John Stuart Mill, the authority on inductive logic, praised the book's argumentation. Mill had cited the *Origin* in his *System of Logic* as an "unimpeachable example of a legitimate hypothesis."[24] Darwin was elated with Mill's comment until Emma read it and frankly remarked, "Why you know nothing about Logic."[25]

Gertrude Himmelfarb notes in her treatment of the Darwinian revolution, "Curiously enough, the reviews [of the *Origin*] written by laymen and clerics . . . tended to be more tolerant and amiable than those of the professional scientists."[26] Among churchmen, Huxley admitted in an 1863 letter, "There has been far less virulence and much more just appreciation of the weight of scientific evidence than I expected."[27]

A landmark book entitled *Essays and Reviews* followed Darwin's publication of the *Origin* by several months. Basil Willey writes that those two powerful books "rocked the fabric of Christendom and sent believers scuttling for shelter."[28] The second explosion contained chapters by seven Anglican scholars, six of whom were influential priests, which revealed some freedom of thought within the Church of England. Essayist Baden Powell, a mathematician and scientist as well as a theologian, found Paley appalling and Darwin appealing. Contrary to Paley's contention, Powell maintained that arguing from miracles that supposedly suspend natural law makes it difficult for reasonable people to find Christianity credible. Powell boldly stated:

> Mr. Darwin's masterly volume on *The Origin of Species* by the law of "natural selection"—which now substantiates on undeniable grounds the very principle so long denounced by the first naturalists— *the origination of new species by natural causes*: a work which must soon bring about an entire evolution of opinion in favour of the grand principle of the self-evolving powers of nature.[29]

Darwin's treatment of the eye's evolution, probably the most controversial point for those believing in special Providence, especially impressed clergyman Powell,[30] one of the first British professionals to attach his name publicly to Darwin's theory.

Frederick Temple, headmaster of Rugby School, and the other avantgarde authors in *Essays and Reviews* gave much attention to "higher criticism," which referred to scrutinizing sacred texts by the historical and literary techniques used for analyzing other documents. It was no accident that major developments in biblical criticism occurred at the same time that geology and biology were being transformed. Those studying ancient documents were concerned with their age of origin and literary development over time, paralleling evolution investigations of scientists. Temple countered the prevailing view that the alleged written "Word of God" should be treated as completely unlike any other book, and he judged fearfulness of scientific findings to be "high treason against the faith." He asserted, "If geology proves to us that we must not interpret the first chapters of Genesis literally, . . . the results should still be welcome."[31]

Benjamin Jowett, recognized for his translation of Plato's dialogues, insisted in his essay that Christianity was not formed on the basis of a Bible presumed to be without error, and that it should be approached by the ordinary methods of classical scholarship.[32] Charles Goodwin frankly recognized that the two distinct Genesis creation accounts by different writers are "erroneous" in providing scientific knowledge of the earth's beginnings, and that "geologists of all religious creeds are agreed" that the earth is millions of years old. He criticized the misguided attempt of "theological geologists," especially William Buckland, to make the opening chapter of Genesis scientifically sophisticated by supposing that a cloud cover obscured the already created sun, moon, and stars until the fourth day, and that a "day" in that context meant an eon.[33]

The public reaction to those questioning the prevailing interpretation of the Bible was more vehement than the reaction to Darwin. The craving for an inerrant source of authority was deeply ingrained in Protestants, for most of them had substituted the claim of an infallible Bible for the Catholic claim of an infallible church. *Essays and Reviews*, which had phenomenal sales, was more controversial than the *Origin*, not because of what it said positively about Darwin's theory but because it disputed the literal truth of parts of the alleged writings of Moses. Bishop Samuel Wilberforce of Oxford viewed the "seven against Christ" as "putters forth of doctrines which seem at least to be altogether incompatible with the Bible and the Christian Faith," and insisted that they resign their positions as priests. With crocodile tears he expressed his "deepest sorrow" that among the infidels was one of Dr. Temple's high position.[34] A petition signed by 10,906 clergymen requested that *Essays and Reviews* be censured.[35] Those bibliolaters were fearful that the validity of all the Bible might be called into question if any part of it was admitted to be in error. In 1864, Wilberforce obtained from the Anglican hierarchy a formal reprimand of the "heretics," and two of them were ousted from their work.

Darwin defended the vilified essayists and contributed money to support the two priests who were dismissed from their positions. He was among the few signatories to this petition:

> We the undersigned have read with surprise and regret a letter in which the Archbishop of Canterbury and the other English Bishops have severely censured the volume of Articles entitled *Essays and Reviews*. Without committing ourselves to the conclusions arrived at in the various Essays, we wish to express our sense of the value which is to be attached to enquiries conducted in a spirit so earnest and reverential, and our belief that such enquiries must tend to elicit truth, and to foster a spirit of sound religion. Feeling as we do that the discoveries in science, and the general progress of thought, have necessitated some modifications of the views generally held on theological matters, we welcome these attempts to establish teaching on a firmer and broader foundation.[36]

Apart from some of the controversial essayists, other churchmen responded favorably to Darwin's theory. American Henry Adams, who lived in London during the 1860s, became aware of the many clergy involved in science. With some hyperbole, he asserted, "Every curate in England dabbled in geology and hunted for vestiges of Creation."[37] In 1860, Rev. Leonard Jenyns, a naturalist friend of Darwin from his student days at Cambridge, found much of Darwin's theory acceptable, although Jenyns doubted if the implications for human evolution could be harmonized with the claim in Genesis that humans were created independently of other animals and in the divine image.[38] Darwin responded: "[I]t is open to everyone to believe that man appeared by separate miracle, though I do not myself see the necessity or probability." He modestly added, "Your going some way with me gives me great confidence that I am not very wrong."[39] That same year Fenton Hort, a distinguished Cambridge biblical scholar, welcomed Darwin's "unanswerable" theory.[40] In addition, Rev. Frederick Maurice, professor of moral philosophy at Cambridge, believed that the truth Darwin discovered was "a revelation to man by God whether the discoverer accepted it in that sense or not." Maurice commended to his students "the spirit of Mr. Darwin's investigations as a lesson and a model for churchmen."[41]

Contrary to common assumptions, no church in Darwin's era officially rejected evolution and his adversaries tended to include more scientists than religious authorities. Priests were Darwin's defenders at the Cambridge meeting and at the British Association for the Advancement of Science (BAAS) that was to meet at Oxford. They generally had a propensity to be open to the new scientific ideas and, for the first quarter century after the BAAS was founded in 1831, forty Anglican priests had been among those presiding over its sessions.

On the opening day of the BAAS meeting in June 1860, Owen again denounced Darwin's theory and coached Wilberforce on how to do the same the next day. He was known as "Soapy Sam" to his detractors because of the smooth but slippery way he handled arguments. Accepting his nickname, Wilberforce unctuously explained: "[T]hough often in hot water, he always came out with clean hands."[42] Although the *Origin* does not directly address human evolution, he contended:

> The principle of natural selection . . . is absolutely incompatible not only with single expressions in the word of God on that subject . . . [but] with the whole representation of that moral and spiritual condition of man which is its proper subject-matter. Man's derived supremacy over the earth; man's power of articulate speech; man's gift of reason; man's free will and responsibility; man's fall and man's redemption; the incarnation of the Eternal Son; the indwelling of the Eternal Spirit,—all are equally and utterly irrec-oncilable with the degrading notion of the brute origin of him who was created in the image of God, and redeemed by the Eternal Son assuming to himself his nature.[43]

Wilberforce's reaction to Darwin was similar to that of Pope Paul V who, in 1616, had condemned the heliocentric theory of Copernicus as "false in theology, and heretical, because absolutely contrary to Holy Scripture."[44] The bishop claimed that Darwin had such credulity that "to him it is just as probable that Dr. Livingstone will find the next tribe of negroes with their heads growing under their arms." Wilberforce admitted that he had not read the *Origin*, and his paucity of understanding can be illustrated by this comment, "If transmutations were rapidly occurring . . . the favourable varieties of turnips are tending to become men."[45]

Being ill—and uninterested in polemics even when well—Darwin learned through his defenders about Wilberforce's diatribe at the BAAS meeting. On the speaker's platform was Henslow, with Wilberforce to his right and Huxley to his left. According to legendary accounts, while the eminent bishop was concluding his speech he turned and asked with his mellifluous voice if Huxley traced his descent from an ape through his grandfather or his grandmother. (Huxley must have found it ironic that Wilberforce belonged to the group of Anglican officials commonly known as "primates.") Some class haughtiness was contained in the bishop's question, because his father William was one of the most famous of British parliamentarians, whereas Huxley came from an undistinguished family. Sensing that Wilberforce's sarcasm was beyond what his audience deemed fair, Huxley gleefully uttered this stage whisper, "The Lord hath delivered him into mine hands," appropriating what an Israelite boy had said of a Philistine giant.[46] Encouraged by the quotation, biographers have compared the Oxford drama to the biblical story. Michael Ruse's treatment is the best:

> This was a David and Goliath encounter, for Huxley was young and vigorous, a morphologist and paleontologist and now professor at the London School of Mines—a worthy home but with virtually no status whatsoever—and Wilberforce was old and established and important and occupying one of the most distinguished of bishoprics—at Oxford, no less, the city of the most venerable and powerful university in the realm.[47]

In his counterattack, Huxley said something like this:

> A man has no reason to be ashamed of having an ape for his grandfather. If there were an ancestor whom I should feel shame in recalling it would rather be a *man*—a man of restless and versatile intellect—who, not content with an equivocal success in his own sphere of activity, plunges into scientific questions with which he has no real acquaintance, only to obscure them by an aimless rhetoric, and distract the attention of his hearers from the real point at issue by eloquent digressions and skilled appeals to religious prejudice.[48]

Surprisingly, the largely clerical audience applauded the debater who hit the Oxford giant in the forehead. The priests may have realized that the issue for Huxley was not religion versus evolution but scientific truth versus an out-of-date prelate. As long as Darwin lived, pugnacious Huxley continued to be his chief protagonist. Describing himself as "Darwin's bulldog," he alerted his gentle master to surrounding foes and sought valiantly to defend him from their attacks. Huxley announced at this time, "Extinguished theologians lie about the cradle of every science as the strangled snakes beside that of Hercules."[49] A year earlier he had written, "True science and true religion are twin-sisters, . . . and religion flourishes in exact proportion to the scientific depth and firmness of its basis."[50]

FitzRoy, now an admiral, was present for the Oxford meeting and he, along with other Tory aristocrats, found Darwin's theory shocking. They had been reared to judge a person by the station of their ancestors, so a simian pedigree was viewed as especially belittling no matter what an individual might accomplish. FitzRoy had been generally cordial to Darwin while at sea, but his subsequent religious conversion influenced him to support Wilberforce at the BAAS meeting. The admiral raised a large Bible over his head, pleading with the audience to accept divine rather than human ideas and "to reject with abhorrence the attempt to substitute human conjecture and human institutions for the explicit revelation which the Almighty has himself made."[51] FitzRoy then sent Darwin an article that attempted to justify the Genesis accounts as geologically sound. About this, Darwin wrote, "I am weary of all these various attempts to reconcile, what I believe to be irreconcilable."[52] Several years later FitzRoy committed suicide, possibly triggered by his angst over having once invited Darwin to accompany him to areas where his views on natural selection were conceived.

Frederick Temple, who was present for the Oxford debate, preached the next day to the BAAS delegates. As would be expected, his sermon was in marked contrast to Wilberforce's speech. Temple insisted that religion must change to find God's wisdom manifested "not in individual acts of will, but in a perfection of legislation . . . which shall have the effect of tender care, though it proceed by an invariable action." He concluded, "The more the Bible is studied [as it was meant to be studied as a spiritual guide], and the more nature is studied, the deeper will be found the harmony between them."[53] One congregant reported that Temple "espoused Darwin's ideas fully!"[54]

The anti-evolutionary goliath that Wilberforce represented was only stunned, not slain, by the Oxford contest. Shortly afterward he published anonymously in the *Quarterly Review*, a Tory journal, the same judgment on the *Origin* that he had loquaciously aired at the BAAS meeting. After reading it, Darwin graciously commented that the review "picks out with skill all the most conjectural parts, and brings forward well all the difficulties." Also he expressed his amusement to Huxley on the presumptuous way the sacerdotal reviler dealt with matters such as the geographical distribution and classification of species: "Is it not grand the way in which the Bishop asserts that all such facts are explained by ideas in God's mind?"[55] Darwin also shared with Asa Gray his reaction to Wilberforce's oratory: "It is uncommonly clever, not worth anything scientifically, but quizzes me in splendid style till I chuckled with laughter at myself."[56]

Unfortunately, Baden Powell died several weeks before the BAAS debate. Had he been present to respond on behalf of the clergy, how different the result might have been! Darwin had informed Powell that he had found his 1855 essay, "The Philosophy of Creation," of great interest. It claimed that new species were introduced in a regular, non-supernatural manner, and that the "Word of God" must bow before the "Works of God." Actually, Powell and Darwin rejected special creation at about the same time, although more than a decade would pass before Darwin would publicize his opinion. In 1845, Powell wrote that science "shows that as successive forms and species of organization from time to time disappeared, NEW *forms* and NEW *species* WERE PRODUCED to supply their places. . . . None of them were at once universal in extent and simultaneous in time."[57] Following Powell's suggestion, Darwin wrote a historical sketch for the third and subsequent editions of the *Origin*, in which he gave credit to predecessors who contributed to evolutionary theorizing, including Powell.[58] In an 1860 letter to him, Darwin clarified what was distinctive in his contribution to evolutionary theory: "No educated person, not even the most ignorant, could suppose that I meant to arrogate to myself the origination of the doctrine that species had not been independently created. The only novelty in my work is the attempt to explain *how* species became modified."[59]

The significance of Huxley's encounter with Wilberforce became exaggerated to the extent that the St. George of evolution was viewed as slaying the dragon of opposition composed primarily of benighted religious leaders. For example, Owen Chadwick writes, "This clash became the symbol of the entire Victorian conflict: empirical and instructed professor versus ignorant, rhetorical and obscurantist bishop."[60] The BAAS exchange wrongly suggests that the scientists of that time were generally accepting of Darwin's theory of evolution, while the theologians were the prime champions of the immutability of species. In 1872, the sixth and last edition of the *Origin* during Darwin's life was issued. There he commented, with exaggeration, about the response to the earliest editions: "I formerly spoke to very many naturalists on the subject of evolution, and never once met with any sympathetic agreement. . . . Authors of the highest eminence seem to be fully satisfied with the view that each species has been independently created." For them he raised these difficult questions:

Do they really believe that at innumerable periods in the earth's history certain elemental atoms have been commanded suddenly to flash into living tissues? Do they believe that at each supposed act of creation one individual or many were produced? Were all the infinitely numerous kinds of animals and plants created as eggs or seed, or as full grown?[61]

But Darwin was confident that rising naturalists would be free from the "load of prejudice" that had encumbered "experienced naturalists."

Several references to the Deity by Darwin during this period of his life seem to be more than a secular way of emphasizing gratitude, since they relate to traditional religious concerns for healing, brotherhood, truth, and suffering. To Joseph Hooker, who had become and would remain Darwin's confidante for the rest of his life, he wrote in 1858: "Thank God, you are one of the few men who dare speak the truth."[62] Later that year he again wrote him, "God bless you, my dear kind friend."[63] In 1862, Darwin commented to Hooker on Emma's scarlet fever: "My wife is almost well, thank God."[64] In 1860, Darwin concluded a long letter to botanist William Harvey with, "We must remain content to be as wide asunder as the poles; but without, thank God, any malice or other ill feeling."[65] That same year, in expressing condolence to Huxley after the death of his child, Darwin alluded first to his grief over a similar loss, and then wrote: "My wife and self deeply sympathise with Mrs. Huxley and yourself. Reflect that your poor little fellow cannot have had much suffering. God Bless you."[66]

Darwin's first book after the *Origin* was *On the Fertilisation of Orchids*. He wrote in its introduction, "This treatise affords me . . . an opportunity of attempting to show that the study of organic beings may be as interesting to an observer who is fully convinced that the structure of each is due to secondary laws, as to one who views every trifling detail of structure as the result of the direct interposition of the Creator." He succinctly stated his main idea: "When I think of my beloved orchids, with rudiments of five anthers, with one pistil converted into a rostellum, with all the cohesion of parts, it really seems to me incredibly monstrous to look at an orchid as created as we now see it. Every part reveals modification on modification."[67]

Kingsley acknowledged that Darwin's orchid study "had opened a new world to him, and made all that he saw around him . . . even more full of divine significance than before." In 1863 he wrote both Darwin and Maurice about how the theory of natural selection was strengthening his faith. To the latter he sounded this triumphant note, "Darwin is conquering everywhere, and rushing in like a flood, by the mere force of truth and fact. . . . [Darwinians] have got rid of an interfering God— a master-magician."[68] Kingsley's response to Darwin's description of the "beautiful contrivances" of orchids was similar to that of another Christian. On reading the orchid book, a writer in *The Literary Churchman* borrowed a psalmist's praise: "O Lord, how manifold are thy works! in wisdom hast thou made them all: the earth is full of thy riches. So is this great and wide sea, wherein are things creeping innumerable, both small and great beasts."[69]

In an 1866 letter, a Mrs. Boole asked if she was right in assuming that Darwin's theory was compatible with her belief that "God is a personal and Infinitely good Being" and that the "direct inspiration of the Spirit of God" can impel humans to act morally. Darwin replied that it is beyond the competence of scientists to answer such questions. Nevertheless, he did venture a comment that had bearing on her conception of God's goodness: "It has always appeared to me more satisfactory to look at the immense amount of pain and suffering in this world as the inevitable result of the natural sequence of events, *i.e.* general laws, rather than from the direct intervention of God, though I am aware this is not logical with reference to an omniscient Deity."[70]

Darwin was sorry that he had referred in the concluding sentence of the *Origin* to organisms having been "breathed" into by the Creator, because the inbreathing metaphor was associated with one origin of life theory. He confided to Hooker: "I have long regretted that I truckled to public opinion and used the Pentateuchal term of creation, by which I really meant 'appeared' by some wholly unknown process. It is mere rubbish thinking, at present, of origin of life; one might as well think of origin of matter."[71] Also, some seemed to interpret Darwin as believing that God breathed his last at the initial creation of animals and Adam before resting in heaven everlastingly.

At the time of the publication of the *Origin*, Louis Pasteur was performing experiments that would disprove an origin-of-life theory that had been advanced from the ancient Greeks onward. Darwin was impressed by the French scientist's proof that bacteria were not spontaneously generated from dirt.[72] However, he continued to be open-minded as to whether aboriginal forms of life could be generated from inorganic matter. Darwin made no public statements on the first production of living organisms, but in 1871 he privately speculated that they might have come about by lightning striking "some warm little pond, with all sorts of ammonia and phosphoric salts," resulting in an organic soup.[73] Darwin stated, "I expect that at some future time the principle of life will be rendered intelligible."[74]

Alfred, Lord Tennyson, who was born the same year as Darwin, had been disturbed by some ideas he found in Robert Chamber's *Vestiges*. Long before the *Origin* was published, he expressed his concern in these lines:

> [Man] trusted God was love indeed
> And love Creation's final law—
> Tho' Nature, red in tooth and claw
> With ravine, shriek'd against his creed—[75]

That harsh appraisal of evolution, contained in Tennyson's poem *In Memoriam*, has been widely quoted. When the poet laureate of England came to call on Darwin in 1868, he observed, "Your theory of evolution does not make against Christianity." Darwin replied, "No, certainly not."[76]

The immensely popular *In Memoriam* contained other lines that could well be applied to Darwin:

> There lives more faith in honest doubt,
> Believe me, than in half the creeds.[77]

If this outlook on faith is valid, then Darwin, who questioned established doctrine in the search for truth, had more faith than Bishop Wilberforce.

Darwin did not see why there should be an adversarial relationship between defenders of religion and science. He evaluated as "monstrous" a newspaper article that portrayed religion and science at fisticuffs, but he appreciated a response in another paper that argued that religion does not attack science.[78] He believed that it was counterproductive to fight for natural selection like an irreligious zealot, and frankly advised Ernst Haeckel, the German popularizer of Darwin's theory, "I do not at all like that you towards whom I feel so much friendship, should unnecessarily make enemies, and there is pain and vexation enough in the world without any more being caused."[79] Peaceful Darwin did not view the issues separating theology and science as a hostile "warfare," a metaphor that others frequently used.

While serving as BAAS president, Hooker declared, "Religion is your opinion on one set of subjects, science your opinion upon another set of subjects." Darwin agreed and stated that religion does not attack science, but he wondered if it would not be wise for scientists to skirt discussing religion.[80] William Irvine, an authority on naturalists of the

Victorian era, has commented on Darwin's preference to remain off-stage theologically:

> Darwin was quick to defend the integrity of his own principles but slow to follow the argument into theology. He was delighted to hear a clergyman [Kingsley] endorse the theism of his book [the *Origin*], but reluctant to do so himself. In an age when everyone talked religion, when atheists dogmatized as boldly as clergymen and agnostics wrote volumes about their ignorance, Darwin maintained for a lifetime a discreet and sensitive reticence.[81]

In serving science, Darwin was fully aware of the appropriate sphere of authentic religion. His father told him of the testimony he had received from an old lady "who suspected him of unorthodoxy," "Doctor, I know that sugar is sweet in my mouth, and I know that my Redeemer liveth." She was alluding to Job 19:25, a verse that a magnificent libretto in Handel's *Messiah* had taught Christians to inwardly sing. Charles Darwin recognized that such statements of personal religious experience were "unanswerable."[82] He did not presume that science can exclude Deity or should have any inherent hostility toward religion. He understood the domain of religion to be moral values and theological meaning.

IN AMERICA

Eager to find acceptance for the *Origin*, Darwin sent Asa Gray a copy upon its publication in November 1859. "I never learned so much from one book as I have from yours," Gray responded.[83] He pointed to some weak points, as Darwin had requested, but at that time expressed no criticism of the work's treatment of theological issues. Gray was an editor of the *American Journal of Science and Arts*, so he immediately published a positive review of the *Origin*. In addition, he gave it a more lengthy treatment, which was published in three *Atlantic Monthly* installments.

Since the first British reactions to the *Origin* had been mostly unfavorable, Darwin expressed his delight to Gray:

> I cannot resist expressing my sincere admiration of your most clear powers of reasoning. As Hooker lately said in a note to me, you are more than *anyone* else the thorough master of the subject. I declare that you know my Book as well as I do myself; and bring to the question new lines of illustration and argument in a manner which excites my astonishment and almost my *envy*!"[84]

In another letter to Gray, Darwin exclaimed: "By Jove, I will tell you what you are, a hybrid, a complex cross of Lawyer, Poet, Naturalist, and Theologian! Was there ever such a monster seen before? I have just looked through the passages which I have marked as appearing to me extra good, but I see that they are too numerous to specify."[85]

Darwin informed Gray that his reviews were "*far* the best Theistic essays" he had ever read.[86] Darwin was profoundly relieved to find a reputable scientist who believed there was no intrinsic incompatibility between his evolutionary theory and liberal religion. He hoped that the public would also realize that divine creation and natural selection need not be treated as opposing ways of explaining the natural world. Gray became the trusted American spokesperson for Darwin, and he paid to have Gray's reviews reprinted in pamphlet form for circulation in Britain, selecting "Natural Selection not Inconsistent with Natural Theology" as part of the title.

In his reviews, the American apostle of Darwin showed that "a theistic view of nature" is declared in the *Origin*. Gray pointed out that Darwin affirms that God is the primary cause of the universe and that natural law is "the human conception of continued and orderly divine action."[87] Since "natural science deals only with secondary or natural causes," Gray thought Darwin's focus was right. Gray recognized that the Genesis account of divine creativity does not exclude the idea of secondary causes, and he perceived that they were suggested by the declarations "the waters brought forth abundantly" and "the earth brought forth" both vegetation and living creatures.[88] Apparently the *Origin* convinced him that his previous categorical separation of species and variations was faulty, because he no longer assigned species to special Providence.[89]

Gray did not accept the view of some of his colleagues that "what science removes from the supernatural to the natural is lost to theism."[90] He thought of Darwin's formulation of evolutionary law in the life sciences as no more subversive to religion than Newton's earlier formulation of gravitational laws. Later, in a jocular way, he wrote Darwin that the University of Cambridge should honor him with a doctor of divinity degree for what he had written about ultimate causality.[91] Darwin's theism was distinguished both from pantheism, which identifies God with evolutionary force, and from atheism, which rejects Deity in every configuration. While admitting that some Darwinists were inclined toward atheism, Gray did not think that such an outcome was inherent in the natural selection hypothesis. He held that an Almighty

Creator has the power to produce a natural order that can reproduce slightly dissimilar organisms without successive supernatural interference. Gray explained why Darwin's science did not collide with theological considerations: "His hypothesis concerns the *order* and not the *cause*, the *how* and not the *why* of the phenomena."[92]

Although Darwin had earlier said that he rejected "revelation" as Paley had used the term, he may have had little difficulty with the way it was used by Gray:

> I take it that religion is based on the idea of a Divine Mind revealing himself to intelligent creatures for moral ends. We shall perhaps agree that the revelation on which our [Christian] religion is based is an example of evolution; that it has been developed by degrees and in stages, much of it in connection with second causes and human actions.... The knowledge of God's character and will which has descended from the fountainhead in the earlier ages has come down to us, through annalists and prophets and psalmists, in a mingled stream, more or less tinged or rendered turbid by the earthly channels through which it has worn its way.[93]

There is a similarity, Gray maintained, between learning the facts of life about one's own species and about all species. When a child is told his infant brother is "a gift of God," further inquiry is usually not stifled during maturation. Rather, this partial understanding stimulates investigation into the complex and delicate sexual way in which the precious gift was bestowed.[94] Gray was more forthright than the *Origin* in acknowledging that "Darwin's hypothesis strongly suggests the evolution of the human no less than the lower animal races out of some simple primordial animal." Gray suggested that it was due to false pride that humans find it difficult to acknowledge such ancestors in our family tree. Also, he recognized "the very first step backward [in natural history] makes the negro and the Hottentot our blood relations— not that reason or Scripture objects to that, though pride may."[95]

While Gray gave strong support to much of Darwin's theory, he retained a theological reservation. In 1860, Darwin wrote Yale geologist James Dana, "No one person understands my views and has defended them so well as A. Gray, though he does not by any means go all the way with me."[96] Darwin selected the main point of dispute from one of Gray's reviews of the *Origin*: "Asa Gray and some others look at each variation, or at least at each beneficial variation (which A. Gray would compare with the rain drops which do not fall on the sea, but on the land to fertilize it) as having been providentially designed."[97] Darwin wrote Gray, "I grieve to say that I cannot honestly go as far as you do about Design. . . . I cannot think that the world, as we see it, is the result of chance; and yet I cannot look at each separate thing as the result of Design."[98]

This argument over design continued for years between the biological geniuses of Britain and America. Darwin wrote of his quandary in 1861:

> What you say about our keeping in our intrenchments and firing long shots about Design has made me laugh. I suspect I am more cowardly than you, as I ought to be, as I do not feel sure of my ground. . . . I feel more inclined to show a white flag than to fire my usual long-range shot. . . . If anything is designed, certainly Man must be. . . . If I was to say I believed this, I should believe it in the same incredible manner as the orthodox believe the Trinity in Unity. You say you are in a haze; I am in thick mud; the orthodox would say in fetid, abominable mud. I believe I am in much the same frame of mind as an old Gorilla would be in if set to learn the first book of Euclid. . . . Yet I cannot keep out of the question.[99]

A year later Darwin tried another amusing figure of speech, "It is really almost a pleasure to receive stabs from so smooth, polished and sharp a dagger as your pen."[100]

Darwin recognized, of course, that *humans* have plans in mind and act to accomplish them, but he did not accept the analogy that God's design can be seen in the details of natural happenings. In 1860, he wrote Gray:

> An innocent and good man stands under tree and is killed by flash of lightning. Do you believe that God *designedly* killed this man? Many or most persons do believe this; I can't and don't. If you believe so, do you believe that when a swallow snaps up a gnat that God designed that that particular swallow should snap up that particular gnat at that particular instant? I believe that the man and the gnat are in the same predicament. If the death of neither man nor gnat are designed, I see no good reason to believe that their *first* birth or production should be necessarily designed. Yet . . . I cannot persuade myself that electricity acts, that the tree grows, that man aspires to loftiest conceptions all from blind, brute force.[101]

Pressing on with his moral problem of special Providence, Darwin repeatedly raised his concerns with Gray. If Deity is directly responsible for mutations, then this suggests that malevolence as well as benevolence is the will of God. For example, does the Creator specially cause some infants to have congenital deformities? Darwin could not believe that God is directly involved in particular situations, either hindering or aiding the innocent. He articulated his struggle in a letter to Gray, which contains, in the opinion of Stephen Gould, Harvard's acclaimed zoologist, "the finest comment ever written on the proper relation of science and religion."[102] In it Darwin said:

> With respect to the theological view of the question; this is always painful to me. I am bewildered. I had no intention to write atheistically. But I own that I cannot see as plainly as others do, and as I should wish to do, evidence of design and beneficence on all sides of us. There seems to me too much misery in the world. I cannot persuade myself that a beneficent and omnipotent God would have designedly created the Ichneumonidae [a parasite] with the express intention of their feeding within the living bodies of caterpillars, or that a cat should play with mice. Not believing this, I see no necessity in the belief that the eye was expressly designed. On the other hand, I cannot anyhow be contented to view this wonderful universe and especially the nature of man, and to conclude that everything is the result of brute force. I am inclined to look at everything as resulting from designed laws, with the details, whether good or bad, left to the working out of what we may call chance. . . . The lightning kills a man, whether a good one or a bad one, owing to the excessively complex action of natural laws,—a child (who may turn out an idiot) is born by the action of even more complex laws, and I can see no reason why a man, or other animals, may not have been aboriginally produced by other laws, and that all these laws may have been expressly designed by an omniscient Creator, who foresaw every future event and consequence.[103]

In 1867, Darwin decided to publish his position on the relation of the Creator to creation, giving this reason: "There have been so many allusions to what I think about the part which God has played in the formation of organic beings that I thought it shabby to evade the question."[104] Accordingly, in the conclusion of his next book, he criticized Gray's notion of God directing variations "along certain beneficial lines." Darwin could not accept Gray's codicil to his theory that God was responsible for favorable variations. To make his point he used an apt analogy of a mason who selects for his construction particular rocks from those that have fallen off a cliff:

The shape of the fragments of stone at the base of our precipice may be called accidental, but this is not strictly correct; for the shape of each depends on a long sequence of events, all obeying natural laws. . . . But in regard to the use to which the fragments may be put, their shape may be strictly said to be accidental. And here we are led to face a great difficulty, in alluding to which I am aware that I am travelling beyond my proper province. An omniscient Creator must have foreseen every consequence which results from the laws imposed by Him. But can it be reasonably maintained that the Creator intentionally ordered, if we use the words in any ordinary sense, that certain fragments of rock should assume certain shapes so that the builder might erect his edifice?[105]

Darwin could not believe that God foreordained that rocks should be released from the face of the cliff in various shapes—wedge formed for arches, elongated for lintels, and flat for roofing—for the purpose of aiding in house construction. In responding to Darwin on this theological issue, Gray admitted, "I found your stone-house argument unanswerable in substance."[106] Gray seems to have recognized theological as well as scientific problems in his beneficial design hypothesis, for would not God also be responsible for what humans regard as malevolent variations? He conceded to Darwin that his earlier conviction, that each variation had been ordained by benevolent Providence for a special end, was without merit. He eventually concluded, "The field which we took to be thickly sown with design seems, under the light of Darwinism, to yield only a crop of accidents."[107]

In addition to Gray's visits with Darwin, the colleagues exchanged several hundred letters over many years. Some of the letters touched on theological issues but most dealt with botanical matters. Gray exemplified not only for Darwin but also for the educated public the compatibility of religion and evolution. When Cambridge conferred upon Gray their highest scientific honors, the citation read: "How cheerfully, many years ago, among his own Western countrymen, was he the first of all to greet the rising sun of our own Darwin, believing his theory of the origin of various forms of life demanded some First Cause, and was in harmony with a faith in a Deity who has created and governs all things."[108] Philosopher John Dewey, in discussing the Darwinism of Asa Gray, stated, "Variation, struggle, and selection simply define the mechanism of 'secondary causes' through which the 'first cause' acts; and the doctrine of design is none the worse off because we know more of its *modus operandi*."[109]

While one Harvard naturalist was Darwin's chief advocate in America, another one was his main adversary. Zoology professor Louis Agassiz stated that species originate not by "laws in nature which were established by the Deity" but by "the immediate intervention of an intelligent Creator." His rather traditional religious outlook contributed to his being the most acclaimed American scientist of his day. Agassiz also declared: "[M]an is not only the last and highest among the living beings" but "is the last term in a series beyond which there is no material progress possible." That position was made known from the beginning, he affirmed: "The history of the earth proclaims its Creator. It tells us that the object and the term of creation is man. He is announced in nature from the first appearance of organized beings."[110] In pummeling Darwin's theory, he quipped, "The resources of the Deity cannot be so meagre that in order to create a human being endowed with reason, he must change a monkey into a man."[111] Agassiz's arrogant approach to data riled Darwin, who found him "confident that he reads Nature through and through, and without the least apparent misgiving that anything will turn up that he cannot explain away."[112] Ironically, Agassiz had a wide reputation for training students to glean inductively and to make generalizations only after patiently and thoroughly recording their observations.

Agassiz had adopted the metaphysical idealism of eighteenth-century British philosopher George Berkeley and fancied that the coming into existence or the perishing of a species was a function of God thinking or not thinking about it.[113] Two months after the *Origin* was published he asserted:

> What has the whale in the arctic regions to do with the lion or the tiger in the tropical Indies? There is no possible connection between them. . . . There is a design according to which they were built, which must have been conceived before they were called into existence. . . . We study the manner in which it has pleased the Creator to express his thought in living realities.[114]

Many North Americans, intellectuals and educated people generally, found the *Origin* provocative. A year after it began to circulate in the United States, a Methodist journal commented, "Perhaps no scientific work has ever been at once so extensively read, not only by the scientific few, but by the reading masses generally, and certainly no one has ever produced such commotion."[115] An unusual American response came from George Frederick Wright, a Calvinist theologian, who argued that to reject Darwin was to impugn God's veracity. Wright had been much influenced by Gray's treatment of natural selection and urged the botanist to publish more that pertained to theology. Darwin informed Wright that he was pleased to learn of his position. James Moore states: "Wright maintained that Darwin's work actually allies itself with the Reformed faith in discouraging romantic, sentimental, and optimistic interpretations of nature. Far from threatening orthodox beliefs, Darwinism and those who represent it, he predicted, will likely lead Christians to an outlook 'eminently favorable to sound doctrine.'"[116]

A Swiss-American botanist of some note, Leo Lesquereux, published articles against the *Origin* but later accepted Darwin's theory for strange reasons. In 1865, Darwin wrote about him to Hooker: "How funny men's minds are! [H]e says he is chiefly converted because my books make the Birth of Christ, Redemption by Grace, etc., plain to him!"[117]

In his book on *Darwinism and the Divine in America,* historian Jon Roberts tells of the ambivalent response to Darwin's theory in the third quarter of the nineteenth century:

> Most American Protestant intellectuals could agree that the evolutionary hypothesis was irreconcilable with the prevailing formulations of numerous Christian doctrines. They differed radically among themselves, however, in the inferences they drew from this conclusion. Some insisted that it constituted sufficient grounds for rejecting the hypothesis. Others just as adamantly maintained that it made theological restatement imperative.[118]

Darwin was well protected from the enraged Bible bangers and other opponents because he was not dependent for his livelihood on employment or on approval by some authority. Without his ample inheritance, his controversial ideas might have resulted in his family being socially ostracized and living in poverty. Situated comfortably at Down House, and accepted by his fellow villagers, Darwin continued his research into other biological matters that related to evolution without disruption from adversaries.

Notes

1. *Correspondence*, 7:434.
2. LLD, 1:551.
3. Thomas Huxley, *Darwiniana* (New York: Appleton, 1896), 22–23.
4. George Dorsey, *The Evolution of Charles Darwin* (New York: Doubleday, 1927), 182–85.
5. Leo Henkin, *Darwinism and the English Novel* (New York: Russell, 1963), 62.

6. Elisabeth Arbuckle, ed., *Harriet Martineau's Letters to Fanny Wedgwood* (Stanford, Calif.: Stanford University Press, 1983), 189.

7. David Hull, *Darwin and His Critics* (Cambridge: Harvard University Press, 1973), 174, 191, 214.

8. *Correspondence*, 10:135.

9. *Autobiography*, 105.

10. *Correspondence*, 7:396–97.

11. Hull, *Darwin*, 166–69.

12. *Correspondence*, 8:200–201.

13. Ibid., 7:423.

14. John Herschel, *Physical Geography* (Edinburgh: Black, 1861), 12.

15. *Correspondence*, 9:135.

16. Ibid., 8:161.

17. Ibid., 8:258.

18. Ibid., 9:226.

19. Ibid., 9:235.

20. Ibid., 9:238.

21. Ibid., 9:96.

22. Hull, *Darwin*, 295.

23. Ibid., 280, 283.

24. *Correspondence*, 9:204–5.

25. Ibid., 9:214.

26. Gertrude Himmelfarb, *Darwin and the Darwinian Revolution* (London: Chatto, 1959), 232.

27. Quoted in Charles Raven, *Science, Religion, and the Future* (London: Cambridge University Press, 1943), 47.

28. Basil Willey, *Darwin and Butler* (London: Chatto, 1960), 9.

29. *Essays and Reviews* (London: Parker, 1860), 139.

30. *Correspondence*, 8:88.

31. *Essays and Reviews*, 47.

32. Ibid., 338.

33. Ibid., 210–48.

34. *Quarterly Review* (January 1861): 248–50.

35. John Brooke, *Science and Religion* (Cambridge: Cambridge University Press, 1991), 274.

36. *Correspondence*, 9:418–19.

37. Henry Adams, *The Education of Henry Adams: An Autobiography* (Boston: Houghton Mifflin, 1918), 225.

38. *Correspondence*, 8:14.

39. Ibid., 8:25.

40. Arthur Hort, *The Life and Letters of Fenton John Anthony Hort* (London: Macmillan, 1896), 1:414.

41. Frederick Maurice, ed., *The Life of Frederick Denison Maurice* (London: Macmillan, 1884), 2:452, 608.

42. *Dictionary of National Biography* (New York: Macmillan, 1900), 61:207.

43. *Quarterly Review* (7 July 1860): 258.

44. Quoted in Andrew White, *A History of the Warfare of Science with Theology in Christendom* (New York: Appleton, 1898), 1:159.

45. *Quarterly Review*, 239.

46. 1 Samuel 17:46.

47. Michael Ruse, *The Evolution War* (Santa Barbara: ABC-CLIO, 2000), 60.

48. Quoted in Leonard Huxley, ed., *Life and Letters of Thomas Henry Huxley* (London: Macmillan, 1900), 1:185.

49. Thomas Huxley, *Collected Essays* (London: Macmillan, 1893), 2:52.

50. Thomas Huxley, "Science and Religion," *Builder* 18 (1859): 35.

51. Quoted in Himmelfarb, *Darwin*, 239.

52. *Correspondence*, 9:138.

53. Frederick Temple, *The Present Relations of Science to Religion* (Oxford: Parker, 1960), 8, 17.

54. Quoted in Brooke, *Science*, 274.

55. *Correspondence*, 8:294.

56. Ibid., 8:299.

57. Baden Powell, "Creation," in *The Cyclopaedia of Biblical Literature* (Edinburgh, 1845).

58. *Correspondence*, 8:39–41; *Origin*, 5.

59. *Notes and Records of the Royal Society* (1959), 14:52.

60. Owen Chadwick, *The Victorian Church* (New York: Oxford University Press, 1970), 2:10.

61. *Origin*, 240, 243.

62. *Correspondence*, 7:102

63. Ibid., 7:121.

64. Ibid., 10:402.

65. Ibid., 8:374.

66. Ibid., 8:366.

67. Ibid., 9:302.

68. Fanny Kingsley, ed., *Charles Kingsley* (London: Macmillan, 1895), 252–53.

69. Psalm 104:24–25; LLD, 2:448.

70. LLD, 2:247.

71. *Correspondence*, 11:278.

72. Ibid., 10:141.

73. LLD, 2:203.

74. MLD, 1:273.

75. Alfred, Lord Tennyson, *In Memoriam* (1850), 56.4.

76. Hallam Tennyson, *Alfred Lord Tennyson* (London: Macmillan, 1905), 464.

77. Alfred, Lord Tennyson, *In Memoriam*, 96.3.

78. MLD, 1:309.

79. LLD, 2:251–52.

80. MLD, 1:309.

81. William Irvine, *Apes, Angels and Victorians* (New York: McGraw-Hill, 1955), 108.

82. *Autobiography*, 96.

83. Ibid., 8:48.

84. Ibid., 8:298.

85. Ibid., 8:350.

86. Ibid., 8:388.

87. Asa Gray, *Darwiniana* (Cambridge: Harvard University Press, 1965), 47.

88. Genesis 1:12, 21, 24.

89. Gray, *Darwiniana*, 106–7.

90. Asa Gray, *Natural Science and Religion* (New York: Scribner's, 1880), 77.

91. Jane Gray, ed., *Letters of Asa Gray* (Boston: Houghton, 1893), 2:478.

92. Gray, *Darwiniana*, 122.

93. Gray, *Natural Science and Religion*, 107.

94. Ibid., 79.

95. Gray, *Darwiniana*, 76.

96. *Correspondence*, 8:303.

97. Ibid., 9:200.

98. Ibid., 8:496.

99. Ibid., 9:302, 369.

100. Ibid., 10:117.

101. Ibid., 8:275.

102. Stephen Gould, *Rocks of Ages* (New York: Ballantine, 1999), 35.

103. *Correspondence*, 8:224.

104. LLD, 2:244–45.

105. Charles Darwin, *The Variation of Animals and Plants under Domestication* (London: Murray, 1868), 2:431.

106. Jane Gray, *Letters*, 2:562.

107. Gray, *Natural Science and Religion*, 85.

108. Jane Gray, *Letters*, 2:800–801.

109. John Dewey, *The Influence of Darwin on Philosophy* (New York: Holt, 1910), 12.

110. Louis Agassiz, *Essay on Classification* (Cambridge: Harvard University Press, 1962), 15, 28.

111. Louis Agassiz, *Methods of Study in Natural History* (Boston: Fields, 1870), iv.

112. *Correspondence*, 6:340.

113. Hull, *Darwin*, 445.

114. *Correspondence*, 8:55.

115. *Methodist Quarterly Review* (1861): 605.

116. James Moore, *The Post-Darwinian Controversies* (London: Cambridge University Press, 1979), 287–89, 292.

117. MLD, 1:260.

118. Jon Roberts, *Darwinism and the Divine in America* (Madison: University of Wisconsin Press, 1988), 87.

CHAPTER SIX
The Homo Sapiens Creation

THE ANIMALITY OF HUMANS

The conclusion of the *Origin* contains a sentence that is pregnant with implications for human culture, including religion. There Darwin predicted "light would be thrown on the origin of man and his history" by his natural selection theory. He hinted at human evolution in the *Origin* by asking, "In the case of mammals, were they created bearing the false marks of nourishment from the mother's womb?" The question was stimulated by the convoluted thesis of Philip Gosse's book entitled *Omphalos*. In order to test the faith of humans, Gosse argued, God deceptively created fossils to resemble animal skeletons and simulated natural birth in creating in the garden of Eden our full-grown first parents with navels. Also in the *Origin*, Darwin prophesied that "the day will come when this [special creation doctrine] will be given as a curious illustration of the blindness of preconceived opinion."[1]

Even though Darwin tried to avoid dealing directly with the issue of human evolution in the *Origin*, it was obvious to thinking readers that humans were, for him, a twig on the primate branch of his "tree of life." As early as 1840, Darwin had recognized a family connection between humans and apes. But he knew that if he published evidence of their similarities, the acceptance of his entire theory would be jeopardized. Accordingly, he waited to discuss its most controversial part until the animosity stimulated by the *Origin* had largely dissipated. By 1870 such had happened—at least among London intellectuals—as Henry Adams reported: "Evolution from lower to higher raged like an epidemic. Darwin was the greatest of prophets."[2] Now that there was considerable acceptance of evolution for nonhuman organisms, Darwin dealt straightforwardly with applying natural selection to humans.

In 1869, Alfred Wallace excluded the human brain from evolution, which did much to undermine the natural selection theory he had co-discovered. He believed that supernatural intervention was necessary for the mental, moral, and religious evolution of humans.[3] Darwin made him aware that they no longer shared a common theory by asserting, "I hope you have not murdered too completely your own and my child."⁴ His dismay over Wallace's scientific apostasy helped motivate him to end his silence on human evolution.

In 1871, Darwin published his second most important work, *The Descent of Man and Selection in Relation to Sex*. His use of "descent" in the title has reference to genealogical lineage rather than to humans being a lower manifestation of what had earlier been more lofty. This work, more than any other, eventually convinced most people of their kinship with all creation. But initially even Emma expressed apprehension over its theological implications. As her husband was writing the *Descent*, she said, "I think it will be very interesting, but that I shall dislike it very much as again putting God further off."⁵

In the *Descent*, Darwin aimed at documenting the continuity between humans and other animals. Clues to their numerous structural similarities can be clearly seen by embryonic comparisons. He showed figures of human and dog embryos that "at a very early period can hardly be distinguished," especially since both have tails (257). As people become aware of the parallels among species in anatomy and in embryonic development, Darwin forecasted, they will be amazed "that naturalists, who were well acquainted with the comparative structure and development of man, as well as other mammals, should have believed that each was the work of a separate act of creation" (265). Moreover, he pointed out that humans are related much more widely than merely to other mammals: "The five great vertebrate classes, namely, mammals, birds, reptiles, amphibians, and fishes, are descended from some one prototype, for they have much in common, especially during their embryonic state" (337).

To firmly establish the animality of humans, Darwin culled data from a variety of sources. The susceptibility of humans and other animals to certain common diseases "proves the close similarity of their tissues and blood" (256). Also, humans are not exempt from what Malthus had described as the plight of organic life: "Man tends to increase at a greater rate than his means of subsistence; consequently he is occasionally subjected to a severe struggle for existence, and natural selection will have effected whatever lies within its scope" (590). Darwin investigated human emotions to test anatomist Charles Bell's contention that humans are uniquely endowed with certain muscles for expressing emotions (254). To show that the emotional life of humans is not basically different from that of other animals, Darwin accumulated much evidence, which he decided to publish later in another book.

In the lengthiest section of the *Descent*, Darwin discussed what most Victorians found revolting, the way in which humans share animal sexuality. He was candid in pointing to similarities among the primates perched together in the tree of life. For example, he wrote: "Male monkeys, like men, are bolder and fiercer than the females. . . . We thus see how close is the parallelism between the sexual differences of man and the Quadrumana" (563), that is, species whose four feet are adapted for use as hands. Darwin noticed even trifling physical similarities: "The colour of our beards seems to have been inherited from an ape-like progenitor; for when there is any difference in tint between the hair of the head and the beard, the latter is lighter coloured in all monkeys and in man" (587).

Several chapters of the *Descent* show "the difference in mind between man and the higher animals, great as it is, certainly is one of degree and not of kind" (319). The discovery of a prehistoric primate with a cranium at least as large as that of Homo sapiens ("man the wise") was sobering for those who had cited the comparative size of brains in species as a sign of human superiority. Darwin called attention to that "well developed and capacious" apelike skull, which was named Neanderthal for the valley in Germany where it had been found in 1856 (281). He showed that some nonhuman species are capable of rational expression as well as of emotional sensibility. While admitting that human mental ability is greater than that of other animals, Darwin argued that there is no categorical difference in the intellectual facility of fishes, apes, savages, and civilized humans (287). "Man differs less from the higher apes," he claimed, "than these do from the lower members of the same order of primates" (253). In other words, humans are of closer kin to chimpanzees than chimpanzees are to monkeys.

Human physical abilities compare poorly to that of many other animals. They have neither great teeth nor claws for defense, and they cannot climb trees quickly to escape from enemies. Their speed and muscular strength is not remarkable and their senses of smell and hearing do not serve them well in avoiding danger or discovering food. So how have puny humans become dominant among animals? Adaptation of bodily structure has contributed much to humans' now commanding role among animals. When their arboreal ancestors came down from trees to search for food in open plains, those with dexterous hands could carry food supplies and make weapons. Also, the upright bipedals could better see carnivorous animals and flee from them (279–80). Their survival can also be attributed to their social qualities and intellectual powers, which compensate for their physical weaknesses (286).

Whereas monkeys have prehensile tails, humans have prehensile minds, enabling some of them to com-*prehend* in the manner of Darwin. He said, "I have had the strongest desire to understand or explain whatever I observed, that is, to group all facts under some general laws."[6]

"Through his powers of intellect," Darwin wrote, "articulate language has been evolved; and on this his wonderful advancement largely depended" (278). Language has been the greatest human discovery and "the largeness of the brain in man relatively to his body, compared with the lower animals, may be attributed in chief part to the early use of some simple form of language" (592). What we call culture is composed of language, art, religion, ethics, clothing, housing, and other folk habits that largely separate Homo sapiens from other species. Transmitting cultural ideas by social inheritance, unlike genetic heredity, can cause rapid changes.

Darwin confronted the problem of humans' believing that they sat on the pinnacle of the species pyramid and were, as a psalmist put it, "a little lower than God." Darwin viewed humans as having dignity, but not because they are a species uniquely separated by their Creator from other organisms. Rather, he attempted to show that all organisms are wonderful and that kinship with all of life was ennobling: "We may, with our present knowledge, approximately recognise our parentage; nor need we feel ashamed of it. The most humble organism is something much higher than the inorganic dust under our feet; and no one with an unbiased mind can study any living creature, however humble, without being struck with enthusiasm at its marvellous structure and properties" (341).

To illustrate the excellence of a "most humble organism," Darwin called attention to the ant whose brain is "not so large as the quarter of a small pin's head." He wrote about the ant's phenomenal perspicacity relative to its size: "The brain of the ant is one of the most marvellous atoms of matter in the world, perhaps more so than the brain of a man" (281, 331). Ant intelligence has caused survival-enhancing social habits. Darwin's perception followed the awareness of a biblical sage who exhorted, "Go to the ant, thou sluggard; consider her ways, and be wise."[7] We share with ants and other invertebrates characteristics such as nonverbal communication and group assistance. Thus, humans should be cautious in boasting that they are more intelligent than other species.

◆ ◆ ◆

For millennia, people of the Judeo-Christian culture had readily accepted the Genesis doctrine that humans were made in the image of God and that they were given the responsibility to increase their numbers and have dominion over the rest of creation. Their theology supported their constructing a vast cognitive chasm separating Homo sapiens from zoological brutes. More than other people, Britons especially prided themselves on being supreme within their species. Had they not produced many of the inventors who ushered in the industrial revolution, and were they not the prime global colonizers who made it possible to claim that the sun never sets on the British Empire?

Educated people with Judeo-Christian commitments were only moderately disturbed by geologists who contradicted the Genesis story of a global flood, and they were not overly troubled by biologists who rejected special creation for nonhuman species. But Darwin's account of the evolution of the human species from earlier species was profoundly disturbing to them. His theory tore at the essential fabric of humankind's view of where they stood in the order of nature. People had presumed that they were as distinct from animals as animals were from plants, and were placed in a separate classification. But Darwin rejected the attempt of some naturalists to divide "the whole organic world into three kingdoms, the Human, the Animal, and the Vegetable" (33).

Most of Darwin's fellow Victorians, regardless of their religious orientation, would have read with scorn and contempt this paragraph from the *Descent*:

> The early progenitors of man must have been once covered with hair, both sexes having beards; their ears were probably pointed, and capable of movement; and their bodies were provided with a tail.... The foot was then prehensile, judging from the condition of the great toe in the foetus; and our progenitors, no doubt, were arboreal in their habits, and frequented some warm, forest-clad land. The males had great canine teeth, which served them as formidable weapons.... At a still earlier period the progenitors of man must have been aquatic in their habits; for morphology plainly tells us that our lungs consist of a modified swimbladder, which once served as a float. The clefts on the neck in the embryo of man show where the branchiae [*gills*] once existed. (339)

Darwin's description of human ancestors was so provocative in his day that it was fortunate that he was semi-retired in rural Downe and unavailable for pillorying by mobs.

One popular misconception of Darwin's theory, and the source of much ridicule, has resulted from quoting out of context what he wrote about human origins. He said, "The Simiadae [primates] then branched off into two great stems, the New World and Old World monkeys, and from the latter, at a remote period, Man, the wonder and the glory of the universe, proceeded" (337). Darwin clarified that he was not saying humans had present-day African monkeys as ancestors: "We must not fall into the error of supposing that the early progenitor of the whole simian stock, including man, was identical with, or even closely resembled, any existing ape or monkey" (336). The human, monkey, chimpanzee, and other primate species are modern outcomes of diverging lines from a common ancestor who was "a hairy, tailed quadruped, probably arboreal in its habits" (591). Men and apes living now are co-descendants of fore parents that have been extinct for millions of years. Humans not only have primate relatives but, exploring further down the "tree of life," they have ancestral ties with creatures much less intelligent. While humans are not directly descended from any extant species, they are distant cousins of all other animals and plants.

THE EVOLUTION OF MORALITY AND RELIGION

According to the *Descent*, the sociality that is basic to morality "is probably an extension of the parental or filial affections." By means of such ties, the earliest humans, along with many other species, were conditioned to look out for the best interests of the extended family. Darwin explained:

> The social instinct seems to be developed by the young remaining for a long time with their parents; and this extension may be attributed in part to habit, but chiefly to natural selection. With those animals which were benefited by living in close association, the individuals which took the greatest pleasure in society would best escape various dangers, whilst those that cared least for their comrades, and lived solitary, would perish in greater numbers. (308)

Some animals develop an "internal monitor" that regulates impulses from their social instinct as well as from their individual "instinct of self-preservation" (305, 311). Altruistic affection, which is inherited in many species, may prove to be stronger in some situations than forces of self-protection and vengeance. Moreover, the beneficence may go beyond the quid pro quo of enlightened self-interest. Some apes, Darwin imagined, "might insist that they were ready to aid their fellow-apes of the same

Dr. Erasmus Darwin who influenced his grandson Charles by his poetic writings about evolution.

Dr. Robert Darwin, Charles's father, was a successful physician and financier in Shrewsbury.

Christ's College, Cambridge where Darwin studied there for three years to prepare for becoming a priest in the Church of England.

Rev. John Henslow, Darwin's most influential professor at Cambridge University, taught him about science and religion.

Fuegians hailing H.M.S. Beagle *in the Straits of Magellan. Darwin spent nearly five years aboard this ninety-foot brig.*

Robert FitzRoy, captain of the Beagle, *invited Darwin to serve as his companion and naturalist.*

"A Bible-reading on board ship" by Beagle artist Augustus Earle

We can allow /satellites/ planets, suns, universes, nay whole systems of universes to be governed by laws, but the smallest insect, we wish to be created at once by special act, provided with its instincts, its place in nature, its range, its—etc. etc.—must be a special act, or result of laws. yet we placidly believe the Astronomer, when he tells us satellites etc. etc. The Savage admires not a steam engine, but a piece of colored glass, is lost in astonishment at the artificer.—Our faculties are more fitted to recognize the wonderful structure of a beetle than a Universe.

This notebook excerpt illustrates Darwin's handwriting, which is difficult to read even when enlarged. He is criticizing the special creation doctrine of natural theology.

Emma Darwin at age thirty-two, soon after her marriage to Charles

Charles Darwin at age thirty-three with William, his firstborn

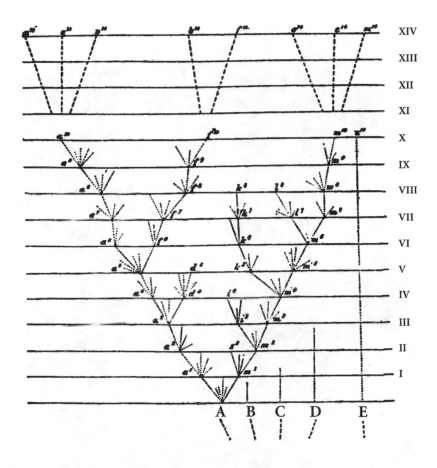

The diagram of "the great tree of life" in Origin. *Each interval between the fifteen horizontal lines represents "a thousand or more generations." A sample is given of the variations radiating from parent species A, which belongs to a genus containing A to E. Most branches and their twigs have "decayed and dropped off." The survivors at the higher levels are winners in the natural selection lottery. At the tenth level the widely divergent surviving variations from A may be labeled three new species.*

Oxford Bishop Samuel Wilberforce versus anatomist Thomas Huxley, Darwin's prime defender, at their 1860 debate. Caricatures by "Ape" in Vanity Fair.

Down House, where the Darwin family resided from 1842 onward. The beginning of the garden path around the eighteen-acre estate is in the foreground. Darwin walked along it daily as he contemplated problems in biology and theology.

Harvard botanist Asa Gray was Darwin's closest American friend and consultant.

troop in many ways, to risk their lives for them, and to take charge of their orphans; but they would be forced to acknowledge that disinterested [impartial] love for all living creatures, the most noble attribute of man, was quite beyond their comprehension" (319).

Animals, and humans in particular, are indebted to their mothers more than to their fathers for the moral disposition most needed for survival. Darwin saw the chief difference between women and men as "her greater tenderness and less selfishness." She not only "displays these qualities towards her infants in an eminent degree" but "often extend[s] them towards her fellow-creatures." By contrast, males are more aggressive: "He delights in competition, and this leads to ambition which passes too easily into selfishness" (556). Philosopher Larry Arnhart recognizes, "Darwin imagines a history of moral progress in which female sympathy could be gradually extended from the family to small tribes, then to large nations, and eventually to all humanity."[8]

Adam Smith's viewpoint on morality, which he expressed in his *Theory of Moral Sentiments*, resonated in Darwin. He found "striking" the emphasis the Scottish philosopher placed on the virtue of sympathy. Smith began his opening chapter with this thesis sentence: "How selfish soever man may be supposed, there are evidently some principles in his nature, which interest him in the fortune of others, and render their happiness necessary to him, though he derives nothing from it, except the pleasure of seeing it." From this treatment by the preeminent capitalist economist, who gave much attention to the pursuit of private interests, Darwin wrote that we are "impelled to relieve the sufferings of another, in order that our own painful feelings may be at the same time relieved" (308–9).

With regard to primeval humans, Darwin recognized that group survival depended on cooperation: "A tribe including many members who, from possessing in a high degree the spirit of patriotism, fidelity, obedience, courage, and sympathy, were always ready to aid one another, and to sacrifice themselves for the common good, would be victorious over most other tribes" (322). Darwin viewed the natural selection process as not favoring the ruthlessly greedy but as rewarding those who aim at group welfare and assisting the weak. He wrote: "[T]hose communities which included the greatest number of the most sympathetic members would flourish best, and rear the greatest number of offspring" (309). The antisocial have less chance of surviving than those who are benevolent and faithful to one another.

Darwin thought of humans more as protectors of one another than as predators on one another. When two tribes are in competition, he stated, the one that warns its members of danger and engages in mutual defense is more likely to succeed (32). The "fittest" are not necessarily the brawniest, nor even those who sire the most offspring, but those who live cooperatively. Darwin defined bad persons as those who permit their social sympathy to atrophy.

Ethicist Paul Farber provides this explication of Darwin's views in the *Descent*:

> A moral sense would likely be of little selective value to the individual; indeed, it might prove harmful. Darwin suggested, however, that a group possessing such individuals would have a significant adaptive advantage. Tribes having members who were willing to risk their own lives for the good of the community would supplant other tribes that lacked such altruistic men. This natural selection of groups, not individuals, served to extend man's moral development. The general advance of man was like the evolution of organic life, not predetermined and with retrogressive as well as progressive moves. . . . What defined a moral action was its contribution to the "general good." The general good was not knowable through a God-given intuition, nor was it action that would promote the "greatest happiness."[9]

According to Darwin, conscience does not arise until human mental development permits reflection upon conduct (304). He said: "A moral being is one who is capable of comparing his past and future actions or motives, and of approving or disapproving of them. We have no reason to suppose that any of the lower animals have this capacity" (311). Darwin declared, "I fully subscribe to the judgment of those writers who maintain that of all the differences between man and the lower animals, the moral sense or conscience is by far the most important."

Darwin buttressed his position by quoting from Sir James Mackintosh's *Dissertation on the Progress of Ethical Philosophy* that conscience "has a rightful supremacy over every other principle of human action" (304). As a teenager Darwin had heard Mackintosh, a member of the Wedgwood clan, discuss morality, and ranked him as the most profound person he had come to know.[10] The philosopher had criticized Thomas Hobbes's claim that humans are naturally amoral, and had developed the theory of eighteenth-century Anglican Bishop Joseph Butler, who established a rational foundation for ethics. In his personal copy of Mackintosh's *Dissertation*, Darwin jotted, "The remarks on Butler contain the cream of Sir J's opinions."

Butler's theme was that the quintessential biblical ethical command, "Love your neighbor as yourself," balances concern for the needs of others with satisfying one's own needs. He followed Jesus and Paul who singled out that command as summarizing the moral law.[11] According to Butler, humans have been created with inclinations toward both self-love and benevolence and they live according to their true nature when they keep those tendencies in equilibrium. Individual conscience is the rational arbiter of conflicts arising between personal interests and social duties.[12]

The ethical outlook of Butler, Mackintosh, and Darwin echoes the famous affirmation of Immanuel Kant, the most outstanding of modern philosophers, who contrasted the insignificance of his body amid vast nature with the dignity he received by acting in accord with the moral law:

> Two things fill the mind with ever new and increasing admiration and awe, the oftener and the more steadily we reflect on them: *the starry heaven above and the moral law within*. . . . The former view of a countless multitude of worlds annihilates as it were my importance as an *animal creature*, which after it has been for a short time provided with vital power, one knows not how, must again give back the matter of which it was formed to the planet it inhabits (a mere speck in the universe). The second, on the contrary, infinitely elevates my worth as an *intelligence* by my personality, in which the moral law reveals to me a life independent of animality and even of the whole sensible world.[13]

Unlike the ancient Greeks who thought of the conscience as only a negative monitor,[14] Darwin's treatment of the term is like that of the apostle who introduced the concept into Christianity. According to Paul, conscience operates apart from biblical commands to regulate impulses of humans and to inform them of their obligations; it has both "accusing" and "excusing" functions. After looking backward, the guilt or good feeling it produces depends on whether or not the individual has acted in accord with an unwritten internal standard.[15] Darwin thought that remorse or repentance is especially dependent on the judgment of peers and on "reverence or fear of the Gods, or Spirits believed in" (313). The mind of a moral person "may occasionally tell him to act in opposition to the opinion of others, whose approbation he will then not receive; but he will still have the solid satisfaction of knowing that he has been faithful to his innermost guide or conscience."[16]

As Darwin viewed it, "[T]he golden rule, 'As ye would that men should do to you, do ye to them likewise' . . . lies at the foundation of morality" (319). Darwin quoted the reciprocity rule from Jesus' Sermon on the Mount, but he did not accept it as a moral law only because it was sanctioned by a religious leader. Rather, he thought, humans have learned of its prudential value in their struggle for survival. Darwin recognized that the moral principle that has been called "golden" for centuries is egoistic in orientation. Before applying the rule, an individual or a group reflects on what treatment it desires from others. The cumulative experience of many generations teaches that those who aid their fellows can generally expect to receive aid in return. Thus, most children are instructed not to make an exception for themselves of conduct they expect from others. They learn that social cooperation and treating others fairly is, in the long run, mutually advantageous. Darwin claimed that the valuing of reciprocity does not change from culture to culture, which explains why the golden rule is found in folk religions throughout the world. Other such universal core values are courage and self-sacrifice, which have been authenticated as heroic values by all people, and no tribe sanctions murder, robbery, and treachery among its own people (314–15).

Science philosopher Robert Richards points out:

> Darwin noticed, of course, that people . . . formed contracts to respect the person and property of others, provided they received the same consideration themselves; they acted, in our terms, as reciprocal altruists. Darwin also observed that his fellow creatures glowed or smarted under the judgments of their peers; accordingly they might at times practice virtue in response to public praise rather than to the inner voice of austere duty. Yet individuals did harken to that voice, which they understood to be authoritative, if not always coercive.[17]

To enhance the virtue of the golden rule, Darwin contrasted it with the vice of retaliation, a common emotion in animal species that is expressed as an unlimited vengeance or as a limited harming of others to the degree that they have been harmed. Darwin thought that revenge, along with some other impulses, witness to our distant fore parents. As he put it in an early notebook, "Our descent, then, is the origin of our evil passions! The Devil under form of Baboon is our grandfather!"[18] Darwin later avoided using religious mythology to describe the conflicts of human conscience. Before Benjamin Disraeli became prime minister, Bishop Wilberforce asked him at an Oxford meeting whether humans are apes or angels. Speaking for Britons generally, he replied, "My Lord, I am on the side of the angels." From his Jewish ancestry, the politician recognized that humans are portrayed in the Bible as, on the one hand, bound with other creatures—including the Eden serpent—as physical dust, and on the other hand, as spiritual beings.[19] Disraeli found more dignity in the latter imagery, in spite of the tradition that the devil was a fallen angel. But Darwin did not refer to angels to account for human conscience. Having little appreciation of Disraeli's Tory views or of his biblical interpretation, Darwin called him "such a poor creature" rather than a heaven-sent messenger.[20]

For Homo sapiens, Darwin believed that natural selection is to some extent overridden by a determination to promote the welfare of all people:

> With savages, the weak in body or mind are soon eliminated; and those that survive commonly exhibit a vigorous state of health. We civilised men, on the other hand, do our utmost to check the process of elimination; we build asylums for the imbecile, the maimed, and the sick; we institute poor-laws; and our medical men exert their utmost skill to save the life of every one to the last moment. There is reason to believe that vaccination has preserved thousands, who from a weak constitution would formerly have succumbed to small-pox.

Darwin realized that neglect of the weak and helpless had frequently been practiced by some species, but for civilized humans it was "an overwhelming present evil" (323).

Higher morality is attained, Darwin believed, when humans break away from a narrow orientation and extend their circle of neighbors beyond the immediate family, to the tribe, the nation, and the international community. In socially evolved people, he wrote, "sympathies become more tender and widely diffused, extending to men of all races, to the imbecile, maimed, and other useless members of society" (318). This higher morality also includes a concern for the welfare and happiness of others, regardless even of species:

> As man advances in civilisation, and small tribes are united into larger communities, the simplest reason would tell each individual that he ought to extend his social instincts and sympathies to all the members of the same nation, though personally unknown to him. This point being once reached, there is only an artificial barrier to

prevent his sympathies extending to the men of all nations and races. If, indeed, such men are separated from him by great differences in appearance or habits, experience unfortunately shews us how long it is, before we look at them as our fellow-creatures. Sympathy beyond the confines of man, that is, humanity to the lower animals, seems to be one of the latest moral acquisitions. (317)

Darwin opposed selfish individualism and admired the person who, without deliberation, risks drowning while trying to save another person's life. In his ode to conscience, he commended individuals who suffer self-deprivation for the welfare of the group: "It is summed up in that short but imperious word *ought*, so full of high significance. It is the most noble of all the attributes of man, leading him without a moment's hesitation to risk his life for that of a fellow-creature; or after due deliberation, impelled simply by the deep feeling of right or duty, to sacrifice it in some great cause" (304).

Darwin took exception to hedonists who argue that humans do not risk their lives for others unless they can rationally calculate some pleasure they will gain for themselves. He praised Kant's categorical imperative, which consists of doing one's duty for duty's sake (304). "The highest possible stage in moral culture," according to Darwin, "is when we recognise that we ought to control our thoughts, and 'not even in inmost thought to think again the sins that made the past so pleasant to us.'"[21] Those lines of Tennyson define what he called "true repentance," and it is in accord with the meaning of the Greek term *metanoia* (literally, "change mind") that English translations of the New Testament render as "repentance." Darwin did not make explicit the source of the "standard of morality" that rises "higher and higher" (317–18), or the content of the pleasant "sins," but they are anchored in his religious culture. He echoed the struggle with sin that the apostle Paul had described, as well as the striving expressed in these lines of Tennyson: "Ah for a man to arise in me, / That the man I am may cease to be!"[22]

About the composition of conscience, Darwin concluded, "Ultimately our moral sense of conscience becomes a highly complex sentiment— originating in the social instincts, largely guided by the approbation of our fellow-men, ruled by reason, self-interest, and in later times by deep religious feelings, and confirmed by instruction and habit" (322). He commended ideals that are difficult to attain: "To do good in return for evil, to love your enemy, is a height of morality to which it may be doubted whether the social instincts would, by themselves, have ever led us." He recognized that religious education is needed for the cultivation of that epitome of the moral teachings of Jesus (312),[23] which contains expectations that far surpass the tit-for-tat conduct characterizing minimal moral behavior.[24] Darwin claimed that humans find high satisfaction when they act for the good of others. This often enables a person to "gain the love of those with whom he lives," which "undoubtedly is the highest pleasure on this earth."[25]

Darwin recognized that modern humans were generally different in their ethical constitution from their prehistoric human and zoological relatives. Having a transcendent enforcer of moral conduct was among those distinctions:

> Man . . . has few or no special instincts. He differs also from the lower animals in the power of expressing his desires by words, which thus become a guide to the aid required and bestowed. The motive to give aid is likewise much modified in man: it no longer consists solely of a blind instinctive impulse. . . . With the more civilised races, the conviction of the existence of an all-seeing Deity has had a potent influence on the advance of morality. Ultimately man does not accept the praise or blame of his fellows as his sole guide. . . . The moral qualities are advanced, either directly or indirectly, much more through the effects of habit, the reasoning powers, instruction, religion, etc., than through natural selection; though to this latter agency may be safely attributed the social instincts, which afforded the basis for the development of the moral sense. (592–93, 596)

William Ritter has discerned the significance that Darwin gave religion as a behavioral force: "He included religion not only as a quality of the species but as one of its most definitive qualities. . . . The case for religion stood with him exactly as the case for language and reason. . . . To Darwin the problem . . . was that of the element of belief in religion (the creedal aspect) rather than that of religion as an experience and a force in human life."[26]

◆ ◆ ◆

For decades Darwin thought over the evolution of religion. In 1838 he jotted, "Hensleigh [Emma's brother] says the love of the deity and thought of him or eternity [are the] only difference between the mind of man and animals—yet how faint in a Fuegian or [aboriginal] Australian! Why not gradation?"[27] Darwin reported on his investigation of the South American tribe, "We could never discover that the Fuegians believed in what we should call a God, or practised any religious rites" (303).

While Darwin was completing the *Descent* he wrote Edward Tylor to praise him for "a most profound work" he had just published, *Primitive Culture*. The tracing of religious development from animism by one of the earliest anthropologists provided Darwin with a new point of view.[28] Homo sapiens could be called a religious animal if the definition of "religious" were broad enough. Tylor hypothesized that dream experiences by early humans led them to believe in a separate soul (*anima*) in themselves. Correspondingly, they came to believe in the existence of surviving souls or spirits that inhabit plants and animals, as well as move about in the air as ghosts. He contributed much to Darwin's sketch on how religion arose among humans:

> Savages do not readily distinguish between subjective and objective impressions. When a savage dreams, the figures which appear before him are believed to have come from a distance, and to stand over him. . . . But until the faculties of imagination, curiosity, reason, etc., had been fairly well developed in the mind of man, his dreams would not have led him to believe in spirits. . . . The belief in spiritual agencies would easily pass into the belief in the existence of one or more gods. For savages would naturally attribute to spirits the same passions, the same love of vengeance or simplest form of justice, and the same affections which they themselves feel. . . . The same high mental faculties which first led man to believe in unseen spiritual agencies, then in fetishism, polytheism, and ultimately in monotheism, would infallibly lead him, as long as his reasoning powers remained poorly developed, to various strange superstitions and customs. Many of these are terrible to think of—such as the sacrifice of human beings to a blood-loving god; the trial of innocent persons by the ordeal of poison or fire; witchcraft, etc. (302–3)

Darwin appears to have seen a parallel between marital and theological development. He believed that marriage gradually evolved from communal marriages—when all in a tribe are husbands and wives to one another—through polygamy to monogamy (579–81). He apparently accepted the standard view of biblical interpreters that the emerging monogamy of the New Testament era was a moral improvement over the marital arrangements of earlier times.

Belief in one or more gods is not instinctive, Darwin discerned, because it is not found among all people. However, "a belief in all-pervading spiritual agencies seems to be universal," and among them are

"many cruel and malignant spirits. . . . The idea of a universal and beneficent Creator does not seem to arise in the mind of man," Darwin opined,
"until he has been elevated by long-continued culture" (593). Displaying
that he was not engaging in historical reductionism, he asserted:

> There is no evidence that man was aboriginally endowed with the
> ennobling belief in the existence of an Omnipotent God. . . . The
> question [of primitive religion] is of course wholly distinct from
> that higher one, whether there exists a Creator and Ruler of the
> universe; and this has been answered in the affirmative by some of
> the highest intellects that have ever existed. . . . The feeling of reli-
> gious devotion is a highly complex one, consisting of love, complete
> submission to an exalted and mysterious superior, a strong sense of
> dependence, fear, reverence, gratitude, hope for the future, and per-
> haps other elements. No being could experience so complex an
> emotion until advanced in his intellectual and moral faculties to at
> least a moderately high level. (302–3)

Darwin was aware of the compulsion of each culture to make gods in
the image of its own people. After describing differences in taste on
matters such as skin and eye color or hair and nose length, he relates
this to anthropomorphism in religion:

> We thus see how widely the different races of man differ in their
> taste for the beautiful. In every nation sufficiently advanced to have
> made effigies of their gods or of their deified rulers, the sculptors
> no doubt have endeavoured to express their highest ideal of beauty
> and grandeur. . . . It is certainly not true that there is in the mind of
> man any universal standard of beauty with respect to the human
> body. (575, 577)

The degeneration theory of religion, which some church leaders
advocated, was rejected by Darwin. He associated the theory with
Richard Whately, the Anglican archbishop of Dublin, an influential figure in Victorian Britain (328). By accepting the historicity of the opening chapters of Genesis, degenerationists argued that the earliest
humans were monotheists and civilized. Adam functioned as the preeminent naturalist, because Holy Writ declares: "[T]he Lord God
formed every beast of the field, and every fowl of the air; and brought
them unto Adam to see what he would call them; and whatsoever Adam
called every living creature, that was the name thereof."[29] Monogamists
Adam and Eve enjoyed a special intimacy with the high God but, after

they ate the forbidden fruit, their pure religion collapsed and they transmitted corrupted theology and ethics to their descendants. Among the consequences of the first parents' "fall" have been polytheism and the worship of a host of demonic powers, as well as savage conduct, including polygamy and slavery. For Whately, the loss of an earlier paradise with divine companionship was an expression of inverted cultural evolution.[30]

Darwin found no evidence that the Fuegians or other savage tribes are decayed remnants of a civilization that worshiped a high God. Rather, the reverse is true, for there are clear vestiges of barbaric customs and beliefs among civilized people. Darwin then made a normative judgment about true religion:

> Many existing superstitions are the remnants of former false religious beliefs. The highest form of religion—the grand idea of God hating sin and loving righteousness—was unknown during primeval times. . . . To believe that man was aboriginally civilised, and then suffered utter degradation in so many regions, is to take a pitiably low view of human nature. It is apparently a truer and more cheerful view that progress has been much more general than retrogression; that man has risen, though by slow and interrupted steps, from a lowly condition to the highest standard as yet attained by him in knowledge, morals, and religion. (329–30)

Darwin did not think there was a straight line of moral or religious progress. In the *Descent* he acknowledged, "[M]any nations, no doubt, have fallen away in civilisation, and some may have lapsed into utter barbarism" (329). For example, incalculable deterioration was caused in the Middle Ages by mandatory celibacy for those aspiring to holy office and by the "Holy" Inquisition's burning of the boldest men (327). Also, pertaining to the commonplace slaughter of babies by their own parents in barbarous tribes, Darwin wrote:

> If we look back to an extremely remote epoch, before man had arrived at the dignity of manhood, he would have been guided more by instinct and less by reason than are the lowest savages at the present time. Our early semi-human progenitors would not have practised infanticide . . . for the instincts of the lower animals are never so perverted as to lead them regularly to destroy their own offspring. (277)

The size of one's family or fortune should not be the measure of achievement, Darwin thought. He regarded primogeniture as an evil and believed that a culture diminishes its mental and productive qualities when it establishes status by birthright (324). The inheritance bestowed by eminent humans is more important: "Great lawgivers, the founders of beneficent religions, great philosophers and discoverers in science, aid the progress of mankind in a far higher degree by their works than by leaving a numerous progeny." Natural selection has but little effect on human progress; more important is advancement in education and morality that is strengthened by "instruction during youth, and religious feelings" (325).

Cultural historians were then divided between monogenists and polygenists, the latter arguing that peoples of different races were separate species by divine creation. Darwin provided much data to demonstrate "all the races ... have sprung from the same primitive stock" (347). He admitted that, due to the incremental change among humanoids, "it would be impossible to fix on any definite point when the term 'man' ought to be used" (349). Finding much lacking scientifically in discussions of different subspecies of humans, Darwin wrote about "the so-called races of man" (253, 342, 347). The ability of all races to interbreed was the most compelling way to support that they were diverging leaves from the same twig of the "tree of life." Darker skin in tropical regions is due, he discerned, to the greater solar protection it provides and the greater resistance it gives to diseases. Likewise, lighter color predominates in colder climates because it has a survival advantage there (258).[31] Darwin deemed it improbable that the "similar inventive or mental powers" of races were independently acquired (349).

Darwin was amazed at how quickly the Fuegian children whom Captain FitzRoy had taken to Europe readily adapted to the new environment. He testified, "The Fuegians rank amongst the lowest barbarians, but I was continually struck with surprise how closely the three natives on board H. M. S. *Beagle*, who had lived some years in England and could talk a little English, resembled us in disposition and in most of our mental faculties" (287). Darwin did not regard even the most uncivilized people he encountered as "a missing link" in some evolutionary chain of ascent between simians and humans. His close contact with both Fuegians and an African living in Britain showed him "how similar their minds were to ours."

The sequel to the *Descent* was a book on *The Expression of the Emotions*, in which Darwin reported on his investigation of racial variation. From the results of a questionnaire he sent to a variety of observers of natives in remote parts of the earth, he stated, "It follows, from the information thus acquired, that the same state of mind is expressed throughout the world with remarkable uniformity; and this fact is in itself interesting as evidence of the close similarity in bodily structure and mental disposition of all the races of mankind.[32] In spite of physical differences, he found striking the similarity among races in dispositions, artistic pleasures, and body language (348). The common mental ability among races was paramount in his rejection of a natural basis for slavery. Darwin, like Abraham Lincoln, believed that since no rational person wants to be enslaved, practitioners of the golden rule must affirm that all other humans have the right to be free.[33]

Perhaps because of residual biblical language in his mind, Darwin did not express his ideas on the originating humans clearly. His view was independent of the mythic story of God creating the first pair of humans in the garden of Eden, or of the story of all races descending from Noah's sons after the great deluge, or of the New Testament assumption that all humans come from a common stock. He did not find evidence that "man has sprung from a single pair of progenitors," even though he held that "all the races agree in so many unimportant details of structure and in so many mental peculiarities that these can be accounted for only by inheritance from a common progenitor" (350, 591). Darwin rejected polygenism but he did not support the Catholic theory that all humans are literally descended from Adam and Eve.[34] Incautiously, he wrote these sentences to Charles Lyell: "All mammals must have descended from a single parent," and "All the races of man are so infinitely closer together than to any ape that . . . I should look at all races of man as having certainly descended from *single* parent."[35] He must have meant "one parental pair," but even that modification does not square with his other statements.

Darwin concluded the *Descent* by recognizing that although many find "highly distasteful" the thought of descent from simians, nevertheless, "he who is not content to look, like a savage, at the phenomena of nature as disconnected, cannot any longer believe that man is the work of a separate act of creation" (590). He admitted that his boast about the immense superiority of the human species had been tempered by his visit with a barbaric tribe on the frigid tip of South America:

> The astonishment which I felt on first seeing a party of Fuegians on a wild and broken shore will never be forgotten by me, for the reflection at once rushed into my mind—such were our ancestors. These men were absolutely naked and bedaubed with paint, their long hair was tangled, their mouths frothed with excitement, and

their expression was wild, startled, and distrustful. They possessed hardly any arts, and like wild animals lived on what they could catch; they had no government, and were merciless to every one not of their own small tribe. (596)

In contrast to such people, Darwin perceived that some nonhuman primates have more virtue. He provided personal anecdotal evidence, relating what a London zookeeper had told him and reporting what had happened in the hills of Abyssinia:

For my own part I would as soon be descended from that heroic little monkey, who braved his dreaded enemy in order to save the life of his keeper, or from that old baboon, who descending from the mountains, carried away in triumph his young comrade from a crowd of astonished dogs—as from a savage who delights to torture his enemies, offers up bloody sacrifices, practices infanticide without remorse, treats his wives like slaves, knows no decency, and is haunted by the grossest superstitions. (306–7, 596–97)

Also, Darwin found the effect of drugs on monkeys and humans was similar except that there was one kind of South American monkey who, "after getting drunk on brandy, would never touch it again, and thus was wiser than many men" (256).

As with the *Origin*, Darwin ends the *Descent* with an attempt to allay concerns of religiously oriented persons:

I am aware that the conclusions arrived at in this work will be denounced by some as highly irreligious; but he who denounces them is bound to show why it is more irreligious to explain the origin of man as a distinct species by descent from some lower form, through the laws of variation and natural selection, than to explain the birth of the individual through the laws of ordinary reproduction. The birth both of the species and of the individual are equally parts of that grand sequence of events, which our minds refuse to accept as the result of blind chance. The understanding revolts at such a conclusion, whether or not we are able to believe that every slight variation of structure,—the union of each pair in marriage,— the dissemination of each seed,—and other such events, have all been ordained for some special purpose. (593)

The birth of a child is generally recognized as awesome, but the event confirms rather than violates natural law. Those who, with the psalmist, say of God, "You knit me together in my mother's womb,"[36] are not denying the facts of life. Similarly, to say God created the species should not require a rejection of the evolutionary method by which it happened. Describing the way nature has developed and currently functions does not deal with questions of human worth. The latter is determined by one's individual life, not by one's ancestral lineage. The primate kin of Homo sapiens do not make them of less value.

Darwin concludes the *Descent* on this upbeat note:

> Man with all his noble qualities, with sympathy which feels for the most debased, with benevolence which extends not only to other men but to the humblest living creature, with his god-like intellect which has penetrated into the movements and constitution of the solar system—with all these exalted powers—Man still bears in his bodily frame the indelible stamp of his lowly origin.

RESPONSES TO *THE DESCENT OF MAN*

Although the *Origin* was a more seminal work than the *Descent*, the latter book focused on human organisms and was more troubling to the common reader. A leading Scottish journal observed that the *Descent* had raised "a storm of mingled wrath, wonder and admiration." If its contents are true, the review stated, then "most earnest-minded men will be compelled to give up these motives by which they have attempted to live noble and virtuous lives, as founded on a mistake; our moral sense will turn out to be a mere developed instinct . . . and the revelation of God to us, and the hope of a future life, pleasurable daydreams." If Darwin's views are proven correct, the review prophesied, they "will shake society to its very foundations by destroying the sanctity of the conscience and the religious sense."[37] Darwin was mistakenly interpreted as saying that the moral and religious standards of civilized people were not significantly different from the instinctual patterns of conduct in animal communities. He had attempted to guard against that caricature by illustrating that what is good for one species might be atrocious conduct in another: "If . . . men were reared under precisely the same conditions as hive-bees, there can hardly be a doubt that our unmarried females would, like the worker-bees, think it a sacred duty to kill their brothers, and mothers would strive to kill their fertile daughters; and no one would think of interfering" (305).

Most of Darwin's contemporaries were doubly appalled at his speculation that all humanity grew from a single taproot in Africa and his idea that they were related to hairy apes. He had suggested, "It is . . .

probable that Africa was formerly inhabited by extinct apes closely allied to the gorilla and chimpanzee; and as these two species are now man's nearest allies, it is somewhat more probable that our early progenitors lived on the African continent than elsewhere" (336). As has been subsequently confirmed, without Africa the chimpanzee, gorilla, and human species might never have arisen, so humans living on all other continents are ultimately immigrants. This notion of African roots of all human races clashed with the conventional wisdom among Caucasians that Adam and Eve looked just like them and that the birthplace of the human species was in Mesopotamia, not far from the mountains for which their race was named. Interpreting the garden of Eden story literally reinforced this ethnocentrism, for the Euphrates is named as one of its rivers.

Thomas Carlyle recommended the silent treatment for the evolutionist's theory about human ancestry, because "if true, it was nothing to be proud of, but rather a humiliating discovery, and the less said about it the better."[38] Even so, when the *Descent* was published, several reviews commended its theology. Sir Alexander Grant assured readers "there is nothing atheistical in Mr. Darwin's work; on the contrary, it might be described as a system of Natural Theology founded on a new basis."[39] Another review claimed that the *Descent* was a "far more wonderful vindication of Theism than Paley's *Natural Theology.*"[40] Darwin's reference to infanticide in some human cultures was used as evidence of historical retrogression, which gave support to a doctrine of the Christian church:

> Mr. Darwin finds himself compelled to reintroduce a new doctrine of the fall of man. He shews that the instincts of the higher animals are far nobler than the habits of savage races of men, and he finds himself, therefore, compelled to re-introduce,—in a form of the substantial orthodoxy of which he appears to be quite unconscious,— and to introduce as a scientific hypothesis the doctrine that man's gain of *knowledge* was the cause of a temporary but long-enduring moral deterioration.[41]

To josh Darwin, Asa Gray combined words of a biblical king with those of the *Descent*: "Almost thou persuadest me to have been 'a hairy quadruped, of arboreal habits, furnished with a tail and pointed ears.'"[42] Gray, an orthodox Christian, had actually become persuaded of Darwin's theme:

> Man, while on the one side a wholly exceptional being, is on the other an object of natural history—a part of the animal kingdom. . . .

He is as certainly and completely an animal as he is certainly something more. We are sharers not only of animal but of vegetable life, sharers with the higher brute animals in common instincts and feelings and affections. It seems to me that there is a sort of meanness in the wish to ignore the tie. I fancy that human beings may be more humane when they realize that, as their dependent associates live a life in which man has a share, so they have rights which man is bound to respect.[43]

Gray found religious significance in recognizing other animals in our family tree and our responsibility to all other family members. Other species should be protected and their sacredness recognized. Gray thought that the divine origin of humans is not diminished by their being the "transformation of a brute mammal."[44] He stated that the evolutionist would agree with the apostle Paul that the spiritual follows the physical, which is first in natural history.[45]

Louis Agassiz continued to oppose Darwin, in large part because Darwin affirmed that all humans are interrelated. Agassiz had spoken of blacks as "a degenerate race" and not of the same blood as Caucasians. He had charmed plantation owners of the American South because he seemed to provide a scientific basis for racism. Agassiz declared that blacks and whites had been separately created and were of different species.[46] He stated that blacks differ from whites as much as blacks differ from orangutans, and he viewed miscegenation as sinful. Although Agassiz used religious vocabulary, his was far from the biblical message that motivated abolitionists—that God "hath made of one blood all nations of men,"[47] and therefore all humankind were ultimately of the same adamic stock. Regarding the race question, Darwin wrote Lyell, "I do not think doctrine . . . of Agassiz that there are several species of man helps *us* in the least."[48]

Charles Hodge, professor at Princeton Theological Seminary and the bellwether of Old School Presbyterians, sided with Agassiz. In one of his widely studied tomes on Christian dogma, he appealed to the much-touted Harvard natural history professor who had attacked Darwin's theory as "untrue in its facts, unscientific in its method, and mischievous in its tendencies."[49] Hodge's repudiation of Darwinism was primarily due to its rejection of Paley's theology of design. He stated in his 1874 book on the subject: "The conclusion of the whole matter is, that the denial of design in nature is virtually the denial of God. Mr. Darwin's theory does deny all design in nature, therefore, his theory is virtually atheistical; his theory, not he himself."[50]

Philosopher James McCosh, another prominent Presbyterian, emigrated from Scotland to become president of what is now Princeton University. Due to Gray's influence, he interpreted Darwinian evolution as compatible with Calvinism.[51] Stressing general rather than special Providence, McCosh treated evolution as simply the means that God uses in creating species.[52] He did not view Darwin's theory, as some had accused, as justifying a selfish pleasure principle for the human species. Rather, he found it in accord with the Christian who invokes "the spirit of Him who stood by the weak against the strong . . . recognizes as brothers and sisters the lowest specimens of humanity, whether found in pagan lands or in the lowest sinks of our cities."[53]

George Mivart, a convert to Catholicism, had been Huxley's anatomy student in the 1860s and accepted evolutionary theory for nonhuman organisms. In his 1871 publication, *On the Genesis of Species*, he faulted Darwin for neglecting to discuss the role of God and the divine soul in natural selection. Mivart viewed the evolutionary process as too regular to be the result of haphazard trial and error. Contrary to Darwin, he insisted that there is a difference of kind and not just of degree between the mental and moral faculties of humans and nonhumans. Mivart was convinced "that a monkey and a mushroom differ less from each other than do a monkey and a man."[54] Darwin concluded a lengthy response to Mivart by saying that to admit his position on sudden transformations of species is "to enter into the realms of miracle, and to leave those of Science."[55]

Mivart had animosity toward Darwin even though Darwin had patiently carried on correspondence with him. Huxley quipped that some were running loose with "Darwinophobia" because of Mivart's bite.[56] Darwin remarked:

> I have almost always been treated honestly by my reviewers, passing over those without scientific knowledge as not worthy of notice. My views have often been grossly misrepresented, bitterly opposed and ridiculed, but this has been generally done, as I believe, in good faith. I must, however, except Mr. Mivart, who as an American expressed it in a letter has acted towards me "like a pettifogger."[57]

Mivart was not only rejected by Darwinians but also by Catholics, who denied him the sacraments for other reasons and did not permit his body to be buried in hallowed ground.

The mixed response of other English Catholics to Darwin is illustrated by the views of two prominent churchmen. Msgr. Henry Manning, later

Cardinal Manning, preached against Darwin's "brutal philosophy," which he represented as declaring "there is no God and the ape is our Adam."[58] But Cardinal John Henry Newman, far from libeling evolutionary science, thought Darwin was deserving of a degree from Oxford, an honor which he declined in 1870.[59]

Pope Pius IX, who had the doctrine of papal infallibility approved during his reign, was in office throughout the period when Darwin's major works were published. Allegedly in defense of authentic science, he wrote to a French Catholic:

> We have received with pleasure, dear son, the work in which you refute so well the aberrations of Darwinism. A system which is repudiated by history, by the traditions of all peoples, by exact science, by the observation of facts, and even by reason itself, would seem to have no need at all of refutation, if alienation from God and the penchant for materialism, both stemming from corruption, were not avidly searching for support in this fabric of fables. . . . But the corruptions of this century, the guile of the depraved, the danger of oversimplification demand that such dreamings, absurd as they are, since they wear the mask of science, be refuted by true science.[60]

But the pope did not proceed beyond this informal attack on Darwin's theory and condemn it officially, nor did he put Darwin's books on the Index of Forbidden Books.

◆ ◆ ◆

Herbert Spencer and Darwin wrote during the same period on the relation between evolution and ethics. David Oldroyd has clarified the way they significantly differed on the subject:

> Darwin himself was one of the first to consider the relationship between ethical theory and evolutionary doctrines, as when he argued that altruism might have had an evolutionary origin. He sought to show how ethical behaviour would have survival value, and thus might become established in human societies. But Darwin did not take the further step and say that one might distinguish between right and wrong by considering what had happened during the course of evolution, or where it was going in the future. Evolution *per se* did not provide an ethical code. Herbert Spencer, however, went beyond Darwin and hinted that this would be a possibility, as when he wrote: "The conduct to which we apply the

name good, is the relatively more evolved conduct; and . . . bad is the name we apply to the conduct which is relatively less evolved."[61]

Spencer's evolutionary philosophy was introduced independently of Darwin's theory and a decade before the *Origin* was published. Late in life Darwin wrote: "I am not conscious of having profited in my own work by Spencer's writings. . . . His fundamental generalisations . . . are of such a nature that they do not seem to me to be of any strictly scientific use."[62] Unfortunately, at Wallace's urging, Darwin introduced into later editions of the *Origin* the "survival of the fittest" phrase that Spencer had coined. Referring to natural selection in that way has caused immense confusion because of the different meanings of "fittest." The term often refers to the most healthy, but in Darwin's theory survival pertains to an organism's success at reproduction, regardless of health. Also, "fittest" pertains to that which is morally best. But the term "evolution" literally means *gradual* change in contrast to "*revolution*," meaning *sudden* change, with no for-better or for-worse direction presumed. Thus, for example, a cockroach need not be designated as one of the morally best creatures, even though it has surpassed virtually all other organisms in surviving with little change for millions of years. Evolution does not imply an automatic improvement; natural history is neither always progressive nor always regressive.

Spencer's "survival of the fittest" philosophy resulted from his presumption that laissez-faire economics was an expression of organic evolution. He believed that nature favored unrestrained capitalism as the means to move societies toward the pinnacle of civilization; therefore, it is wrong to interfere publicly with the pursuit of private interests on which a free enterprise system is based. Spencer advocated private charity to ameliorate poverty but he opposed governmental assumption of responsibility for below-subsistence wages. Progress is threatened when state aid is provided for the "unfit," who would otherwise be eliminated. Spencer thought that the example of trampled-down underachievers would motivate others to avoid their lifestyles and thereby gain success. Following Jean Lamarck, Spencer believed that such personal achievement would be inherited and spur on future generations. In 1851, Spencer wrote that ethical strength came through conforming to the harshness of the evolutionary order:

It seems hard that a laborer incapacitated by sickness from competing with his stronger fellows, should have to bear the resulting privations. It seems hard that widows and orphans should be left to struggle for life or death. Nevertheless, when regarded not separately, but in connection with the interests of universal humanity, these harsh fatalities are seen to be full of the highest beneficence. . . . Under the natural order of things, society is constantly excreting its unhealthy, imbecile, slow, vacillating, faithless members.[63]

The popularity of Spencer's theory in the late-nineteenth-century era of the robber barons on both sides of the Atlantic caused many to associate it wrongly with Darwin's theory. For instance, philosopher Will Durant has stated that because of Darwin, "[I]n this battle we call life, what we need is not goodness but strength, not humility but pride, not altruism but resolute intelligence."[64] What has been called social Darwinism should more accurately be called social Spencerism, because, as has been frequently noted by science historians, evolutionary ethics originated more with Spencer than with Darwin. The social Darwinism label is a libel on Darwin and on the religious values of social justice for which he stood. Theologian John Raines points out the confusion:

Darwin knew, but the Social Darwinists didn't, that evolution awards *social* species with survival if and only if they modify in the direction of greater social collaboration. Among social species, it is their evolving of capacities to cooperate that displays their successful journey through life. . . . The division of labor, as Emil Durkheim saw, is the way our species differentiates its work and so is able to occupy a confined space more densely, accommodating the competition to which new members give rise by increasing our ways of being useful to one another.[65]

The most egregious preacher of social Spencerism was John D. Rockefeller, who built the world's largest monopoly. The tycoon, who used cutthroat competition to destroy his rivals and to increase his personal wealth, illustrates that American pietists "swallowed 'social Darwinism' tail and hooves."[66] Rockefeller defended his Standard Oil Company to his Sunday school class in this manner: "The growth of a large business is merely a survival of the fittest. . . . The American Beauty rose can be produced in the splendor and fragrance which bring cheer to its beholder only by sacrificing the early buds which grow up around it. This is not an evil tendency in business. It is merely the working-out of a law of nature and a law of God.[67]

In his outspoken manner, Huxley gave expression to a viewpoint that is similar to that contained in the *Descent*. Whereas Spencer tended to equate what is good with what he presumed was natural, Huxley rejected

"Might makes right" as a guide for moral practice. In an Oxford lecture, he stated what would become one of the most widely quoted paragraphs by an evolutionist:

> The practice of that which is ethically best—what we call goodness or virtue—involves a course of conduct which, in all respects, is opposed to that which leads to success in the cosmic struggle for existence. In place of ruthless self-assertion it demands self-restraint; in place of thrusting aside, or treading down, all competitors, it requires that the individual shall not merely respect, but shall help his fellows; its influence is directed, not so much to the survival of the fittest, as to the fitting of as many as possible to survive. It repudiates the gladiatorial theory of existence.[68]

Ethical norms, Huxley contended, cannot be derived from the carnival of carnage in nature's coliseum. His understanding of human nature is similar to that of contemporary sociobiologist Richard Dawkins, who thinks that moral nurture is necessary but is contrary to our entire natural history. He exhorts, "Let us try to *teach* generosity and altruism, because we are born selfish."[69] But where can such nurture be found that can enable humans to act counter to their brutal forebears? To what standards can they appeal for resisting the crude policies associated with either the unrestrained individualism of pure capitalism or the total collectivism of unalloyed communism?

Huxley acknowledged that his culture was living off the moral interest of its religious heritage and recommended non-natural sanctions for curbing the cosmic process. Accordingly, when he was chair of the London School Board in 1870, he insisted that Bible study should be part of the school curriculum. He admired that ancient text for the quality of its literary expression and for its morality, if used selectively. Huxley advised:

> Take the Bible as a whole; make the severest deductions which fair criticism can dictate for shortcomings and positive errors . . . and there still remains in this old literature a vast residuum of moral beauty and grandeur. . . . I am in favour of reading the Bible, with such grammatical, geographical and historical explanations by a lay-teacher as may be needful, with rigid exclusion of any further theological teaching than that contained in the Bible itself.[70]

Much to the disappointment of the irreligious, who liked to think of Huxley as their champion, he favored Bible instruction because it can inculcate "the religious feeling, which is the essential basis of conduct." In 1871 Huxley advocated a church in which "services should be devoted, not to the iteration of abstract propositions in theology, but to the setting before men's minds of an ideal of true, just, and pure living."[71] Huxley admired these qualities of normative Christianity: "Its justice and its pity for human frailty; its helpfulness, to the extremity of self-sacrifice; its ethical purity and nobility; which apostles have pictured, in which armies of martyrs have placed their unshakable faith, and whence obscure men and women, like Catherine of Sienna and John Knox, have derived the courage to rebuke popes and kings."[72]

"The glory of Judaism and of Christianity," according to Huxley, was "that one should rejoice in the good man; forgive the bad man; and pity and help all men to the best of one's ability."[73] In his lecture on "The Evolution of Theology," the Hebrew prophets who lived eight centuries before the Christian era were cited as superb spokespersons of human duty. He saw them as "constantly striving to free the moral ideal from the stifling embrace of the current theology and its concomitant ritual." The essence of religion, Darwin's bulldog concluded, is best expressed in Micah's saying, "What doth the Lord require of thee, but to do justly, and to love mercy, and to walk humbly with thy God?" Huxley gave the last phrase this paraphrase, "and to bear himself as humbly as befits his insignificance in the face of the Infinite."[74]

Huxley shared the general ethical outlook that historian Owen Chadwick describes: "Everyone, agnostic or not, assumed that the morality which they inherited was absolute and must be preserved, even though the creed linked with it might be dropped. . . . The complicating fact for the late nineteenth century was the claim that you could have morality without Christianity while the morality which you must have was Christian morality."[75]

Huxley had a spirit akin to that of Matthew Arnold, a leading literary figure of the day, who defined religion as "morality touched by emotion."[76] Both appealed to the Hebrew prophets in judging good conduct to be the object of religion. Arnold thought that those with a scientific mind who interpret figuratively the biblical accounts of creation, miracles, and the afterlife gain more true insights on religion than literalists. He described the apostle Paul as having a scientific outlook because he interpreted resurrection as a spiritual experience of those who identify with what preceded and followed Jesus' death.[77] Arnold wrote: "To popular religion, the real kingdom of God is the New Jerusalem with its jaspers and emeralds; righteousness and peace and joy are only the kingdom of God figuratively. . . . Science exactly reverses this process; for science, the spiritual notion is the real one, the materialist notion is figurative."[78]

Darwin shared with Huxley and Arnold an earnestness in the pursuit of Victorian righteousness. Arnhart notes that Huxley's contrast between biological nature and human duty develops one theme of the *Descent*: "Darwin's appeal to universal humanitarianism can only be explained as a utopian yearning for an ideal moral realm that transcends nature." Arnhart thinks Huxley's position is unrealistic in invoking "some transcendental norm of impartial justice (such as Christian charity) that is beyond the order of nature."[79]

Exiled Russian Prince Petr Kropotkin, a younger contemporary of Darwin, disagreed with Huxley's emphasis on evolution as involving a vicious clash among antisocial creatures. He emphasized that altruism as described in the *Descent* has done the most to enhance the survival of the sociable animals, which make up the vast majority of species.[80] Anthropologist Paul Heyer writes:

Full of insight from his field experiences [in Eurasia], Kropotkin elaborated in depth this previously unacknowledged aspect of Darwin's work. He saw sociability rather than a life-and-death struggle between individuals as typifying the animal world. . . . Kropotkin helped to entrench Darwin's contention that the social is not a secondary but a primary and deeply rooted aspect of human nature.[81]

Several positions on evolutionary ethics originated in this period. For Spencer, competition was primary in natural selection and consequently is stressed by the good person. Kropotkin took the opposite position, and Huxley curiously agreed with Spencer on the primacy of competition in biological evolution but with Kropotkin in stressing cooperation as the moral way to behave. Darwin's position avoided those extremes, which seemed intent on reading values into nature, and found guidance from the ethical teachings of Jesus and Kant.

Anthropologist Ashley Montagu, in writing about competition and cooperation in Darwin's writings, concludes: "Though Darwin is somewhat ambivalent in his attitude toward cultural factors as agencies in the evolution of man, it is reasonably clear that he considered man's future development to be dependent largely, if not entirely, upon the improvement in his morality through cultural means."[82] It is not a corollary of natural selection that the future for humans necessarily belongs, on the one hand, to the strongest, the swiftest, and the cleverest, nor, on the other hand, to the weakest, the slowest, and the stupidest. Humans are irresponsible if they assume they will be moral if they passively follow nature's way. Darwin understood morality as a concept that applied to creatures who can choose between alternatives, and he was convinced that cooperative behavior among humans assists survival more than does bloody competition.

Rev. Henry Drummond, professor of natural science at the Free Church College in Glasgow and a participant in Dwight Moody's evangelistic efforts, attempted to correct a misunderstanding of Darwin's writings. He pointed out that Darwin explained that he used his "struggle for existence" phrase "in a large and metaphorical sense including dependence of one being on another, and including (which is more important) not only the life of the individual, but success in leaving progeny."[83] Drummond also correctly noted that Darwin amplified that interdependence comment in the *Origin* by stating and illustrating in the *Descent* the way "those communities which included the greatest number of the most sympathetic members would flourish best."[84]

Based on Darwinism, Drummond focused on the dual forces that play prominent parts in evolution: "There are *two* Struggles for Life in every living thing—the Struggle for Life, and the Struggle for the Life of Others. The web is woven upon a double set of threads, the second thread distinct in color from the first, and giving a totally different pattern to the finished fabric." He illustrated the way in which "other-regarding" is of at least as much importance as "self-regarding": "Without some rudimentary maternal solicitude for the egg in the humblest forms of life, or for the young among the higher forms, the living world would not only suffer, but would cease." Especially among humans, "co-operation is stronger than competition" because their infants have the longest period of helplessness of any species before they can fend for themselves and arrive at maturity. They are dependent for their very existence on the unrewarded personal care of others that sometimes has a sacrificial dimension. Drummond, like Joseph Butler, related those qualities to the basic moral imperatives of the biblical religion, to love both others and one's self.[85] He criticized theologians who claim to discover evidence for God in the "missing links" of paleontology, who "ceaselessly scan the fields of Nature and the books of Science in search of gaps—gaps which they will fill up with God."[86] Drummond's stress on continuity between the theological and biological realms was well received among British and American Christians in the late nineteenth century.[87]

At Darwin's university, ethicist George Moore followed up on evolutionary issues by discussing, at the beginning of the twentieth century, what he called the "naturalistic fallacy."[88] He was questioning what eighteenth-century poet Alexander Pope affirmed when extolling nature: "One truth is clear, Whatever is, is right."[89] Moore singled out Herbert Spencer as the principal offender, because Spencer tended to define moral good in terms of what conforms to empirical understandings of natural processes. Moore soundly reasoned that it is fallacious to attempt to deduce what ought to be done from describing the way the evolutionary world has been operating. Normative prescriptions or proscriptions cannot be derived from behavioral descriptions. For example, it is a statement of natural fact that stronger animals often devour weaker ones, but that does not imply that humans cannot and ought not improve upon zoological practices. Even though descriptive data may contribute to forming norms, the latter cannot be reduced to the former. "What ought to be" is derived from qualities of ideal humanity found in such sources as literary and religious texts.

Robert Millikan, the Nobel prize-winning physicist, singled out three ideas that stand out above all others in the influence they have had on human development: the golden rule, natural law, and evolution.[90] If his assessment is correct, Darwin can be credited for promoting all three in *Descent*, which threw a multifaceted light on previous mysteries.

Notes

1. *Origin*, 240.
2. Henry Adams, *The Education of Henry Adams: An Autobiography* (Boston: Houghton Mifflin, 1918), 284.
3. *Quarterly Review* (April 1869): 391–94.
4. Quoted in Paul Heyer, *Nature, Human Nature, and Society* (Westport, Conn.: Greenwood, 1982), 176.
5. Henrietta Litchfield, ed., *Emma Darwin* (New York: Appleton, 1915), 2:196.
6. *Autobiography*, 141.
7. Proverbs 6:6.
8. Larry Arnhart, *Darwinian Natural Right* (Albany: State University of New York, 1998), 144.
9. Paul Farber, *The Temptations of Evolutionary Ethics* (Berkeley: University of California Press, 1994), 19–20.
10. *Autobiography*, 55, 66.
11. Mark 12:13; Romans 13:10.
12. Joseph Butler, *Sermons* (London: Tegg, 1836), 29, 118–24.
13. Immanuel Kant, "Conclusion," in *Critique of Practical Reason* (1788).

14. Euripides, *Orestes*, 395–98; Plato, *Apology*, 40.

15. Romans 2:14–15.

16. *Autobiography*, 94–95.

17. Robert Richards, *Darwin and the Emergence of Evolutionary Theories of Mind and Behavior* (Chicago: University of Chicago Press, 1987), 800.

18. *Notebooks*, 550.

19. Genesis 2:6–7; 6:4; 19:1, 12; Ecclesiastes 3:19–20.

20. *Correspondence*, 7:214.

21. Alfred, Lord Tennyson, "Guinevere," 372–73.

23. Matthew 5:44.

24. William Phipps, *The Wisdom and Wit of Rabbi Jesus* (Louisville: Westminster/John Knox, 1993), 189–99.

25. *Autobiography*, 94.

26. William Ritter, *Charles Darwin and the Golden Rule* (New York: Storm, 1954), 102.

27. *Notebooks*, 316.

28. LLD, 2:331.

29. Genesis 2:19.

30. Richard Whately, *A General View of the Rise, Progress, and Corruption of Christianity* (New York: Gowans, 1860), 14–33.

31. *Origin*, 2.

32. Charles Darwin, *The Expression of the Emotions in Man and Animals* (Chicago: University of Chicago Press, 1965), 17.

33. Arnhart, *Darwinian*, 192–95.

34. Pius XII, *Humani Generis*, 1950 encyclical.

35. *Correspondence*, 8:377–78.

36. Psalm 139:13 (New Revised Standard Version).

37. *The Edinburgh Review* (July 1871): 195.

38. Quoted in David Wilson, *Carlyle in Old Age* (London: K. Paul, 1934), 328.

39. *Contemporary Review* 17 (1871): 275.

40. *The Spectator* (18 March 1871), 320.

41. Quoted from *The Spectator* in a footnote of the *Descent*, 277.

42. Jane Gray, ed., *Letters of Asa Gray* (Boston: Houghton, 1893), 2:615; Acts 26:28.

43. Asa Gray, *Natural Science and Religion* (New York: Scribner's, 1880), 54.

44. Ibid., 99.

45. Ibid., 55; 1 Corinthians 15:46.

46. Edward Lurie, *Louis Agassiz* (Chicago: Chicago University Press, 1960), 257.

47. Acts 17:26.

48. *Correspondence*, 7:358.

49. Charles Hodge, *Systematic Theology* (New York: Scribner's, 1871), 2:31; *The American Journal of Science and Arts* (July 1860): 154.

50. Charles Hodge, *What Is Darwinism?* (New York: Scribner's, 1874), 173.

51. William Phipps, "Asa Gray's Theology of Nature," *American Presbyterians* (fall 1988): 171–72.

52. James McCosh, *Religious Aspects of Evolution* (New York: Scribner's, 1890), 58.

53. James McCosh, *Christianity and Positivism* (New York: Carter, 1871), 67.

54. George Mivart, "Ape Resemblances to Man," *Nature* (20 April 1871): 481.

55. *Origin*, 118.

56. Ronald Clark, *The Survival of Charles Darwin* (New York: Random House, 1984), 194.

57. *Autobiography*, 125–26.

58. Henry Manning, *Essays on Religion and Literature* (London, 1865), 51.

59. Gregory Elder, *Chronic Vigour* (Lanham, Md.: University Press of America, 1996), 75.

60. Quoted in Philip Appleman, ed., *Darwin* (New York: Norton, 1979), 536.

61. David Oldroyd, *Darwinian Impacts* (Kensington, Australia: New South Wales University Press, 1980), 270; Herbert Spencer, *The Data of Ethics* (London: Williams, 1907), 19.

62. *Autobiography*, 109.

63. Hebert Spencer, *Social Statics* (New York: Appleton, 1896), 150–51.

64. Will Durant, *The Story of Philosophy* (New York: Simon and Schuster, 1926), 436.

65. John Raines, "Darwin, Death, and Hope," *Cross Currents* (summer 1994): 243.

66. James Nicols, *History of Christianity* (New York: Ronald, 1956), 281.

67. Quoted in Richard Hofstadter, *Social Darwinism in American Thought* (Boston: Beacon, 1955), 45.

68. "The 1893 Romanes Lecture," in *The Essence of T. H. Huxley*, ed. Cyril Bibby (New York: Macmillan, 1967), 173.

69. Richard Dawkins, *The Selfish Gene* (New York: Oxford University Press, 1989), 3.

70. Bibby, *Huxley*, 198–99.

71. Thomas Huxley, *Methods and Results* (New York: Appleton, 1896), 284.

72. Thomas Huxley et al., *Christianity and Agnosticism* (New York: Appleton, 1889), 50.

73. Ibid., 52.

74. Thomas Huxley, *Science and Hebrew Tradition* (New York: Appleton, 1894), 161, 361.

75. Owen Chadwick, *The Secularization of the European Mind in the Nineteenth Century* (Cambridge: Cambridge University Press, 1975), 231, 237.

76. Matthew Arnold, *Literature and Dogma* (London: Nelson, 1873), 47.

77. Romans 6:5–6; Colossians 3:1–3.

78. Matthew Arnold, *St. Paul and Protestantism* (New York: Macmillan, 1883), 75–76.

79. Arnhart, *Darwinian*, 146–49.

80. Petr Kropotkin, *Mutual Aid, a Factor of Evolution* (Boston: Horizons, 1902), x, 110–11, 293.

81. Heyer, *Human Nature*, 156–57.

82. Ashley Montagu, *Darwin: Competition and Cooperation* (Westport, Conn.: Greenwood, 1975), 94–95.

83. *Origin*, 33.

84. Henry Drummond, *The Lowell Lectures on the Ascent of Man* (New York: Pott, 1894), 217, 238.

85. Drummond, *Ascent*, 17, 219, 222.

86. Ibid., 426.

87. David Livingstone, *Darwin's Forgotten Defenders* (Edinburgh: Scottish Academic Press, 1987), 97.

88. George Moore, *Principia Ethica* (Cambridge: Cambridge University Press, 1902), 10.

89. Alexander Pope, *An Essay on Man*, 1:289.

90. Robert Millikan, *Science and the New Civilization* (New York: Scribner's, 1930), 167.

CHAPTER SEVEN

Final Personal Considerations

Darwin's seventy-three years spanned a time of enormous intellectual, technical, and cultural change. As a result of the industrial revolution, the railroad and steamship were rapidly replacing transportation powered by the horse and wind. Convulsive shifts in physics, geology, and biology were paralleled by the application of methods of literary and historical criticism to interpret the heretofore presumed inerrant Bible. The intellectual horizons of most educated people were vastly enlarged, and many were caught in confusion, trying to integrate the new ideas with an old worldview.

After Darwin gained his evolutionary understanding of biology, he struggled for the rest of his life with the question of whether and how religion could be reconciled with it. In the autobiography Darwin wrote during his final years, he devoted much attention to his problems with religious doctrine. He had called himself a Christian until about 1845, and a theist for most of the last half of his life. James Moore, who has made the deepest probe into Darwin's life in the Downe village, states that "he remained a muddled theist to the end."[1] Stephen Gould surmises that Darwin, in his last years, "probably retained a belief in some kind of personal god—but he did not grant his deity a directly and continuously intervening role in the evolutionary process."[2] Darwin's residual theism was "a part of his total vision of reality up until the end," because it made his science possible: "For him, the rationality and moral probity of God underlay the rationality and meaningfulness of science: it was a metaphysical basis, a remnant of natural theology . . . that Darwin required but acknowledged only by implication. It assured him that the laws of nature and the universe which they described were a genuine world."[3]

In his metaphysical quandary, Darwin:

> [N]ever made up his mind in any final sense. It so baffled him that he could only set it in the category of the unanswerable ultimates (like the conflict between free will and determinism, only worse). . . .

He was always reticent; if one could not speak with authority, and to console, silence were the better part. . . . In the end he hung his doubt in the all-concealing cloak of a freely-admitted ignorance. . . . He frankly didn't know whether Design or Choice, God or No-God, ruled the universe.[4]

But Darwin was not so open-minded that he indiscriminately tolerated any theology in his inner sanctum. He was in line with traditional Christianity in rejecting the alleged supernaturalism that was then a fad in Britain. George Bernard Shaw noted that during the late nineteenth century the British were "addicted to table-rapping, materialization séances, clairvoyance, palmistry, crystal-gazing and the like."[5] Janet Oppenheim writes: "Spiritualism appeared to solve that most agonizing of Victorian problems: how to synthesize modern scientific knowledge and time-honored religious traditions concerning man, God, and the universe."[6] Evolutionist Alfred Wallace was among those who were convinced of the reality of such phenomena.[7] But Darwin acknowledged to his pastor, Brodie Innes, "I am a complete skeptic about . . . stories one hears about the spirit-tapping now-a-days—the old saying to believe nothing one hears and only half of what one sees is a golden rule."[8] When dilettante Erasmus Darwin indulged in a séance where clients of a medium awaited reassuring communications with disembodied spirits of the dead, his exasperated brother said, "The Lord have mercy on us all, if we have to believe in such rubbish."[9]

TWO SIMILAR AGNOSTICS

In the last decade of life, Darwin moved toward an outlook on ultimate concerns that had recently been given a name—"agnostic." According to the *Oxford English Dictionary*, it was originally an epistemological term to express that God is beyond what humans can know by their empirical and rational facilities. A few years after Thomas Huxley introduced the Greek word into English in 1869, Darwin applied it to himself in an effort to deal with some theological difficulties:

Can the mind of man, which has, as I fully believe, been developed from a mind as low as that possessed by the lowest animal, be trusted when it draws such grand [theistic] conclusions? May not these be the result of the connection between cause and effect which strikes us as a necessary one, but probably depends merely on inherited experience? Nor must we overlook the probability of the constant inculcation in a belief in God on the minds of children producing so strong and perhaps an inherited effect on their brains not yet fully developed, that it would be as difficult for them to throw off their belief in God, as for a monkey to throw off its instinctive fear and hatred of a snake. I cannot pretend to throw the least light on such abstruse problems. The mystery of the beginning of all things is insoluble by us; and I for one must be content to remain an Agnostic.[10]

Huxley used the term "agnostic" in a distinctive way. He endorsed the advice of the apostle Paul, "Prove all things; hold fast to that which is good."[11] Huxley realized that there was a heretical group known as Gnostics in the New Testament era who were disdainful of those who did not claim to have received special *gnosis* (knowledge) from God.[12] Their claim of exclusive enlightenment caused them to abstain from marriage, alcohol, and other allegedly defiling worldly enjoyments. The majority of early Christians, who became known as the orthodox, doubted their truth claims. Those Christians were anti-gnostic or a-gnostic because they rejected the presumption of esoteric knowledge derived from special revelations. Huxley informed his fellow members of the Metaphysical Society that his use of agnostic was "antithetic to the 'gnostic' of Church history, who professed to know so much about the very things of which I was ignorant."[13] Interestingly, he allied himself on this point with mainline early Christians.

Huxley had been influenced by the 1858 Bampton Lecture entitled "The Limits of Religious Thought" by Henry Mansel, an orthodox Oxford theologian who became the dean of St. Paul's Cathedral. "A piece of clear and unanswerable reasoning" was the way Huxley described it to Charles Lyell.[14] Mansel introduced into English religious thought the epistemology of Immanuel Kant contained in *The Critique of Pure Reason*. The German philosopher argued that our knowledge is restricted to the "phenomenal world," the realm humans construct in accord with patterns provided by their minds. Accordingly, we can have belief in, but no certain knowledge of, the external world as it really is, whether considering matter, God, or immortality of the soul. According to Kant, absolute proof of the existence *or* nonexistence of God is not possible. Huxley agreed with Mansel and Kant that knowledge of the transcendent God was beyond the limits of human cognition. Huxley recalled that on reading Mansel's book, he felt "as orthodox as a dignitary of the Church."[15]

Huxley advised: "Follow your reason as far as it will take you . . . [and] do not pretend that conclusions are certain which are not demonstrated or demonstrable. That I take to be the agnostic faith."[16] Agnosticism is closely related to skepticism, which suspends judgment on the existence of anything beyond and behind natural phenomena. Scorned by Huxley were theologians who pretended to be absolutely certain about the nature of God and the way Deity operated in daily life. But he also applied his agnostic outlook to science, maintaining that there are likewise limits on what scientists can explain. He wrote to Charles Kingsley, "I don't know that atoms are anything but pure myths."[17] Moreover, Huxley always had some doubt as to the validity of Darwin's natural selection hypothesis.[18]

Huxley opposed atheists as well as many theologians. He viewed agnosticism as undermining "not only the greater part of popular theology but also the greater part of popular antitheology."[19] In Huxley's day atheism was especially associated with the dialectical materialism of Marx and Engels. Huxley declared, "I, individually, am no materialist, but on the contrary believe materialism to involve grave philosophical error."[20]

For Darwin as well as Huxley, the problem of belief without sufficient evidence was not just a problem in religion. Darwin wrote: "[N]othing is so difficult to decide as where to draw a just line between skepticism and credulity" and that caution is "almost the soul of science."[21] Frequently, he was frank in admitting doubts in his scientific judgments, which should not be interpreted to mean that he was about to reject them.

Huxley and Darwin steered between the reductive naturalism of the atheist philosophers and the superstitious supernaturalism of the biblical literalists. Thinking that it was wrong to believe without sufficient evidence, Huxley resisted the "God of the gaps" approach. The approach can be damaging to religion because when a previous ignorance gap is eliminated, it appears that God's rule has shrunk. Darwin, likewise, when ignorant of a natural explanation, did not find it honest or helpful to posit that God was responsible.

Darwin did not view Huxley as antireligious and was sincere when, in 1864, he said of Huxley, "You are so good a Christian."[22] In 1860, Darwin became the godfather of Huxley's son, Leonard.[23] Huxley can be distinguished from the practical atheists who in later times would call themselves agnostics. In 1875, he learned to read Greek and then frequently used his knowledge of the original language of the New Testament to debate religious issues. He probably acquired more understanding of the literary structure of the New Testament than most clergymen of his day. Adrian Desmond, in his unexcelled biography of Huxley, calls him "a Manichaean Calvinist,"[24] emphasizing the puritanical, anticlerical, and rationally cautious aspects of Protestant theology.

A great deal of traditional religious morality was embedded in Victorian agnosticism: "The agnostics were not trying to destroy all forms of religion when they launched their onslaught on Christianity. The new reformation represented for Huxley the building of a new religion that would recover what had been lost by Christianity when it perverted the pure ideals of its founder."[25] According to Huxley, agnosticism does not touch religion that is defined as "reverence and love for the ethical ideal, and the desire to realise that ideal in life."[26] The moral dimension of Jesus' life and teachings resonated in Huxley, who saw in the founder of Christianity an expression of the ethical teachings of the prophets of Judaism, shorn of priest-craft and dogma.

Darwin, like Huxley, thought it would have been arrogant for him to claim to know the mind of One who moves in a mysterious way. Agnostic musings can be traced through most of Darwin's adult life. In 1838 he wrote, "We know nothing of the will of the Deity, how it acts and whether constant or inconstant like that of man."[27] "In his later years Darwin tended to an agnosticism that vacillated between a vague hope that evolution might eventually be reconciled with belief in God and a pessimistic fear that no purpose whatsoever could be discerned in the history of life."[28] His agnosticism pertained to a lack of certainty, not to a denial of Deity. "Darwin's agnosticism does not entirely eradicate his theistic belief, which seems to him almost innate; it questions whether the belief is backed by appropriate evidence."[29] Gavin De Beer, director of the British Museum, asserts, "For all his agnosticism, Darwin was not devoid of faith, but it was the faith of a scientist, that the laws of nature are consistent and that fundamentally order prevails in the universe."[30]

Lyman Abbott, who edited a leading American religious journal entitled *Outlook*, commended Huxley and Darwin for calling themselves agnostics. In his 1897 book, *Theology of an Evolutionist*, he viewed their agnosticism as "an indication of their frank recognition that the universe cannot be comprehended by finite man."[31] Those biologists, along with some orthodox Christians, recognized that the more they increased the diameter of their knowledge, the more they became aware of the circumference of their ignorance.

Darwin was aware of what Christians believed about immortality and the soul, but he suspended judgment on their existence. He described himself as "a man who has no assured and ever present belief in the existence of a personal God or of a future existence with retribution and reward."[32] Several years before his death, Darwin reflected on the idea of personal immortality: "Believing as I do that man in the distant future will be a far more perfect creature than he now is, it is an intolerable thought that he and all other sentient beings are doomed to complete annihilation after such long-continued slow progress. To those who fully admit the immortality of the human soul, the destruction of our world will not appear so dreadful."[33]

Darwin had a "pet horror," but it was not the prospect of there being no immortality for humans. He had become aware of the recently discovered second law of thermodynamics and accepted its implication that the solar system would eventually become too cold to sustain life. The gloomy prospect of a universe that was running down prompted this reflection: "Personal annihilation sinks in my mind into insignificance compared with the idea or rather I presume certainty of the sun some day cooling and we all freezing. To think of the progress of millions of years, with every continent swarming with good and enlightened men, all ending in this. . . . *Sic transit gloria mundi*."[34]

Darwin was repelled by the outspokenness of atheists. He had appreciated atheist Auguste Comte's distinction between the theological stage of thought and the subsequent stage that searched for laws, but he was uninterested in other aspects of Comte's philosophy. In 1869 he told Joseph Hooker that he once "had a vague wish to read Comte," but Huxley's devastating article "The Scientific Aspects of Positivism" had cured him of the desire.[35] Comte developed a religion of humanity with a ritual that affirmed "Glory to humans in the highest." Huxley was incensed by Comte's authoritarian pseudoreligion, which he satirized as "Catholicism minus Christianity."[36] Darwin said that he liked reading what Huxley had written about Comte's "propounding solemn nonsense."[37]

In 1877, when Charles Bradlaugh was elected to Parliament but denied a seat there because of his antireligious views, he wrote Darwin to request his support. He refused to testify on Bradlaugh's behalf at a trial because, as James Moore points out, his "social sympathies lay, as usual, with Christians, not atheists."[38] Darwin was a closet agnostic; he was careful to make no public disclosure of his position. By way of partially explaining his shyness in publicizing his religious views, Moore states: "Darwin's reluctance to speak out on religion arose from growing uncertainty about whether he had any good grounds for still believing in God and personal immortality. It was altogether easier, and certainly much more respectable, to keep one's views to oneself and be judged by one's deeds as an eminent Christian gentleman."[39]

In 1880, Edward Aveling, Marx's son-in-law, was eager to obtain Darwin's permission to dedicate to him a book on Darwinian evolution that an antireligious press would publish. In refusing his request, Darwin stated:

> Though I am a strong advocate for free thought on all subjects, yet it appears to me (whether rightly or wrongly) that direct arguments against christianity and theism produce hardly any effect on the public; and freedom of thought is best promoted by the gradual illumination of men's minds, which follow from the advance of science. It has, therefore, been always my object to avoid writing on religion [for publication], I have confined myself to science."[40]

Darwin did permit Aveling, in the company of German physiologist Ludwig Buchner, to interview him in 1881 at Down House. Aveling later reported that Darwin initiated a conversation about religion:

> Almost the first thing he said was, "Why do you call yourselves Atheists? . . . I should prefer the word Agnostic to the word Atheist." . . . [Aveling replied] that 'Agnostic' was but 'Atheist' writ respectable, and 'Atheist' was only 'Agnostic' writ aggressive. . . . [Darwin] asked: "Why should you be so aggressive? Is anything gained by trying to force these new ideas upon the mass of mankind?"[41]

In response to John Fordyce's inquiry, Darwin stated about his religion: "What my own views may be is a question of no consequence to any one but myself."[42] But he did disclose: "My judgment often fluctuates. . . . In my most extreme fluctuations I have never been an Atheist in the sense of denying the existence of a God. I think that generally (and more and more as I grow older), but not always, that an Agnostic would be the more correct description of my state of mind." Darwin's final outlook was similar to Gould's, who called himself an agnostic but was convinced that evolution is "both true and entirely consistent with religious belief."[43]

For Darwin, agnosticism was an expression of metaphysical modesty over against the dogmatists. He distrusted that the human mind had the capability to understand questions of ultimate origin. He made fun of the anthropomorphizing of persons who seem to think "God is a man, rather cleverer than us."[44] For them, Darwin's ideas could enlarge awareness of God's greatness by rejecting a naïve identification of commonly accepted ideas with the order established by the Creator. He claimed that he did not have a conviction about the purpose of the universe.

During the century after Darwin, the ordinary meaning of the term agnostic changed. In practice, the style of life of contemporary agnostics is often the same as that of an atheist, and, unlike Darwin, they often enjoy pummeling religion.

LATTER-DAY RELIGION

On many occasions during his final years in Downe, through personal contact or by letter, Darwin interacted with various people with religious interests. He gave regular financial support to the South American Missionary Society and commended the progress of mission work on that continent. Admiral James Sullivan, once a *Beagle* officer, told of the change in Darwin's outlook on the Fuegians. When on their island he thought it was useless to send missionaries there because they could not be changed from savagery, but later he wrote Sullivan that he had underestimated the potential of the natives.[45]

Darwin was the overseer of a former schoolroom in the Downe parish and his family set up a temperance reading room there to diminish the alcoholism that was a major social problem in Britain at the time. James Fegan, a local evangelist, requested in 1880 to use the room so that his tent revival could be brought indoors.[46] In a letter granting Fegan permission, Darwin added: "Your services have done more for the village in a few months than all our efforts for many years. . . . Through your services I do not know that there is a drunkard left in the village."[47]

George Romanes came to work with Darwin in 1874 as a young research consultant and became his strongest supporter. Romanes had planned to follow the career of his theologian father, and received a prize at Christ's College in Cambridge for his essay on the relationship between Christian prayer and natural law.[48] Darwin expressed appreciation for being given a copy of the published essay, which concluded that science and religion are not "antagonistic but complementary." Romanes used a verse from the Torah to garnish his position: "The secret things belong unto the Lord our God, but those things which are revealed belong unto us and to our children forever."[49] Darwin and Romanes had a close mentor-disciple relationship for the rest of the Darwin's life. He read carefully Romanes's 1878 publication *A Candid Examination of Theism*, and found it "very eloquently written."[50] It stimulated Darwin to recognize that different approaches in religions and sciences can enable one to move further along the road toward total truth. Referring to God's existence, Darwin commented, "Reason may not be the only instrument for ascertaining its truth."[51] Darwin asked Romanes how he would respond to a theologian who maintained that matter "was created by God with the most marvelous affinities, leading to complex definite compounds and with polarities leading to beautiful crystals." Darwin admitted that he could not criticize the hypothetical theologian.[52] Romanes came to share Darwin's agnostic outlook, which did not keep him from being ever sensitive to the moral and literary qualities of the Bible.

In an 1874 letter to Lyell, Darwin recognized that many accept the existence of a personal God and immortality by "intuition," but he said, "I do not feel any innate conviction on any such points."[53] He later wrote: "If we consider the whole universe, the mind refuses to look at it as the outcome of chance—that is, without design or purpose. The whole question seems to me insoluble, for I cannot put much or any faith in the so-called intuitions of the human mind."[54] Darwin's ambivalence was like that of the Gospel's Thomas, who testified, "Lord, I believe; help thou mine unbelief."[55]

Darwin corresponded occasionally with Francis Abbot, a Unitarian clergyman and editor of *The Index*, the organ of the Free Religious Association based in America. Darwin subscribed to the journal from 1871 onward, which prompted Abbot to solicit literary contributions from him. But Darwin responded that his poor health had prevented him from feeling "equal to deep reflection on the deepest subject which can fill a man's mind."[56] He also confided to Abbot: "I was strongly advised by a friend never to introduce anything about religion in my works, if I wished to advance science in England; and this led me not to consider the mutual bearings of the two subjects."[57] In 1876, he sent Abbot the same generous donation for his organization that he gave to the Downe Vicarage Endowment Fund. Abbot was permitted to reproduce in his periodical that Darwin, after reading his pamphlet *Truths for the Times*, replied: "I admire them from my inmost heart, and I believe that I agree to every word."[58] In an effort to reconcile science and religion, Abbot published *Scientific Theism* in 1885. At the end of his life he stated that the purpose of his writings had been to help his fellows "know God better, and make this world more noble, pure, and just."[59]

Frequently during his last years, Darwin received international letters inquiring about his religion. Sometimes he replied, "I am sorry to have to inform you that I do not believe in the Bible as a divine revelation, and therefore not in Jesus Christ as the Son of God."[60] Darwin distanced himself from discussions about religious matters, but he admired the ability of some scholars to establish a rapprochement between science and theology. In response to a letter in 1879, he cited the ability of "Asa Gray the eminent botanist" and Charles Kingsley to harmonize evolution and theology as well as to show that it is "absurd to doubt that a man may be an ardent theist and an evolutionist."[61] Darwin's inability to resolve the question of the relationship between God and particular organic processes did not lead him to conclude that discussion of such relationship was meaningless. Rather, he realized that religion was not within the scope of empirical science.

To a German student who inquired about his religious views, Darwin first had a family member respond, "He considers that the theory of Evolution is quite compatible with belief in a God; but that you must remember that different persons have different definitions of what they mean by God." When the student wrote again, Darwin penned this reply: "Science has nothing to do with Christ, except in so far as the habit of scientific research makes a man cautious in admitting evidence. For myself, I do not believe that there ever has been any revelation. As for a future life, every man must judge for himself between conflicting vague probabilities."[62] These letters have been "seized upon by some as evidence that Darwin was a complete atheist, which is a grave misreading of his character as a scientist."[63]

Darwin's seasoned religious disposition is well displayed in his response to a Dutch student:

> The impossibility of conceiving that this grand and wondrous universe, with our conscious selves, arose through chance, seems to me the chief argument for the existence of God; but whether this is an argument of real value, I have never been able to decide. I am aware that if we admit a first cause, the mind still craves to know whence it came, and how it arose. Nor can I overlook the difficulty from the immense amount of suffering through the world. I am, also, induced to defer to a certain extent to the judgment of many able men who have fully believed in God; but here again I see how poor an argument this is. The safest conclusion seems to be that the whole subject is beyond the scope of man's intellect; but man can do his duty.[64]

Stated here is the logical flaw of the first cause argument: namely, if everything has a cause, then what caused God? The infinite regress argument fails on its own premise, so it has been given little attention in the modern era by reasoning people. Also, Darwin shared the problem that both the simple and the wise have always found baffling—how can a good and almighty God permit the innocent to suffer?

When George Darwin asked for comment on a religion essay he had written, his father provided this reminder, "I am not a good critic as I have not read much on such subjects."[65] About publishing the essay, George's father urged, "My advice is pause, pause, pause." He confided, "[I]t is a fearfully difficult moral problem about the speaking out on religion, and I have never been able to make up my mind."[66]

In 1878, Rev. Edward Pusey, a conservative Anglo-Catholic leader, preached a sermon entitled "Un-Science, Not Science, Adverse to Faith." It charged that Darwin inconsistently introduced the Creator to avoid the eternity of matter but then excluded God "from all interference with the works which He has made." Pusey quoted Cardinal Newman's remark, "[A]ny one study . . . . exclusively pursued, deadens in the mind the interest, nay the perception, of any other."[67]

About Darwin's theory, Pusey wrote, "It is an enormous theory without the basis of a single fact for these 6,000 years."[68] After reading Pusey's sermon, Darwin wrote: "When I was collecting facts for the *Origin* my belief in what is called a personal God was as firm as that of Dr. Pusey himself." Darwin thought Pusey should not have faulted him for not attempting to solve theological puzzles; moreover, Pusey was wrong in imagining that he "wrote the *Origin* with any relation whatever to theology."[69]

Newman's psychological insight is germane because Darwin's inability to find religious meaning in later life paralleled his loss of finding meaning in other areas of the humanities. He recognized that poetry seeks imaginative truth while science seeks factual truth, and that both types of truth can enlarge one's understandings. Darwin lamented that his brain had atrophied to "become a kind of machine for grinding general laws out of large collections of facts."[70] After becoming absorbed in his doctrine of natural selection, he lost his former appreciation for the liberal arts, with the exception of history, biography, and travel books. He acknowledged that until he was about thirty, he received "great pleasure" from Milton and some other figures in English literature. "But now for many years I cannot endure to read a line of poetry," he confessed. "I have tried lately to read Shakespeare and found it so intolerably dull that it nauseated me."[71] Frances Wedgwood, his sister-in-law, spoke to him around 1875 about his loss of interest in Wordsworth's poems. She observed that he was focused on "some different kind of understanding from what poetry admits of." Darwin admitted, "The habit of looking for one kind of meaning I suppose deadens the perception of another."[72]

There was a corresponding situation with fine art and music, which, Darwin recalled, had once given him "very great delight."[73] After hearing Haydn's *Creation* oratorio on returning to Cambridge in 1838, he wrote: "In the evening attended Trinity Chapel, and heard 'The Heavens are telling the Glory of God,' in magnificent style; the last chorus seemed to shake the very walls of the College."[74] By contrast, thirty years later he wrote Hooker, "I am glad you were at the 'Messiah,' it is the one thing that I should like to hear again, but I dare say I should find my soul too dried up to appreciate it as in old days; and then I should feel very flat, for it is a horrid bore to feel as I constantly do, that I am a withered leaf for every subject except Science."[75] He regretted that oratorios had become noise and empty words in his later years because his single-minded concentration on science had eclipsed interest in all else. Darwin called the esthetic loss an "atrophy of that part of the brain . . . on which the higher tastes depend." He went on to ruminate on how the enfeebling of this important emotional part of his nature might have been prevented: "If I had to live my life again I would have made a rule to read some poetry and listen to some music at least once every week."[76]

Darwin's personal view of music affected his description of human evolution. Since birds use music as a means of courtship, he reasoned that humans, "before acquiring the power of expressing their mutual love in articulate language, endeavoured to charm each other with musical notes and rhythm." Darwin thus thought "musical sounds afforded one of the bases for the development of language." He then added a surprising twist to a common observation: "Women are generally thought to possess sweeter voices than men, [so] we may infer that they first acquired musical powers in order to attract the other sex. But if so, this must have occurred long ago, before our ancestors had become sufficiently human to treat and value their women merely as useful slaves." Darwin was aware of the recent Cro-Magnon discovery in France where flutes of primeval cave dwellers had been found. He baldly stated that songs no longer have a useful function: "Neither the enjoyment nor the capacity of producing musical notes are faculties of the least use to man in reference to his daily habits of life."[77]

Tone deafness or color blindness, Darwin realized, is not the fault of the external source but the internal defect of the subject. He compared his loss of appreciation for the fine arts with his loss of ability to worship:

Formerly I was led by feelings [of beauty] . . . to the firm conviction of the existence of God and of the immortality of the soul. . . . But now the grandest scenes would not cause any such convictions of feelings to rise in my mind. It may be truly said that I am like a man who has become colour-blind, and the universal belief by men of the existence of redness makes my present loss of perception of not the least value as evidence. . . . The state of mind which grand scenes formerly excited in me, and which was intimately connected with a belief in God, did not essentially differ from that which is often called the sense of sublimity . . . excited by music."[78]

Darwin's almost perpetual illness may also have affected his religious disposition. His maladies were mostly gastrointestinal, which might have been in part caused by his inner conflict over unresolved theological issues. Darwin focused his diminished energy on making careful biological observations and drawing ideas on evolution from them.

Darwin's caution in affirming or denying God in that last year of his life was displayed in an exchange he had with George Campbell, duke of Argyll. As they discussed orchids, Campbell remarked that he found it impossible to contemplate their exquisite design "without seeing that they were the effect and the expression of mind." After reflecting on his judgment, Darwin said, "Well, that often comes over me with overwhelming force; but at other times, it seems to go away."[79]

A few weeks before his death, Darwin wrote Daniel Mackintosh, a naturalist, "Whether the existence of a conscious God can be proved from the existence of the so-called laws of nature (*i.e.* fixed sequence of events) is a perplexing subject, on which I have often thought, but cannot see my way clearly."[80] Darwin found he did not know of any way to construct an inductive argument that would clearly affirm or deny the existence of a Creator.

During his last days, Darwin puttered in his extensive garden and continued to engage in research. He was among the loving family that had given him much happiness in life, and was especially blessed with a devoted and understanding wife. In spite of his having to cope with opponents to his theory and with his semi-invalid body, his life had generally been pleasant. He had always been comfortably financed by parental wealth, and in the end he was widely respected by scientists he respected. Darwin gave this evaluation of his lengthy life: "I believe that I have acted rightly in steadily following and devoting my life to science. I feel no remorse from having committed any great sin, but have often and often regretted that I have not done more direct good to my fellow creatures."[81]

Regarding their nearly forty years of marriage, Charles gave Emma this sincere tribute: "I marvel at my good fortune that she, so infinitely my superior in every single moral quality, consented to be my wife. She has been my wise adviser and cheerful comforter throughout life, which without her would have been during a very long period a miserable one from ill-health."[82] He could hardly function when absent from his "greatest blessing," who kept him from working his frail body to death. The sentiments Darwin expressed to his new American daughter-in-law show that he had not lost all ability to worship: "Judging from my own experience life would be a most dreary blank without a dear wife to love with all one's soul."[83] Emma, who was always a steadfast Victorian Christian, was admired by her husband not only for her compassion and patience toward him but also because she never "missed an opportunity of doing a kind action to anyone near her."[84] Moore writes perceptively:

> She had been so much more than the bearer of his children and a nurse to his physical suffering. When at last he relinquished the comforts and terrors of Christianity, she became his means of grace. Like a saintly mother, she felt for him, prayed for him. Insensibly, he grew to depend on her faith and intuitions; they made up for that part of his religious sentiment eroded by reason and bitter grief.[85]

Distressed by seeing her husband often "miserably uncomfortable," Emma jotted down for him her belief that prayer is a means of relief. She acknowledged that she often thought of a biblical assurance: "Thou [God] shalt keep him in perfect peace whose mind is stayed on thee," and she tried to accept "that all suffering and illness is meant to help us to exalt our minds and to look forward with hope to a future state." She observed, "When I see your patience, deep compassion for others, self command and above all gratitude for the smallest thing done to help you I cannot help longing that these precious feelings should be offered to Heaven for the sake of your daily happiness." On the bottom of this note, Charles scribbled "God Bless you."[86]

After his death, numerous tracts circulated widely containing made-in-America fabrications about Darwin's deathbed conversion.[87] For example, Oswald Smith claims that Darwin, just before entering "into the presence of God and Eternity," deplored that he "destroyed Biblical faith in multitudes."[88] Smith received the story from Lady Hope who allegedly visited at Down House. According to her report, she saw Darwin sitting up in bed and studying his Bible. When she alluded to his treatment of its creation account, "his fingers twitched nervously, and a look of agony came over his face." Darwin showed his repentance for the damage his immature ideas had done by asking Lady Hope to return the next day to read the Bible to villagers who would gather outside his bedroom window. He promised that he would join in the singing when the evangelical service was conducted.

To a Canadian who had written Huxley in 1887 to verify a sermon anecdote, he responded: "The statement . . . that 'Mr. Darwin, when on his deathbed, abjectly whined for a minister and renouncing Evolution, sought safety in the blood of the Saviour' is totally false."[89] The actual fact is that several family members heard Darwin whisper "I am not in the least afraid to die" before he succumbed to a heart attack at age seventy-three.[90] Those last words probably had less to do with his reflection on what might await him after death as to his satisfaction over a fulfilled life that had already exceeded the customary span of threescore and ten years. He had made his life's contribution so fully that there was little left for death to take away.

MEMORIALIZING THE SCIENTIFIC SAINT

Darwin had intended to be buried without pomp in the Downe parish graveyard where months earlier the remains of his brother had been interred, and Brodie Innes offered to conduct the funeral. Emma had also decided that her burial would be appropriate there, alongside the graves of two of their children. But simple final rites were not to be.

Frederic Farrar, canon of Westminster Abbey, took the initiative to suggest to Huxley that a funeral in the great historic abbey would be appropriate for Darwin. The mutual admiration that Farrar and Darwin had for one another began when Farrar was present for the famed Oxford meeting, decades earlier, and made a reliable record of the Wilberforce-Huxley encounter. Darwin had written Farrar, then a Harrow schoolteacher, in support of his proposal to permit instruction in science for some students instead of drilling them in classic languages. In the *Descent*, Farrar is commended for his "most interesting" study of the origin of language.[91] Darwin so appreciated his contributions to evolutionary philology that he obtained for him membership in the Royal Society. Huxley had hesitated to request the highest of British funeral honors because he was sure the religious establishment would refuse it. But his friend Farrar assured him, "[W]e clergy were not all so bigoted as he supposed."[92] Farrar contacted the dean of the abbey, who was in France, and he responded positively to a petition by twenty members of Parliament for a state funeral. Virtually no controversy arose over the decision to place Darwin's body among the illustrious dead of Britain.

The shift in burial place signified that British leaders had generally come to realize that Darwin's theory need not be interpreted as detrimental to religious faith and hope. At last, the British establishment gave full recognition to the most significant citizen of Queen Victoria's long reign. John Lewis, the Downe carpenter, testified: "I made his coffin just the way he wanted it, all rough, just as it left the bench, no polish, no nothin'. But they agreed to send him to Westminster. . . . My coffin wasn't wanted and they sent it back. This other one you could see to shave in."[93] In 1882, seven years after geologist Sir Charles Lyell was buried in London's Westminster Abbey, Darwin was accorded the same high honor even though he had never been knighted. Since Darwin had been pleased with the tribute in death paid to his principal mentor, his children were open to the state church's atoning for the shabby treatment previously accorded their father.

The majestic ritual at the place where British sovereigns are crowned and where heroes are buried was a dramatic contrast to Darwin's modest lifestyle. At high noon on April 26, while Beethoven's Funeral March was reverberating, pallbearers Hooker, Huxley, Wallace, Farrar, and other dignitaries, including American Ambassador James Russell Lowell, carried Darwin's coffin up the nave of Westminster Abbey for the state funeral. (Lowell had aided in gaining acceptance for Darwin's theory by publishing Gray's reviews of the *Origin* while he was editor of the *Atlantic Monthly*.) The choir processed singing, "His body is buried in peace, but his name liveth evermore," and following them were diplomats from six European nations, as well as representatives from universities and learned societies. The abbey's organist composed the anthem by adapting words from the third chapter of the Book of Proverbs:

> Happy is the man that findeth wisdom and getteth understanding. . . .
> She is more precious than rubies, and all that thou hast cannot be compared unto her.
> Length of days is in her right hand; and in her left hand riches and honor.
> Her ways are ways of pleasantness, and all her paths are peace.

Had the composer realized that the "tree of life" was Darwin's basic metaphor for natural selection, he might have included the next verse in that Proverbs passage: "She is a tree of life to them that lay hold upon her."

The service was concluded for the "Newton of biology" by laying his body to rest in Britain's most hallowed ground. His remains were placed next to those of his revered teacher, Sir John Herschel, and at the foot of the monument to Isaac Newton, the other English scientist of similar importance. It was also appropriate that Darwin was buried in the company of Dr. David Livingstone, who had been outspoken against slavery in European colonies. The honor he received approximates for the Anglican Church what the canonization of a saint connotes in the Catholic Church. Ironically, if Darwin had pursued a career as a priest, he probably would not have achieved such high religious status at his death.

Had Darwin not requested that there be no epitaph on his gravestone, a line from Ralph Waldo Emerson that Huxley had suggested might have been inscribed on it: "Beware when the great God lets loose a thinker on this planet."[94] Or again, the couplet that Alexander Pope wrote for astrophysicist Newton might have been given a name change and applied just as appropriately to another Cambridge alumnus:

> Nature and nature's laws lay hid in night;
> God said, "Let Darwin be!" and all was light.

In his sermon that Sunday evening, Farrar gave this tribute to Darwin:

> This man, on whom for years bigotry and ignorance poured out their scorn, has been called a materialist. I do not see in all his writings one trace of materialism. I read in every line the healthy, noble, well balanced wonder of a spirit profoundly reverent, kindled into deepest admiration for the works of God. . . . Calm in the consciousness of integrity; happy in sweetness of home life; profoundly modest; utterly unselfish; exquisitely genial; . . . Darwin will take his place . . . with Newton and Pascal . . . among those who have not only served humanity by their genius, but have also brightened its ideal by holy lives.

Farrar reminded his congregation that the Bible indicates that candidates for the future life are not those "saying 'Lord, Lord' and, wearing the broadest of phylacteries, show very faint conceptions of honor, kindness, or the love of truth." Rather, Darwin met the biblical standard as announced by the prophet Micah, "to do justly, and to love mercy, and to walk humbly with Him."[95]

Emma did not attend the funeral, but her absence was not a protest to the appropriateness of the church ceremony. She stated that her husband had "religious friends who are deeply attached to him,"[96] and was gratified for this opportunity for a fitting Anglican memorial. Both Darwins were reluctant to appear in public, so she remained in Down House and probably consoled herself with the poem par excellence of the Victorian era by Alfred, Lord Tennyson. She had copied verses into her notebook from *In Memoriam* that, in the opinion of her daughter Henrietta, contained "an epitome of her life."[97]

Having Christian rites performed over Darwin was not a sacrilege, because he always had an open mind toward belief in God and was ever a practicer of religious duty. After rejecting in life the opportunity to become a priest in the Anglican Church, in death he became an integral part of the Church of England. In a sermon preached at the abbey on the Sunday after Darwin's death, Harvey Goodwin, bishop of Carlisle, spoke of "the foolish notion which some have diligently propagated, but for which Mr. Darwin was not responsible, that there is a necessary conflict between a knowledge of Nature and a belief in God."[98]

Although some thought the abbey funeral was as unfitting as "giving of that which is holy to the dogs," most Britons took pride in the occasion, and appreciated that the nation had expressed gratitude for the steadfast quester for scientific understanding.[99] Across the Atlantic, Rev. John Chadwick appropriated psalmist imagery to describe the event at the abbey: "The nation's grandest temple of religion opened its gates and lifted up its everlasting doors and bade the king of science come in."[100]

Darwin was posthumously treated as a saint: "Religious writers of all persuasions now testified to his 'noble character and his ardent pursuit of truth.' The *Church Times* was lost for epithets—patience, ingenuity, calmness, industry, moderation. Others added the Pauline graces perseverance and faith, and depicted him as a 'true Christian gentleman.'"[101]

In 1885, a statue of Darwin was placed in the Natural History Museum, which the *Times* of London called the "Temple of Nature." Visitors entered under a towering statue of Adam to view the figure of Darwin inside![102] In New York a half century later, a statue of Darwin was placed in the grand Gothic Riverside Church, witnessing that mainline liberal Protestants in America had also integrated his theory into their worldview.

REVERENT CHARLES DARWIN

Darwin did not complete his theological study by becoming ordained, so he was not referred to as a "divine" nor entitled to be addressed as "Reverend." The absence of these outward signs of piety did not separate him from the spiritual leaders of the biblical era; the only use of "reverend" in the English Bible refers to God, not clergy.[103] Although he abandoned his intention to take holy orders, he displayed throughout life some characteristics that are often used to describe holy persons. Darwin exhibited reverence toward whoever was responsible for originating and developing the universe and a concomitant humility toward his own position within it. William Darwin commented on his father's deep respect for the laws of nature: "It might be called reverence if not a religious feeling. No man could feel more intensely the vastness or the inviolability of the laws of nature, and especially the helplessness of mankind except so far as the laws were obeyed."[104]

Shortly after publishing the *Origin*, Darwin shared with Gray the way in which Calvinist foreordination theology transcended comprehension: "It has always seemed to me that for an omnipotent and omniscient Creator to foresee is the same as to preordain; but then when I come to think over this I get into an uncomfortable puzzle *something* analogous with 'necessity and Free-will' or the 'Origin of evil,' or other such subject quite beyond the scope of the human intellect."[105]

In recognizing that God is beyond human understanding, Darwin was in line with the outlook of pivotal leaders of his religious tradition. They maintained that God's truth is much greater than human ideas of God, in keeping with the prophecy of Isaiah: "My thoughts are not your thoughts, neither are your ways my ways, saith the Lord. For as the heavens are higher than the earth, so are my ways higher than your ways, and my thoughts than your thoughts."[106]

Following the Hebrew epistemological outlook, Paul might be called a reverent agnostic. In spite of being the foremost theologian of Christianity, he exclaimed: "Oh the depth of the riches both of the wisdom and knowledge of God! how unsearchable are his judgments, and his ways past finding out! For who hath known the mind of the Lord?"[107] According to Paul, humans are but dimly aware of God's essence, and complete insight into ultimate reality on this side of death is not possible.[108] Unlike dogmatic agnostics who claim that no one can ever have knowledge of God, the stance of reverent agnostics, including Darwin, is that knowledge is lacking but openness is expressed toward removing some theological ignorance in the future.

Continuing in the Judeo-Christian tradition, Reformed theologian John Calvin claimed that God is "incomprehensible," a doctrine of monotheistic religions also found in Islam.[109] Calvinism profoundly affected British Protestantism from the sixteenth century onward. Calvin interpreted as baby talk the biblical anthropomorphism that describes God as having human form, to "accommodate . . . our slight capacity."[110] When people think of God literally acting like a good Father, using his hand to uphold the godly, the problem of evil is exacerbated. Since finite minds cannot define the infinite, full disclosure of the divine is not possible even in God's self-revelation.

Newton expressed well the view that the totality of truth about God and the universe is far beyond human grasp. A devout Christian, he testified shortly before his death: "I do not know what I may appear to the world, but to myself I seem to have been only like a boy playing on the seashore, and diverting myself in now and then finding a smoother pebble or a prettier shell than ordinary, whilst the great ocean of truth lay all undiscovered before me."[111] Newton recognized the humility that is needed for opening doors to greater illumination.

Darwin's awareness of nature's vastness also freed him from delusions of grandeur and increased in him what religions regard as a prime virtue—humility. This was not self-abrogation, but a realistic assessment of where he stood in his physical and social environment. To someone who thought that his views explained the universe, Darwin replied that such an assumption was "a most monstrous exaggeration." He continued, "The more one thinks the more one feels the hopeless immensity of man's ignorance."[112] He used this figure: "It strikes me that all our knowledge about the structure of our earth is very much like what an old hen would know of a hundred acre field, in a corner of which she is scratching."[113] Observing that the dogmatic tend to be those who actually know little, Darwin supplied this aphorism: "Ignorance more frequently begets confidence than does knowledge."[114] His characteristic lack of pretense can be contrasted to the hypocrites who are cited in the Gospels as irreverent. Modest self-esteem has ever been a hallmark of both good science and good religion.

In a chapter on Darwin's religion, psychologist Robert Wright analyzes the subtleties of self-mockery:

> Martin Luther . . . said a saint is someone who understands that everything he does is egotistical. This definition of sainthood reflects favorably on Darwin. Here is a characteristic utterance: "But what a horridly egotistical letter, I am writing; I am so tired, that nothing short of the pleasant stimulus of vanity and writing about one's own dear self would have sufficed." . . . (He had been voicing anxiety, not confidence, about how his work aboard the Beagle would be received.)[115]

Leonard Darwin told how his father tended "to concentrate his attention on possible defects in his own character and to ignore probable merits."[116]

Darwin's devotion to nature was similar to the attitude Huxley expressed:

> Science seems to me to teach in the highest and strongest manner the great truth which is embodied in the Christian conception of entire surrender to the will of God. Sit down before fact as a little

child, be prepared to give up every preconceived notion, follow
humbly wherever and to whatever abysses nature leads, or you shall
learn nothing. I have only begun to learn content and peace of
mind since I have resolved at all risks to do this.[117]

Owen Chadwick thinks that it was because of Darwin's admiration of
John Henslow's qualities as a practicing Christian and scientist that "he
retained all his life a respect for good religion where it could be
found."[118] Chadwick states: "Darwin helped the adjustment of English
minds to new truth because he, who became the symbol of the conflict,
had almost no pugnacity. In his background was the Reverend Dr.
Henslow, at his side was a Christian wife, and his personality lacked all
wish to demolish religion. He was a direct, humble and reverent seeker
after truth."[119]

Moore writes that Darwin always thought that humility toward
human mental acumen was in order:

> The lowliness of human reason is the principal handicap of theo-
> logical speculation on origins. . . . One has no right to assume that
> the Creator works by intellectual powers like one's own. Indeed,
> since these powers have been evolved from unreasoning lower ani-
> mals by fixed biological laws, one cannot help but experience a
> "horrid doubt" as to the trustworthiness of every metaphysical
> conviction.[120]

Darwin was never convinced of his genius—which paradoxically may
have contributed to its increase. In contrast to Thomas Carlyle's "great
man" theory of history, he wrote Herbert Spencer late in life: "I never
believed in the reigning influence of great men on the World's
progress."[121] Darwin's intellectual modesty is well illustrated by the
concluding sentences of two of his books. The *Descent* closes with an
openness to the flaws of his theory: "Many of the views which have
been advanced are highly speculative, and some no doubt will prove
erroneous."[122] Likewise, his autobiography ends: "With such moderate
abilities as I possess, it is truly surprising that thus I should have influenced to a considerable extent the beliefs of scientific men on some
important points."

Throughout his life Darwin maintained a childlike wonder, demonstrated in his last years by his fascination with the habits of earthworms.
In 1881 he published his final work, *The Formation of Vegetable Mould
through the Action of Worms.* An unperceptive Down House gardener
commented that his doting employer was so confused that he made

long pauses on his walk to stare at a single flower. Darwin was giving a clue to his genius, because it was by means of patient observation and concentrated reflection that he was able to make inspired guesses. Also, like St. Francis, he had an affection for organisms. Regarding his garden, one of his sons recalled that he had "a kind of gratitude to the flower itself, and a personal love for its delicate form and colour."[123]

Darwin had the "holy curiosity" that Albert Einstein said was needed for the study of nature.[124] The biologist's intense search for patterns of biological orderliness had a quality of reverence that is conveyed in a poem by one of his English contemporaries. Reflecting on Moses' initiating religious experience, Elizabeth Browning wrote:

> Earth's crammed with heaven,
> And every common bush afire with God;
> But only he who sees, takes off his shoes,
> The rest sit round it and pluck blackberries.[125]

♦ ♦ ♦

Although Darwin rejected some Christian doctrines, he carried out many of the duties associated with traditional Christianity. After indulging in youthful leisure, the adult Darwin took the Protestant work ethic seriously. When he learned while on the *Beagle* that one of his teachers had come to recognize that he had given up idle pursuits, Charles declared to his sisters, "A man who dares waste one hour of time, has not discovered the value of life."[126] Near the end of life he affirmed, "It has been my greatest comfort to say hundreds of times to myself that 'I have worked as hard and as well as I could, and no man can do more than this.'"[127] Because he usually did not feel well, he was able to average only several good hours of concentrated work a day. The remainder of the day was ordinarily spent with members of his family inside and outside their house. His schedule was unchanged every day, including Sunday, and when his wife managed to pry him away for a vacation, he often fretted until he could return to his research. The work was unrelated to economic advancement, because the Darwins lived throughout life almost completely on the wealth their fathers had shared with them.

Darwin derived his standards for living not from the predatory law of the jungle, but, to a large extent, from the rule of reciprocity.

Deep in his character there was a warm humanitarianism and a strong holdover of the Christian ethic in which he had been trained.

Although he thought the moral sense had originated by natural selection of those tribes in whom the social instinct was strongest, he recognized that this primitive ethic had been gradually developed into a "higher morality" through the effects of habit, rational reflection, religious instruction, and the like. . . . Not "the survival of the fittest" but "do unto others as you would have them do unto you" had come to be regarded as the true maxim of human conduct.[128]

In the *Descent*, Darwin concluded his comments on "man a social animal" with this statement:

As love, sympathy and self-command become strengthened by habit, and as the power of reasoning becomes clearer, so that man can value justly the judgments of his fellows, he will feel himself impelled, apart from any transitory pleasure or pain, to certain lines of conduct. He might then declare . . . in the words of Kant, I will not in my own person violate the dignity of humanity.[129]

Darwin measured social progress by how far moral concern reached beyond family and nation to all people. In expressing his core value of social justice, he contributed to the prosecution of the governor of Jamaica who had suppressed a black rebellion by vindictive capital punishment.[130] Son William spoke of his father's character in this way: "The quality which stands out in my mind most preeminently is his abhorrence of anything approaching to oppression or cruelty, and especially of slavery; combined with this he had an enthusiasm for liberty of the individual and for liberal principles."[131] Darwin's repugnance toward harshness was displayed by his preference for "happy ending" novels that featured some "person one can thoroughly love, and if it be a pretty woman all the better."[132] He was an advocate for the handicapped and for humane treatment of all creatures.

Because of his desire to reduce unnecessary suffering of creatures, Darwin supported the Society for the Prevention of Cruelty to Animals. He dealt with the public issue of vivisectioning by joining with animal rights advocates who insisted on proper anaesthetization.[133] But realizing that biological research necessitated killing, he had a balanced approach to conflicting values:

I have all my life been a strong advocate for humanity to animals, and have done what I could in my writings to enforce this duty. . . . [Yet] I know that physiology cannot possibly progress except by means of experiments on living animals, and I feel the deepest conviction that he who retards the progress of physiology commits a crime against mankind.[134]

◆ ◆ ◆

Some interpreters of Darwin have been insensitive to "the varieties of religious experience"—to borrow the title of philosopher William James's book about fellow Victorians. Those calling Darwin irreligious are guilty of the illogic of equating disbelief in one form of Christianity with the rejection of all religion. By narrowly assuming that being a religious person means being an orthodox Christian, a scriptural literalist, or a pietistic churchman, those interpreters claim that he was not religious for most of his life. If criticism of a nation's dominant theology makes someone irreligious, then those who raise for reexamination prevailing values in every era—from Moses to Martin Luther King—would not be religious. If being religious is defined as pledging allegiance to the world's largest Christian church, Roman Catholicism, then Darwin, along with other Protestants, was irreligious. But the scope of religion is much wider than Christianity of either a standard or heretical variety.

To some, religion is defined mainly as belief in the supernatural, often limited to local worship of one or more beings. Socrates, who was devoted to the god of wisdom, was sentenced to death by the democratic assembly of Athens in part because he did not pledge allegiance to the city gods. To others, religion is defined principally as participation in certain awe-inspiring, guilt-arousing, or comfort-producing rituals. To still others, religion is measured by the depth of a person's mental involvement in the meaning of his or her existence. Of the many other definitions remaining, there is an ethical one: living by a moral code believed to be sanctioned by a divine power. Depending on the definition or definitions one selects, Darwin can be classified as either religious or nonreligious.

In the nineteenth century, many people saw Christian faith as a verbal acceptance of orthodoxy—that is, "correct" (*orthos*) "doctrine" (*doxa*). The general measure of being a Christian was the affirming of creedal propositions approved by the church. For example, an orthodox person believed in Genesis's one week of creation and rejected geological data that creation has been continuous over millions of years. Even though Darwin rejected Christian orthodoxy, he retained Christian orthopraxy (correct practice). From that standpoint, he may have had more religion than many conventional religionists.

A glance at some biblical views of religion should assist us in avoiding caricatures. The term "religion" is found in the King James Version—the one that Darwin used—only in the Letter of James. There it pertains not to doctrine but to social welfare and clean habits. "Pure religion," it states, "is this, to visit the fatherless and widows in their affliction, and to keep himself unspotted from the world."[135] The writer denounced the pious who do not help the needy, much as Jesus did in his parable of the good Samaritan.[136] That famous story, as well as Jesus' parable of the Last Judgment,[137] illustrates that the essence of New Testament religion is acting with compassion toward others.

Close companions of Darwin testified that he had qualities often associated with Christian morality. Huxley, who did not often indulge in superlatives, remarked, "I never knew any one of his intellectual rank who showed himself so tolerant to opponents, great and small, as Darwin did. . . . I never knew any one less easily hurt by fair criticism, or who less needed to be soothed by those who opposed him with good reason."[138] Romanes added other Christian virtues:

> Mr. Darwin's character was chiefly marked by a certain grand and cheerful simplicity, strangely and beautifully united with a deep and thoughtful wisdom, which, together with his illimitable kindness to others and complete forgetfulness of himself, made a combination as lovable as it was venerable. . . . No man ever passed away leaving behind him a greater void of enmity, or a depth of adoring friendship more profound.[139]

In a similar manner, naturalist Charles Holder, an early biographer of Darwin, wrote:

> He was in theory an agnostic, in practice an orthodox Christian of the broadest type. Honorable in the smallest things in life, thoughtful of others, doing as he would be done by, sensitive to others to an extreme that was often injustice to himself, kind, lovable, ready to help the young, charitable, and possessed of extreme modesty,— such was the greatest naturalist of the age.[140]

Anthropologist George Dorsey defends Darwin as a Christian if he is measured by some of the principles of the Sermon on the Mount. He recognizes, however, "from the point of view of the modern fundamentalist,

Darwin was not a Christian at all," because "he had none of their blind intolerance" or bibliolatry.[141] Dorsey describes Darwin's patience and understanding as well as "his never-failing kindliness and gentleness" in dealing with his many children.[142] Darwin was "powerful in his humility and mighty in his gentleness;"[143] he was "as lovable, genial, and humane a human being as ever lived."[144]

The description that Henrietta Darwin has given of her mother's religion might also apply to her father: "She kept a sorrowful wish to believe more, and I know that it was an abiding sadness to her that her faith was less vivid than it had been in her youth. . . . Her perfect unselfishness and active goodness gave her rest, peace and happiness.[145]

Because of Darwin's sensitivity to the plight of others, one might take as autobiographical his description of what he regarded as the most humanizing emotion: "It is not a little remarkable that sympathy with the distresses of others should excite tears more freely than our own distress; and this certainly is the case. Many a man, from whose eyes no suffering of his own could wring a tear, has shed tears at the sufferings of a beloved friend."[146]

Darwin's religious odyssey, as the chapter titles of this book indicate, went through several stages. The orthodox Christianity of his first third of his life gradually shifted into unorthodox theism for the next forty years. In his last decade, that theism was mingled with agnosticism. Reverent Darwin had a humble disposition toward *agnosto theo* (the unknown God)—to use the way some skeptical ancient Athenians referred to ultimate reality.[147] His friends and biographers discerned in his character qualities labeled by the apostle Paul as "the fruit of the Spirit," namely, "love, joy, peace, longsuffering, gentleness, goodness, faith, meekness, temperance."[148]

Notes

1. David Kohn, ed., *The Darwinian Heritage* (Princeton: Princeton University Press, 1985), 438.

2. Quoted in *Discovery* (February 1982): 24.

3. Neal Gillespie, *Charles Darwin and the Problem of Creation* (Chicago: University of Chicago Press, 1979), 144–45.

4. Geoffrey West, *Charles Darwin* (New Haven: Yale University Press, 1938), 309–10.

5. George Bernard Shaw, *Collected Plays* (New York: Dodd, 1972), 5:20.

6. Janet Oppenheim, *The Other World* (Cambridge: Cambridge University Press, 1985), 59.

7. Paul Farber, *The Temptations of Evolutionary Ethics* (Berkeley: University of California Press, 1994), 71–77.

8. *Correspondence*, 8:347.

9. LLD, 2:365.

10. *Autobiography*, 93–94.

11. Thomas Huxley et al., *Christianity and Agnosticism* (New York: Appleton, 1889), 43; 1 Thessalonians 5:21.

12. 1 Timothy 6:20.

13. Huxley, *Agnosticism*, 38.

14. Mrs. Charles Lyell, ed., *Life, Letters and Journals of Sir Charles Lyell* (London: Murray, 1888), 2:322.

15. *Nineteenth Century* (March 1895): 53.

16. Huxley, *Agnosticism*, 43.

17. Leonard Huxley, ed., *Life and Letters of Thomas Henry Huxley* (London: Macmillan, 1900), 1:242.

18. Thomas Huxley, *Science and Christian Tradition* (London: Macmillan, 1909), 41.

19. Quoted in Adrian Desmond, *Huxley* (Reading, Mass.: Addison-Wesley, 1997), 528.

20. Thomas Huxley, *Methods and Results* (New York: Appleton, 1896), 155.

21. MLD, 2:443–44.

22. Ibid., 1:247.

23. Ibid., 1:313.

24. Desmond, *Huxley*, 407.

25. Bernard Lightman, *The Origins of Agnosticism* (Baltimore: Johns Hopkins University Press, 1987), 125.

26. Huxley, *Science and Christian Tradition*, 249.

27. *Notebooks*, 635.

28. Peter Bowler, *Darwinism* (New York: Twayne, 1993), 42.

29. Frank Brown, *The Evolution of Darwin's Religious Views* (Macon, Ga.: Mercer, 1986), 31.

30. Gavin De Beer, *Charles Darwin* (London: Nelson, 1963), 270.

31. Lyman Abbott, *The Theology of an Evolutionist* (New York: Outlook, 1925), vi.

32. *Autobiography*, 94.

33. Ibid., 92.

34. MLD, 1:260–61.

35. Kohn, *Darwinian*, 480.

36. Huxley, *Methods and Results*, 158.

37. MLD, 1:382; Thomas Huxley, *Hume* (New York: Harper, 1879), 50.

38. James Moore, *The Darwin Legend* (Grand Rapids, Mich.: Baker, 1994), 48.

39. Gerald Parsons, ed., *Religion in Victorian Britain* (Manchester, England: Manchester University Press, 1988), 1:303.

40. Quoted in Parsons, *Victorian*, 1:310.

41. Edward Aveling, *The Religious Views of Charles Darwin* (London: Freethought, 1883), 4–5.

42. LLD, 1:274.

43. *Natural History* (March 1997): 16; LLD, 1:274.

44. LLD, 2:245.

45. Ibid., 2:308.

46. Moore, *Darwin Legend*, 86–87.

47. W. Fullerton, *J. W. C. Fegan* (London: Marshall, 1930), 30.

48. Joel Schwartz, "Romanes's Defense of Darwin," *Journal of the History of Biology* (summer 1995): 285.

49. Deuteronomy 29:29; George Romanes, *On Christian Prayer and General Law* (London: Macmillan, 1874), 196.

50. Ethel Romanes, ed., *The Life and Letters of George John Romanes* (London: Longmans, 1908), 85.

51. Quoted in Adrian Desmond and James Moore, *Darwin* (New York: Warner, 1992), 614. Hamlet's outlook captures an aspect of this theory of knowledge, "There are more things in heaven and earth, Horatio, / Than are dreamt of in your philosophy" (William Shakespeare, *Hamlet,* 1.5.166–67).

52. Ethel Romanes, *George Romanes*, 88.

53. MLD, 2:237.

54. Ibid., 1:395.

55. Mark 9:24.

56. LLD, 1:275.

57. Darwin Papers, box 139, folio 12.

58. Parsons, *Victorian*, 1:304.

59. Quoted in Sydney Ahlstrom and Robert Mullin, *The Scientific Theist* (Macon, Ga.: Mercer, 1987), 154.

60. Quoted in Desmond and Moore, *Darwin*, 634–35.

61. Charles Darwin to John Fordyce, 7 May 1879, quoted in *New York Times*, 27 December 1981, p. 48.

62. LLD, 1:277.

63. De Beer, *Darwin*, 268.

64. LLD, 1:276.

65. Quoted in Peter Brent, *Charles Darwin* (New York: Harper, 1981), 453.

66. Quoted in Frederick Burkhardt et al., *A Calendar of Correspondence of Charles Darwin* (New York: Garland, 1985), 393.

67. Quoted in Basil Willey, *Darwin and Butler* (London: Chatto, 1960), 29–30.

68. Quoted in Gregory Elder, *Chronic Vigour* (Lanham, Md.: University Press of America, 1996), 36.

69. LLD, 2:412.

70. *Autobiography*, 139.

71. Ibid., 138.

72. Quoted in Ronald Clark, *The Survival of Charles Darwin* (New York: Random House, 1984), 195.

73. *Autobiography*, 138.

74. *Correspondence*, 2:86.

75. LLD, 2:273.

76. *Autobiography*, 139.

77. *Descent*, 569–71.

78. *Autobiography*, 90–92.

79. Quoted in Owen Chadwick, *The Secularization of the European Mind in the Nineteenth Century* (Cambridge: Cambridge University Press, 1975), 2:19.

80. MLD, 2:171.

81. *Autobiography*, 97.

82. Ibid., 95.

83. Ibid., 96.

84. Henrietta Litchfield, ed., *Emma Darwin* (New York: Appleton, 1915), 2:229.

85. Moore, *Darwin Legend*, 58.

86. *Autobiography*, 238; Isaiah 26:3.

87. Moore, *Darwin Legend*, 91–111.

88. Oswald Smith, *Darwin the Believer* (Independence, Mo.: Gospel Tract Society, n.d.), 3.

89. Huxley Papers, Imperial College of Science and Technology, London, 8:138.

90. LLD, 2:529.

91. *Descent*, 298.

92. Reginald Farrar, *The Life of Frederic William Farrar* (New York: Crowell, 1904), 103–8.

93. Quoted in Ronald Clark, *The Survival of Charles Darwin* (New York: Random House, 1984), 197.

94. Ralph Waldo Emerson, "Circles," *Essays*. In the paragraph begun by that sentence, Emerson goes on to say: "The religion of nations, the manners and morals of mankind, are all at the mercy of a new generalization. Generalization is always a new influx of the divinity into the mind."

95. Farrar, *Life*, 109–10.

96. *Autobiography*, 93.

97. Litchfield, *Emma*, 2:49, 307. The verses Emma copied into her notebook from Tennyson's *In Memoriam* (25, 116):

> I know that this was Life,—the track
> Whereon with equal feet we fared;
> And then, as now, the day prepared
> The daily burden for the back.
>
> But this it was that made me move
> As light as carrier-birds in air;
> I loved the weight I had to bear,
> Because it needed help of Love:

When mighty Love would cleave in twain
The lading of a single pain,
And part it, giving half to him.

. . . .

Not all regret: the face will shine
Upon me, while I muse alone;
And that dear voice, I once have known,
Still speak to me of me and mine: Nor could I weary, heart or limb,

Yet less of sorrow lives in me
For days of happy commune dead;
Less yearning for the friendship fled,
Than some strong bond which is to be.

98. Harvey Goodwin, "Funeral Sermon for Charles Darwin," *Walks in the Regions of Science and Faith* (London: Murray, 1883).

99. Chadwick, *Secularization*, 2:28.

100. Quoted in Desmond and Moore, *Darwin*, 676; compare Psalm 24:7.

101. Desmond and Moore, *Darwin*, 675.

102. Ibid., 675.

103. Psalm 111:9.

104. Kohn, *Darwinian*, 475–76.

105. *Correspondence*, 8:106.

106. Isaiah 55:8–9.

107. Romans 11:33–34.

108. 1 Corinthians 13:12.

109. Quran 2:255.

110. John Calvin, *Institutes of the Christian Religion* (1559), 1:13.

111. David Brewster, *Memoirs of Sir Isaac Newton* (Edinburgh, Scotland: Constable, 1855), 2:407.

112. MLD, 1:394.

113. LLD, 2:140.

114. *Descent*, 253.

115. Robert Wright, *The Moral Animal* (New York: Pantheon, 1994), 375–76.

116. Quoted in John Bowlby, *Charles Darwin* (New York: Norton, 1991), 73.

117. Leonard Huxley, *Life*, 1:219.

118. Chadwick, *Secularization*, 2:17.

119. Ibid., 2:20–21.

120. James Moore, *The Post-Darwinian Controversies* (London: Cambridge University Press, 1979), 321.

121. LLD, 2:344.

122. *Descent*, 590.

123. Quoted in David Livingstone, *Darwin's Forgotten Defenders* (Edinburgh: Scottish Academic Press, 1987), 36.

124. Quoted in Ronald Clark, *Einstein* (New York: World Publishing Company, 1971), 622.

125. Elizabeth Browning, *Aurora Leigh*, 7.

126. *Correspondence*, 1:503.

127. *Autobiography*, 126.

128. John Greene, *The Death of Adam* (Ames: Iowa State University Press, 1959), 333.

129. *Descent*, 310.

130. LLD, 2:236.

131. Litchfield, *Emma*, 2:168.

132. *Autobiography*, 138–39.

133. Litchfield, *Emma* 2:219–21.

134. Paul Barrett, ed., *The Collected Papers of Charles Darwin* (Chicago: Chicago University Press, 1977), 2:226.

135. James 1:27.

136. Luke 10:31.

137. Matthew 25:31–46.

138. Leonard Huxley, *Life*, 2:113.

139. Quoted in George Dorsey, *The Evolution of Charles Darwin* (New York: Doubleday, 1927), vii.

140. Charles Holder, *Charles Darwin* (New York: Putnam, 1899), 148.

141. Dorsey, *Darwin*, 257.

142. Ibid., 104.

143. Ibid., 269.

144. Ibid., 277.

145. Litchfield, *Emma*, 2:175.

146. Charles Darwin, *The Expression of the Emotions in Man and Animals* (Chicago: University of Chicago Press, 1965), 216.

147. Acts 17:23.

148. Galatians 5:22–23.

CHAPTER EIGHT

Theological Conclusions

THE DESIGN ARGUMENT TRANSFORMED

Darwin reminisced, "The old argument from design in nature, as given by Paley, which formerly seemed to me so conclusive, fails, now that the law of natural selection has been discovered."[1] The classical argument, which Paley had cogently stated, was based on this analogy: since the awareness of artifacts such as books and libraries compels a rational person to infer that they were produced by authors and architects for particular purposes, so the observation of natural objects such as planets in orderly orbit or beetles with well-functioning body parts requires one to conclude that nature also must have a Designer.

Darwin found it impossible, on the one hand, to conceive of the orderliness of nature as arising accidentally or, on the other hand, to believe that natural selection is due to direct intervention by God. He admitted his dilemma to Joseph Hooker:

> My theology is a simple muddle; I cannot look at the universe as the result of blind chance, yet I can see no evidence of beneficent design, or indeed a design of any kind in the details. As for each variation that ever occurred having been preordained for a special end, I can no more believe in it than that the spot on which each drop of rain falls has been specially ordained.[2]

Darwin noted that most of the moisture raised by the sun's heat over oceans does not benefit vegetation in the vast areas of thirsty land, because the rain that forms there falls back into the ocean.[3] The weather cycle operates independently of benefiting organic needs, and Darwin thought that for the good of the whole, God does not tamper with natural causality.

The design doctrine of natural theology was changed rather than destroyed by Darwin because his theory was based on the idea of order in nature. He discovered that *both* regular order *and* accidental randomness are needed for evolutionary functioning. Georgetown theology professor John Haught has recognized that "the benign, ordering deity of traditional natural theology, as Darwin himself rightly concluded, scarcely accommodates the contingency and turmoil in the life process."[4] There is no predetermination, Darwin hypothesized; randomly generated variations are continued in future generations if they happen to confer a survival advantage, while disadvantageous variations are eliminated. By leaving the details to chance, one's concept of God could be nobler. For Darwin, it was not a matter of an all-design teleology or a mindless all-chance process. Lasting changes come about as random variations are accepted by the environment.

Kenneth Miller, Brown University's distinguished biochemistry professor, writes in *Finding Darwin's God*: "The Western Deity, God of the Jews, the Christians, and the Muslims, has always been regarded more as the architect of the universe than the magician of nature. . . . The very Western idea of God as supreme lawgiver and cosmic planner helped to give the scientific enterprise its start."[5] Monotheistic religions have played a crucial role in the belief in an orderly universe, and by their rejection of nature godlings, scientific probing of depersonalized nature has become acceptable. Miller, who calls himself both an orthodox Christian and an orthodox Darwinist, is a contemporary exponent of Asa Gray's viewpoint.[6]

Philosopher of biology Michael Ruse suggests, "Darwin became an evolutionist because of his religious beliefs, rather than despite them."[7] According to Ruse, there has been too sharp a distinction between Darwin's view and that of the Cambridge naturalists who preceded him: "Darwin argued that, thanks to natural selection, we will have the formation or evolution of features like the hand and the eye, those very organs of which the natural theologians made so much. Darwin regarded the features as adaptations, as did the theologians. . . . The metaphor of design is just as much a feature of Darwin's *Origin* as it is of Paley's *Natural Theology*."[8]

Darwin contributed to a revitalized design argument by showing that his culture had been unscientific in conceiving of God as an intervener in natural processes. Viewing God as indirectly creating the myriad particular species rather than as occasionally tinkering with relative trivia was "far grander," Darwin contended. He approved of thinking of God's laws as the creative agency, and he quoted approvingly a saying of Thomas Browne, "Nature is the art of God."[9] Each new individual or species can be thought of as a divine creation, but no supernatural intervention is called for on God's part. Loren Eiseley comments on the replacement of the naïve special creation design argument with a more sophisticated theology: "Darwin had delivered a death blow to a simple ... form of the design argument but ... it is still possible to argue for directivity in the process of life even though that directivity may be without finality in a human sense."[10] Darwin posited that the general order was designed even though the processes for its accomplishment are nonpurposeful. The design that has been built into the structure of evolution can explain the movement from simple to complex organisms.

In the new design argument, special Providence is rejected and general Providence has reference to the belief that God operates in nature through the universality of law and order. As Neal Gillespie concludes, "While Darwin acknowledged the theological origin of the laws of nature, the operation and end of those laws were not predetermined by divine will nor executed under any kind of divine supervision."[11] Darwin thought that both science and religion are truer if supernatural intervention is not used to account for organic development. Living systems have adapted to their environment by a natural process that enhances survival.

Darwin accepted a cosmic intelligence operating through natural law. Such would be null and void if God, like the comic book Superman, swooped down to save a person who was falling from the force of gravity. Darwin could not accept that minute details of life on Earth were specially guided by divine Providence. He had moral reservations about the notion that God is involved in the determination of every event. Peter Bowler states: "Darwin did not abandon design but realized that the Creator had decided to work in a less directly obvious way. His references to the laws of nature achieving a higher purpose through evolution are genuine expressions of his faith that, despite its superficial air of harshness, natural selection does work for the good of all living things."[12]

German scholar David Strauss, who initiated the modern quest for the historical Jesus by attempting to explain how the so-called miracle stories of the Gospels arose, reflected decades later, in 1872, on Darwin's greater effectiveness in emancipating religion from supernatural lore than he and fellow biblical critics achieved:

> Theologians over and over again decree the extermination of miracles; our ineffectual sentence died away. ... Darwin has demonstrated this force, this process of Nature; he has opened the door by which a happier coming race will finally cast out miracles, never to return. Every one who knows what miracles imply will praise him, in consequence, as one of the greatest benefactors of the human race.[13]

Strauss appreciated Darwin's appeal to the evolutionary law of nature that, as Victorian poet James Thomson put it, "never had for man a special clause of cruelty or kindness, love or hate."[14]

In *The History of the Warfare of Science with Theology in Christendom*, which Cornell University president Andrew White wrote more than a century ago, science is portrayed as engaging and vanquishing its adversary: "The theory of an evolution process in the formation of the universe and of animated nature is established, and the old theory of direct creation is gone forever. In place of it science has given us conceptions far more noble, and opened the way to an argument for design infinitely more beautiful than any ever developed by theology."[15]

Unlike White, Darwin biographer Gertrude Himmelfarb does not view theology as typically a warring counterforce to science:

> Theology has always been more accommodating to the demands of science than is generally thought. Much of the time, both before and after Darwin, the relations between science and religion were entirely amicable—and genuinely so, not as an armed truce, or a grudging concession to an unpleasant reality. "Natural theology"— the search for the "evidences" of Christianity and God in the facts of nature—was not a device invented by shrewd theologians to make science subservient to religion. It was, rather, an attempt to explore nature in the only way that seemed to make nature, as well as God, intelligible: in terms of design. Paley set down the first principle of the creed: "There cannot be design without a designer, contrivance without a contriver." And although he himself preferred to look for illustrations of design where he could find no evidence of natural or mechanical laws, others found design precisely in the operation of such laws. Thus scientists were able to devote themselves to their calling, confident that they could not but enhance the glory of God.[16]

◆ ◆ ◆

The notion of design for the primary benefit of humans was so pervasive in Western civilization that Darwin had difficulty separating himself from it. A heavy emphasis on "final cause" had dominated philosophy and theology from Aristotle onward. "Nature has made all animals for the sake of man," said the ancient Greek. His bias was reinforced by subsequent Greco-Roman philosophy and by the Judeo-Christian belief that humanity is "the apple of God's eye."[17] Aquinas, who baptized much of Aristotle's thought into Christianity, wrote: "The ultimate end of the whole process of generation is the human soul, and to it matter tends as toward its final form."[18] As has been shown, Paley also assumed that everything exists for the good of humankind. Likewise, Darwin's early notebooks on natural selection and, to a lesser extent, the *Origin*, contain references to humans achieving perfected adaptation.

For Darwin, when thinking consistently, organic evolution was not headed toward a goal other than ever-increasing complexity. He led a shift away from inquiry into the purposes lying behind and beyond natural processes. Concomitantly he recognized that natural selection cannot explain the whole of human experience. While purpose is not intrinsic to nature, it has a profound significance for humans. Thus, Platonists have aimed at being like Socrates, Buddhists strive to inculcate values of the Buddha, and democratic people share the hope of "liberty and justice for all." The question of purpose belongs to those who search for future direction, often in the context of religion. Modern religion does not intend to supplant science, but to supplement it by inspiring humans with a vision. As the eminent twentieth-century British-American philosopher Alfred North Whitehead put it, the worship of God is "an adventure of the spirit, a flight after the unattainable."[19]

Although we are products of a cosmic process, it in no way prevents us from being purposeful. To the extent that we comprehend nature, we have the ability to transcend it to some extent. The combination of chance, determinism, and choice can be compared to playing the game of bridge. The randomly distributed cards determine to some extent the outcome, but the skill with which one plays cooperatively with a partner can make a decisive difference. The interplay between individual endowment and purpose can also be illustrated by comparing two sons of Robert Darwin, Erasmus and Charles. They shared a similar heredity and environment; both studied medicine in Edinburgh and resided in the vicinity of London for most of their lives. But Charles's bachelor brother used his share of the family wealth for indulging in idle pleasures throughout life, and achieved nothing of social significance through either offspring or career.

Humans are ambivalently a part of nature and uniquely distinctive in their potential. Unlike other animals, Darwin pointed out, they transmit their past history, first orally and subsequently also in writing. Their capacity for conveying from one generation to another what was learned has a great cumulative effect, which can be illustrated by comparing primitive with civilized societies. Because of such communication, the wheel needed to be invented only once. A blindly operating biological process was intrinsic to natural selection, but Darwin allowed for progress or regress in human culture (including education, art, religion, production methods, and social relationships). Cultures are helped or harmed through human effort that is socially inherited. Homo sapiens now participates in genetic selection and manipulates its own evolution. Due to developments in medicine and technology, survival is no longer a matter of having genes with the best survival potential. Physical and mental defects can be, at least partially, corrected.

Progress was fundamental to some atheistic as well as in the theistic philosophies of Darwin's time. For example, Marxists believed in an inevitable movement toward a utopia similar to what early Christians had hoped to achieve. Their slogan was "From each according to his ability, to each according to his needs."[20] Supplementing a similar social agenda, Calvinists believed that "man's chief end is to glorify God and to enjoy him forever."[21] Monotheists have believed that a progressive struggle to effect deliverance from evil is possible by the cooperation of humans with God's plan.

THE THEODICY ISSUE REFORMULATED

Theodicy, literally "God's justice," is concerned with solving the problem of evil in the world in light of the presumption that its Creator is altogether good. Justifying the ways of God becomes more acute for monotheists who believe in a benevolent being who is also all-powerful and all-knowing. In contrast to the polytheists, they cannot accept a rival satanic god to whom the responsibility for evil happenings can be assigned. Darwin frequently expressed his unease over the undeserved suffering of organisms that have allegedly been created by a loving God:

> A being so powerful and so full of knowledge as a God who could create the universe, is to our finite minds omnipotent and omniscient, and it revolts our understanding to suppose that his benevolence is not unbounded, for what advantage can there be in the sufferings of millions of the lower animals throughout almost endless time? This very old argument from the existence of suffering against the existence of an intelligent first cause seems to me a strong one.[22]

When considering doctrines promulgated by church authorities that made no sense, Darwin said that he refused to affirm "*credo quia incredible*" (I believe because it is absurd).[23] That total credulity slogan goes back to Tertullian, the earliest Latin church leader, who associated devoutness with assenting to irrational creedal statements. One such doctrine is that it is always God's will when particular persons suffer and die; for example, such is the case whether those persons are suicidal terrorists or their victims.

As he grew older, Darwin's diminishing faith was due more to moral than to metaphysical considerations. He did not prefer to conceive of ultimate reality as material rather than as spiritual. The theological issue that most concerned him was not whether God existed, but what kind of God a reasonable person can accept. Also, although Darwin viewed science as being at fisticuffs with supernatural miracles, his alienation from religion was not caused by his seeing it as fundamentally incompatible with biology. Rather, he was perturbed by the age-old problem of attributing bad things to the work of God. If all that happens is divinely caused, such occurrences as gross congenital deformities must be attributed to God. Darwin rejected the traditional view that a great God would either ordain or permit vast suffering to fall upon those having no choice to act otherwise.

Darwin did not reflect on an imaginative alternative universe lacking features such as fire, earthquakes, or viruses that often cause great suffering and death. For example, would the world have been a better place had fire not been created? Geologists point out that much of the oxygen needed for life has been released from the earth's crust by earthquakes, so what would move about on its surface without them? Microbiologists indicate that there are many benefits from viruses, even though most people associate them only with infectious diseases. Cellular growth that can destroy is evident in malignant cancers, but that may be the price to pay for an orderly cosmos.

One step toward resolving the theodicy issue came with the distinction between primary or divine causation and secondary or scientific causation. Naturalists preceding Darwin found such classification useful in dealing with astronomical and geological matters. For them, removing God from direct celestial or terrestrial actions did not take away the natural world's dependence on the continual sustaining presence of God. Secondary or derivative causation diminishes the concept of an anthropomorphic deity, but retains the notion of a Creator beyond scientific investigation. Darwin's acceptance of a dual causation, as asserted in his conclusion of the *Origin*, made the problem of senseless suffering less burdensome. His theology provided an explanation of an overall plan in nature while allowing for the sufficiency of secondary causes. Agonizing death from AIDs need not be regarded as God's punishment for sins committed by particular individuals, but rather as a puzzling outcome of the evolutionary web of life. The pain of backaches so common in humans can be attributed to the adaptation of hominoids from four legs to two in order to gain height to better locate food and to see dangerous animals, rather than to the inept skeletal design by a deity.

Reverent agnostic Darwin may be less a blasphemer than the zealot who insists that God directly causes individuals to be killed by a disease, flood, war, or the like. His culture had identified "acts of God" with natural catastrophes that maim and kill, an entrenched view that continues to be found in insurance policies. To conceive of Deity as an almighty power in charge of every detail implicates God in deliberately unleashing epidemics and hurricanes. But Darwin would have agreed with Einstein that "God is subtle, but he is not malicious."[24] It is unreasonable to accuse nature of being cruel, because it is mindless and does not know; to be cruel requires conscious intent. Biologist Relis Brown's comments are germane here:

> Considering Darwin's worries over the problem of natural evil, one is struck by the fact that an overarching order designed by a distant God could potentially ameliorate those "natural" and "chance" effects of suffering and tragedy that appear to mar the world's beauty and that threaten any sanguine outlook on life. Indirectly their cause, Darwin's kind of God could also indirectly be their cure—not, of course, through active intervention but, rather, simply from having had an orderly plan that would, all things considered, turn out for the good.[25]

Darwin thought that there was a preponderance of pleasure over pain in organisms, and he could see that pain has a protective intent:

> Some . . . are so much impressed with the amount of suffering in the world, that they doubt if we look to all sentient beings, whether there is more of misery or of happiness;—whether the world as a whole is a good or a bad one. According to my judgment . . . all sentient beings have been formed so as to enjoy, as a general rule, happiness. . . . Pain or suffering of any kind, if long continued, causes depression and lessens the power of action; yet is well adapted to make a creature guard itself against any great or sudden evil. Pleasurable sensations, on the other hand, . . . stimulate the whole system to increased action. Hence it has come to pass that most or

all sentient beings have been developed in such a manner through natural selection, that pleasurable sensations serve as their habitual guides. We see this in . . . the pleasure of our daily meals, and especially in the pleasure derived from sociability and from loving our families.[26]

Ironically, although Darwin was theologically disturbed by the perpetual carnage that is a by-product of natural selection, his theory provides a way for understanding why a good God would allow agonizing suffering in the world. The harsh facts of nature are a given in Darwin's theory and in traditional theology. Darwinists have a conceptual basis for being the better apologists for a God who expresses liberty and justice within creation. They can defend the idea that pain and suffering are intrinsic to the Creator's law of evolution that generates complex organisms. Frank Brown comments:

> Once having gone so far as to conceive of God as a being removed from direct control over natural events, Darwin had not only made room for a relatively autonomous science but had also blunted the sharpness of the theodicy question. . . . He noted that he found it more acceptable to think that God was the creator of laws governing natural phenomena than to believe God would directly cause a particular bolt of lightning to kill a particular person. The only God conceivable to Darwin would thus be, at most, responsible only for the overall design of things; the details, and hence much of the suffering, would be left to chance.[27]

Gray found in Darwin's theory, which includes endemic pain and waste, a more satisfactory solution for the problem of evil than Christian orthodoxy had provided. If suffering is necessary for the functioning of evolution, the problem of justifying a good God instigating such a scheme is made easier. Gray wrote about the superior way evolutionary theory accounts for both the failures and the successes of nature: "It explains the seeming waste as being part and parcel of a great economical process. Without the competing multitude, no struggle for life, and without this, no natural selection and the survival of the fittest, no continuous adaptation to changing surroundings, no diversification, and improvement."[28]

Darwin was unable to grasp as clearly as Gray that a by-product of his natural selection theory was a more humane theodicy. This theological outlook might have helped Darwin cope with the problem of evil in general, and with the death by disease of his virtuous young daughter in particular. But this perspective did not console him sufficiently for him to give it full endorsement.

BIBLICAL INTERPRETATION

Christian orthodoxy has not always been associated with a static view of creation. The pivotal Catholic theologians Augustine and Aquinas, on the basis of scriptural interpretation, did not sanction a doctrine of the immutability of the species. As Gray realized, "Mediate creation is just what the thoughtful and thorough observer of the ways of God in Nature would expect, and is what some of the most illustrious of the philosophic saints and fathers of the church have more or less believed in."[29] Henry Osborn, curator of the American Museum of Natural History, also recognized that Augustine "handed down to his followers opinions which closely conform to the progressive views of those theologians of the present day who have accepted the evolution theory."[30]

Augustine of Africa, the foremost Latin theologian, formulated some aspects of evolutionary theology in the fifth century. He perceived the world's initial and continued existence as depending on God; the universe minus God equals nothing, but God minus the universe equals God. Augustine viewed God as the author, producer, and audience of the cosmic drama that has played out across the span of history, with a multitude of organic actors who come on stage and then depart.

Augustine fought to rescue Christianity from the heresy of Mani, a third-century Persian cult leader. The Manicheans rejected much of the Bible because it associated God with material creation. They thought earthly organisms incarnate the principle of darkness; accordingly, salvation comes through abstaining from the physical. By contrast, Augustine conceived of God as eternal and spaceless, but God created both time and space as well as the stuff that fills the world. Being outside time, God is no more connected with one point on Earth's timeline than another. Not limited to a unique event at primeval creation, divine creativity is expressed in the temporal development of organisms. From the human perspective, it may appear that God planned all beforehand and then let it happen, but God is the timeless now, overseeing that things occur as they ought.

Rather than *special* creation, Augustine conceived of *potential* creation: "All development takes its natural course through the powers imparted to matter by the Creator. He believed that God created matter at the beginning of time and commanded the earth to generate various forms by gradual natural processes. Even the corporeal structure of man himself is according to this plan."[31] Augustine suggested that "the possibility of the development of complex animals was established when the universe began, but the realization of this potentiality followed only much later, after plants and simpler animals had gradually developed."[32]

Augustine's dictum for Bible interpretation was to follow its literal and obvious sense except where reason makes it untenable. He interpreted the Genesis creation story as encompassing not six solar days, but six periods of time.[33] Rather than directly making everything at the beginning, God implanted a germinal principle in primeval stuff that caused organic development. Prior to plants yielding seeds, as described in the opening chapter of Genesis, Augustine claimed there was invisible causal activity: "The water brought forth the first swimming things and the winged fowl, and the earth brought forth the first birds according to their kinds, and the first animals according to their kinds." The dormant seeds did not burst forth when matter was created because "conditions suitable for their proper development were lacking." Augustine used this analogy: "As mothers are pregnant with unborn offspring, so the world itself is pregnant with the causes of unborn beings, which are not created in it except from that highest essence."[34]

Along with some theologians coming before and after him in church history, Augustine thought of God as giving the earth power to produce flora and fauna. He regarded a process of "becoming" in the universe as a sign of divine sublimity, not of weakness or absence of Deity. Darwin's concept of a "tree of life," in which some branches are constantly developing while others are withering, is in line with Augustine's portrayal of creation as a tree growing from seed over many years and maturing in the fullness of time. The speed with which the potential becomes actual in this continuous creation is determined by environmental conditions.[35]

The biblical interpretations of Augustine became generally accepted by Christians in the Middle Ages. Aquinas endorsed Augustine's doctrine of continuous creation, saying that God governs "even to this day the work of propagation."[36] The medieval theologian used the terms "primary" and "secondary" to distinguish between ultimate and contingent causes.[37] He criticized those who exclude scientific causation: "Some have made the mistake of attributing all action exclusively to God and denying that natural things perform by their proper powers, as though fire did not heat, but that God creates heat."[38] Pertaining to the Genesis creation account, Aquinas said: "Some say that on the third day plants were actually produced, in their various species, but Augustine says that the earth . . . received power to produce them."[39]

Augustine's doctrine predominated in church teaching during many more centuries than did the special or direct creation theory, which became the standard view only with the coming of Protestant literalism. John Milton's treatment of special creation in *Paradise Lost* provided reinforcement for literalists who accepted as truth what he had intended as imaginative interpretation. The exalting of the poem to inspired literal word status in the English culture precipitated a rejection of the idea of gradual development. Belief in the fixity of the species by the Creator from the earth's beginnings was subsequently reinforced, as we have seen, by Carolus Linnaeus's *Systema Naturae*. In that eighteenth-century classification manual, each life form is assumed to have been individually created by God and subsequently to have remained unchanged. Rev. Aubrey Moore, curator of the Oxford Botanical Gardens, observed that once special creation was generally accepted, "Christians in all good faith set to work to defend a view which has neither Biblical, nor patristic, nor medieval authority."[40] Young Darwin found Milton's works especially appealing, and he may have thought that the telling of God making each species through personal exertion in *Paradise Lost* was an official pronouncement of the church. If the medieval view of active nature as an instrument of God had prevailed, the conflict over Darwin's theory would have been less traumatic.

◆ ◆ ◆

Without realizing it, John Greene notes, Darwin's new ideas gave impetus to the acceptance of a critical understanding of the Bible:

> Darwin was not indispensable to the rethinking of traditional ideas concerning revelation and inspiration that has taken place since his time. Biblical scholarship would have brought it about eventually quite apart from his influence. But Darwin does seem to have played the role of a catalytic agent, helping to precipitate the reaction. The challenge he presented to continued belief in the historicity of Genesis was too grave to be ignored. Adam and Eve taken literally could not be reconciled with *The Descent of Man*; something had to give. Generally speaking, it has been the doctrine of absolute inerrancy that has yielded, rapidly in some quarters, slowly, grudgingly, and covertly in others, but inevitably in all. Yet, strangely enough, Scripture seems to have weathered the ordeal remarkably well.[41]

More recently, Sir John Polkinghorne, a theoretical physicist and Anglican priest at Darwin's university, has written:

Darwin offered a healthy corrective to unjustified claims that the Bible had foreclosed the answers to purely scientific questions. The resultant gain was not merely scientific but also theological. Thereby the early chapters of Genesis were released to serve their valid purpose as mythical statements about man's creaturely dependence and his experience of alienation from God, the true ground of his being. In the symbolic form these ancient stories retain remarkable power to speak to us.[42]

Scientific discovery and literary scholarship have subsequently been a threat only to those religionists who use the Bible for purposes never intended. In the opening chapters of Genesis, the portrayal of God as making an orderly cosmos out of formless stuff is in harmony with the assumption that evolutionary law has converted the chaotic totality into differentiated complexity. The two myths, the older primarily in Genesis 2 and the younger primarily in Genesis 1, affirm similarities between human and other organisms: all are made from earthly elements and are declared to be good/beautiful (*tov*, a Hebrew term that has both an esthetic and a moral meaning). *Adam*, the generic Hebrew term for humankind, is seen to be distinctive in sharing attributes of God and in being assigned the responsibility of caring for the earth. Those early stories contain symbolic truth about human relationships but, like Aesop's fables, they were never intended to state literal facts.[43] Even their composers and their first readers realized that God does not actually walk around physically and that snakes never spoke a human language.

A good case can be made that Darwin demonstrated more wisdom than such self-appointed biblical interpreters as demagogue William Jennings Bryan, who was determined to heighten conflict between the religious and scientific understanding of the organic world. In a 1904 speech, given during the interval between his second and third nominations for president of the United States, he twisted Darwin's ideas: "The Darwinian theory represents man as reaching his present perfection by the operation of the law of hate—the merciless law by which the strong crowd out and kill off the weak. . . . I prefer to believe that love rather than hatred is the law of development."[44] Due especially to Bishop Wilberforce and bigot Bryan, there has often been the presumption of an opposition between science and religion. Bryan presumed a dichotomy that was false when he cleverly stated this choice of values, "It is better to trust in the Rock of Ages than to know the age of the rocks."[45]

Bryan's distortion of the biblical outlook peaked at the Scopes trial in Tennessee when he asserted: "[T]he Christian believes that man comes from above whereas the evolutionist believes that he must have come from below."[46] He failed to see that Genesis states that both humans and other creatures are a *mixture* of divine "breath" and earthy "dust."[47] Darwin's discussion of what he called the "plan of creation" in the conclusion of the *Origin* is more perceptive. Utilizing the Genesis metaphor, he referred to earthy forms as "having been originally breathed [into] by the Creator." Darwin's refusal to isolate humans from the animality category was in harmony with the biblical creation stories that viewed them as modified mud.

The *Oxford English Dictionary* traces the first use of the word "creationist" to Darwin. In sketching his theory in 1844, he criticized the "creationist," meaning the naturalist who believed in a special creation for each species. When the *Origin* was published, he encouraged Huxley to "attack some immovable creationist,"[48] having geologist Sedgwick especially in mind. Aubrey Moore aptly commented that "immutables" would be a better label for those who deny the transmutation of species.[49] Since Darwin, in the *Origin*, expressed belief in the Creator, the term "creationist" could accurately be used to refer to him and to Newton and Galileo as well. To make this point, and to counter current anti-evolutionist fundamentalists who brazenly call themselves "scientific creationists," I wrote an article entitled "Darwin, the Scientific Creationist," in which his outlook was contrasted with pseudo-science and reactionary religion.[50]

It is interesting to look at Darwin's religion against the backdrop of biblical stories. The shift in his religious focus after his *Beagle* voyage was similar to that contained in the Elijah saga. The Hebrew prophet had associated the Lord of Israel with the cause of weather phenomena that, in a contest, bested the Canaanite storm god Baal. But when he retreated to Mount Sinai he discovered that God's presence was found in the "still small voice," often identified with the conscience, rather than in the earthquake, tempest, and lightning.[51] From that internal whisper Elijah was able to gain confidence and make courageous plans to carry out the will of God. Darwin also came to realize that conscience—rather than in alleged irregularities of nature—was the place to discern matters of ultimate significance.

Darwin asked the perennial question: How can one believe in a just and merciful Omnipotence who allows personal tragedy to the undeserving? Had he studied the Book of Job, he might have gained insight into relating unmerited suffering to theology and to natural selection. Job found it impossible to give an adequate moral explanation for either the good or bad fortune of individuals. He yearned for a God who was more just than was found in the traditional theology that his unhelpful "friends" represented. In the end, Job became aware that the ways of God are vastly more complex than he had naïvely assumed, and that a person cannot expect to find rewards matched with merit on an individual basis. To operate the natural order, Job learned, God needs to attend to matters that are bewildering to those whose primary concern is to secure justice in their particular situation. Job saw that an individual's notion of how Providence should operate might be at odds with the general Providence needed to run the universe.

◆ ◆ ◆

Darwin's ideas are also related to some New Testament teachings. Jesus taught that God "maketh his sun to rise on the evil and on the good, and sendeth rain on the just and on the unjust," thus good behavior does not guarantee ample harvests. His Sermon on the Mount goes on to illustrate the impartiality of nature by pointing out that a destructive flood hits all in its path, indiscriminately.[52] The natural order operates independently of human "just desserts," so life-sustaining or life-destructive forces are no respecters of persons. Jesus appears to have thought that the disassociation of special Providence from weather phenomena—an association that Elijah had prior to his enlightenment— is a heightening of God's glory.

Darwin expressed himself vigorously on the presumed doctrine that God would torture eternally all who did not believe in Jesus as their personal Savior. He vented his indignation: "I can indeed hardly see how anyone ought to wish Christianity to be true; for if so the plain language of the text [of the Gospels] seems to show that the men who do not believe, and this would include my Father, Brother and almost all my best friends, will be everlastingly punished. And this is a damnable doctrine."

After her husband's death, Emma marked for omission from his autobiography those sentences on hell. She explained: "It seems to me raw. Nothing can be said too severe upon the doctrine of everlasting punishment for disbelief—but very few now would call that 'Christianity,' (tho' the words are there)."[53] Both Emma and Charles agreed that what was "damnable" was not the unbelievers but the vindictive doctrine itself!

The Darwins were not atypical in their opposition to the traditional outlook on hell, because no doctrine in orthodoxy was more widely repudiated by Victorians.[54] In an 1877 Westminster Abbey sermon, Darwin's friend Frederic Farrar repudiated the "intolerable ghastliness" of the "loveless conception" contained in the popular conception of hell. According to the doctrine, apart from those few whom God "elects" from those who profess Jesus Christ as Lord, the vast majority of humans are tortured for eternity in the devil's furnace. Farrar argued that metaphors in the New Testament had been misinterpreted to support a theology that gloried in suffering and that the true hope expressed there is that "in Christ shall all be made alive."[55] It is surprising that Darwin had not joined his wife in separating from authentic Christianity a doctrine that was defunct among his liberal Anglican and Unitarian companions.

The apostle Paul, who did not write about either hell or supernatural violations of the natural order,[56] had some ideas that are relevant to those of Darwin. Christians who are disturbed by the *Descent* describing humankind as having brutish ancestors may not realize that Paul stated that God's method is to choose "base things of the world and things which are despised" for accomplishing divine purposes.[57] Darwin told of our simian family relations even as St. Francis extolled our kinship with birds and beasts. But if humans are nothing more than dust or flesh, then dignity is lost.

Darwin rejected the Christian doctrine of foreordination, that God's eternal purposes have determined all events, but some of its treatment in the New Testament does not conflict with Darwin's theory. According to the King James Version of Romans 8:28, "All things work together for good to them that love God," but that is a mistranslation of the earliest extant Greek text. To traditional English-speaking readers the verse has seemed to imply that in some fated manner everything will turn out all right in the end, so it encourages the devout to passively await the inevitable happy ending. However, the discovery of a text closer to the original has resulted in this more accurate rendering: "In everything God works for good with those who love him." (The Revised Standard Version restores the subject "God" (*theos*) that some medieval textual copier had omitted.) God, who is persuasive, not coercive, works as a senior partner *with* devotees to make the best of any situation. Paul asserted that God cooperates with everyone who wants to see the divine will achieved. He believed that religion does not change "things," but that it can transform people's attitudes toward situations. God is dependent on humans of all religions to share in the struggle to overcome evil and establish a just and merciful global community. The hope that Paul expressed is that even the worst that happens can be transformed into an unexpected good by divine and human forces working in concert.

The God of the Bible and of the Quran works in history, and not only at a remote beginning.[58] "When God began to create heaven and earth," the translation of the opening words of Genesis by the New Jewish Publication Society, is appropriate for the continuous Creator. This conception of Deity stands in contrast with the view of those called deists, who presume that God withdrew from the world after the initial creation, leaving it to follow a predetermined trajectory. They view God as in splendid isolation from the ongoing activity of the world, having an honorary emeritus title but with nothing to do. Darwin's concept of the mutability of species was to prove fatal to the deists' view of nature.

The theists' acceptance of God as creator of continually changing forms is arguably more worshipful than the deists' belief in everlastingly static entities. The unpredictability of events in the physical sphere can be viewed as part of the will of God. If the almightiness of God is diminished, randomness in the physical realm and freedom in the human sphere can be allowed. Biblical writers, aware of divine omnipresence, spoke of God fashioning limbs in a mother's womb, making grass grow, clothing lilies, and feeding ravens. Those sane writers did not think that such language presumes that natural processes are obliterated.

The term "panentheism," coined by Karl Krause, a nineteenth-century German, is appropriate for labeling an outlook that is contained in some comments of Darwin as well as in some early Christian theology. The three Greek terms that compose pan-en-theism (literally, "all [is] in God") come from the New Testament affirmation that "God . . . is above all and through all and in all."[59] It can be distinguished from pantheism (literally, "all [is] God"), the belief that God is totally immanent in the cosmic processes, a view accepted by some ancient Stoics and by some Hindus. Panentheism is also distinct from deism, the belief that God is totally transcendent. It is a middle way on the continuum between the view that the natural world is identified with the divine and the view that God has not been associated with the world since the beginning of the cosmos. It avoids the determinism that has often characterized religious philosophies at either extreme. Panentheism is the belief that God is the one in whom all organisms live and move and have their being. It allows for the emergence of novelty by a Creator who continuously penetrates every aspect of the universe. As Augustine clarified, God is both beyond and within the universe; the Creator is independent of, and is not exhausted by, the creation.

Some images of God that can be found in religious texts were injured badly by Darwin's theory: the interfering God, the remote Deity, the God of the gaps in human knowledge. But natural selection made more plausible the concept of God championed by Whitehead, who stressed the inclusiveness of God who knows all and empowers all in the world. A genuine freedom of choice is intrinsic to Whiteheadian religion because the future is open for both Creator and creature. "God is the great companion—the fellow-sufferer who understands," wrote Whitehead.[60] In an Augustinian manner, he asserted, "God is that non-temporal actuality which has to be taken account of in every creative phase."[61]

DARWIN'S RELIGIOUS LEGACY

James Moore's discussion on religion in Victorian Britain uses the case of Darwin to illustrate the general shift in what educated people found believable, using the half-century between 1830 and 1880 as a benchmark. The basic changes he notes include: 1) natural law replaces Providence in explaining natural evil; 2) freethinking liberals supplant doctrinal conservatives; 3) authority is vested in scientific interpretations rather than in clerical exegesis of biblical revelation; 4) theology is separated from ethics and worldly moral improvement is stressed instead of otherworldly salvation; and 5) history is viewed as evolutionary rather than static. Moore describes the spirit of the late nineteenth century in this way: "To be scientific does not preclude belief in God, for the natural order may be a divine order after all."[62] The extensive effect of the *Origin* and the *Descent* was basic to all those changes, which were as significant for religion in the nineteenth century as the Protestant Reformation had been three centuries earlier.

Miller likewise tells of the transforming effect of Darwin's work on nineteenth-century natural theology:

> Western religions generally agree on the existence of an active, personal, involved Creator. The retired clockmaker envisioned by deism could hardly be more removed from these traditions, and each emphatically rejected such a passive God. . . . Deism is satisfying only when we visualize a static, controlled, finished creation, a mechanism of precise laws and well-kept orbits. . . . But by the time the nineteenth century drew to a close, that view was gone forever.[63]

Darwin's "tree of life" figure contributed to the view of George Tyrell, a younger contemporary of Darwin and a Catholic theologian:

[The universe] teems with aims and meanings, although it has no *one* aim or meaning. It is like a great tree, that pushes out its branches, however and wherever it can, seeking to realise its whole nature, as far as possible, in every one of them, but aiming at no collective effect. . . . God seems to throw Himself wholly into the very least of His acts and creations, as though it were His sole care and interest. . . . The world grows in all senses and directions and in obedience to His pressure from within. Its branches thwart and strangle and overshadow one another. He cares not which prevails.[64]

In 1884, Anglican Bishop Frederick Temple argued that Darwin's theory had improved the design argument for the existence of God. Paley's argument did not exclude a designer team for the invention and production of a telescope or, by analogy, for the eye. But a single natural law and a Lawgiver are necessary for the evolutionary process. Moreover, Paley's way of expressing the argument had been discredited because he posited that each adaptation had been an instantaneous act rather than a lengthy unfolding of potentialities implanted in physical elements. Temple stated: "[T]he doctrine of Evolution leaves the argument for an intelligent Creator and Governor of the world stronger than it was before" because "there is more divine foresight, there is less divine interposition." He did not find a theological problem in the gory operations of evolution:

There is no waste like the waste of life that is to be seen in nature. Living creatures are destroyed by lack of fit nourishment, by lack of means of reproduction, by accidents, by enemies. The inevitable operation of this waste, as Darwin's investigations showed, has been to destroy all those varieties which were not well-fitted to their surroundings, and to help those that were.[65]

In 1896, Temple was named archbishop of Canterbury, the highest position in the Church of England, signaling that Darwinism had been sanctified in the Anglican Church.

Aubrey Moore argued in the 1880s that Darwin had a positive influence on reinstating the biblical roots of Christian theology:

Science had pushed the deist's God farther and farther away. . . . Darwinism appeared and . . . has conferred upon philosophy and religion an inestimable benefit, by shewing us that we must choose between two alternatives. Either God is everywhere present in nature, or He is nowhere. . . . We must frankly return to . . . the belief in a God in Whom not only we, but all things, have their being.[66]

In contrast to Newton's mechanism, Darwin's theory allowed for spontaneity. It effected a shift from determinism to an open universe where innovation is possible. Aubrey Moore told how the theory of a progressive introduction of new species by the Creator affected Christian thought:

> It is infinitely more Christian than the theory of "special creation" for it implies the immanence of God in nature, and the omnipresence of His creative power. . . . Deism, even when it struggled to be orthodox, constantly spoke of God as we might speak of an absentee landlord, who cares nothing for his property so long as he gets his rent. Yet anything more opposed to the language of the Bible and the [church] Fathers can hardly be imagined. . . . For Christians the *facts of nature* are the *acts of God*. Religion relates these facts to God as their Author, science relates them to one another as integral parts of a visible order. Religion *does not* tell us of their interrelations, science *cannot* speak of their relation to God. Yet the religious view of the world is infinitely deepened and enriched when we not only recognize it as the work of God but are able to trace the relation of part to part.

According to Aubrey Moore, the efforts of Darwin have enabled Christians to focus on God, "with whom is no variableness, neither shadow or turning,"[67] and eliminate, as much as possible, "all that is arbitrary, capricious, unreasonable, even where as yet we cannot explain, to go on in faith and hope."[68]

When Darwin was writing his major books, Henry Ward Beecher was America's preeminent preacher. In support of Darwin's theory, he stated: "I regard evolution as being the discovery of the Divine method in creation. . . . I hold that Evolution, so far from being in antagonism with true religion, will develop it with more power than any other presentation of science that ever has occurred in this world. The day will come when men will render thanks for that which now they deprecate."[69] Evolution gave Beecher a broader understanding of God's creation, and in *Evolution and Religion* he published this aphorism: "Design by wholesale is grander than design by retail." He asked, "If to reject God's revelation of the Book is infidelity, what is it to reject God's revelation of himself in the structure of the whole globe?"[70] Beecher's use of the term "reveal" is similar to that of Einstein, who affirmed that he believed in God "who is revealed in the harmony of the universe."[71]

Calvinist Lyman Abbott, who succeeded Beecher as pastor of Plymouth Church in Brooklyn, described the Bible as containing "the history of a progressive revelation." At the beginning of the unveiling, Abbott acknowledged in his address on "The Evolution of Revelation," Israelites presumed that their God commanded them to massacre the indigenous people of the land where they settled. But when God's will was more fully disclosed, Christians were taught to love their enemies.[72] Abbott's position was informed by Darwin's view that the evolution of religion ran in tandem with the evolution of culture. Darwin, who had attributed revengefulness to the God of the Israelites, would have appreciated the idea of biblical people displaying more refinement in knowledge of God as they moved from barbarity to civility.

In 1901, William James joined those who thought of Darwin's theory as a benefit to mature religion, and built on Beecher's merchandising metaphor:

> The Darwinian notion of chance production, and subsequent destruction, speedy or deferred, applies to the largest as well as to the smallest facts. . . . The God whom science recognizes must be a God of universal laws exclusively, a God who does a wholesale, not a retail business. He cannot accommodate his processes to the convenience of individuals. . . . To coerce the spiritual powers, or to square them and get them on our side, was, during enormous tracts of time, the one great object in our dealings with the natural world. . . . The practical needs and experiences of religion seem to me sufficiently met by the belief that beyond each man and in a fashion continuous with him there exists a larger power which is friendly to him and to his ideals.[73]

Some cultural leaders have thought that a reasonable person could not accept both evolutionary ideas and theological doctrines. For example, Porter Barnard, the acclaimed president of Columbia University, declared in 1873 that God's existence is impossible if Darwin's theory is true, and that he would rather live on in ignorance than to learn that the theory was validated.[74] Magisterial British historian George Trevelyan shifted in the opposite direction, accepting Christian indoctrination about an immutable world until he was taught as a teenager that Darwin had disproved the Bible, and then disbelief immediately ensued.[75] The diverse responses of Barnard and Trevelyan are a typical sampling of the way in which a number of cultural leaders have responded to Darwin's theory in the generations since it was promulgated. The credibility of creation in six days, the edibility of Jonah, and other biblical accounts that seem to contradict scientific findings have often precipitated polarized thinking. A case can be made that the narrow-mindedness of those determined to preserve an outdated rigid theology does much to cause the well educated to reject religion. Also, Michael Denton thinks "the decline in religious belief can probably be attributed more to the propagation and advocacy by the intellectual and scientific community of the Darwinian version of evolution than to any other single factor."[76]

Victorian humor captured the British anxiety over the implications of Darwin's theory. A cartoonist showed a gorilla carrying the abolitionist's logo, "Am I a man and a brother?" Another rendering of this parody depicted a chimpanzee in London's Regent's Park who had learned to read. He paced about in his cage with the Bible under one arm and the *Descent* under the other while muttering, "Am I my keeper's brother?" In 1861, *Punch* carried a poem spoofing natural selection:

> Let pigeons and doves
> Select their own loves,
> And grant them a million of ages,
> Then doubtless you'll find
> They've altered their kind,
> And changed into prophets and sages.[77]

Similarly, a couplet from the operetta lyrics composed by William Gilbert poked fun: "Darwinian Man, though well-behaved, / At best is only a monkey shaved!"[78]

During the past century Darwin has been the scientist that fundamentalists have most loved to scorn, sometimes by sketching his face, with protruding forehead, on an ape's body. They have indulged in such false dichotomies as declaring that God rather than a gorilla is the creator, and that Adam rather than an ape is the father of humankind. According to a 1997 Gallup Poll, nearly half of Americans agree with this anti-evolution statement: "God created human beings pretty much in their present form at one time within the last 10,000 years or so."[79] Another survey by Gallup shows that most Americans believe that the Bible contains no scientific errors.[80] Darwin would probably find current fundamentalists in Christianity, Judaism, and Islam easy to understand, for they have changed little in their bibliolatry since his day.

Malcolm Bowden, a "scientific creationist," illustrates fundamentalism's contemporary no-holds-barred attack on Darwin:

> I would suggest that the root cause of Darwin's illness was the stress generated in him when he was writing about a theory *which he*

knew was basically false. All his symptoms are those of a man who is under prolonged emotional stress—stress due to his continual mental acrobatics as he sought to "wriggle" (a word he used to describe his arguments) around a whole series of facts against his theory. What inner promptings could have driven him to continue along this course, regardless of its effect upon his mental and physical state? Not a desire to avoid God, but an inordinate hunger for fame and recognition.[81]

In contrast to such calumnious drivel, Darwin was encouraged by historical and literary specialists who, beginning during his lifetime, aimed at understanding scriptural texts in their ancient cultural contexts. In his lecture on the bearing of natural selection on religion, historian Basil Willey concludes:

> Darwin has positively (though unwittingly) helped to restore buoyancy to religion by forcing it to abandon some of its more untenable defences. Though scriptural fundamentalism was undermined by historical and textual criticism far more than by any direct attack from natural science, Darwin contributed his share to the weakening of that bibliolatry which was the bane of popular Protestantism. And in so far as he reduced the prestige of the old argument from design, he was discrediting what had always been, in reality, a precarious line of defence. As Pascal had long ago said, Nature proves God only to those who already believe in Him on other grounds.[82]

◆ ◆ ◆

Darwin's theory, along with other scientific theories, can lessen self-centeredness and thereby focus the faith of religious persons outwardly. Accepting that they live on a minor planet that revolves about a minor star, they become aware that their particular species and religion may not have a most favored status with the Orderer of nature. Religion as well as science can advance by the suppression of human arrogance.

Historian John Brooke has suggested a possible cause for Darwin's alienation from establishment religion and from the science of his day: "For Darwin the very enterprise of natural theology had become incurably anthropocentric, reflecting man's arrogance in believing himself the product of special creation."[83] Darwin provided insights that could have extricated untrue conceptual forms from his culture. Yet drinking from the old wineskin of anthropocentrism is found by many to be more satisfying, even though it explodes after the fermenting juice of evolution is poured in.

Anthropocentrism continues to be a major problem for both theology and science. From infancy onward, according to Sigmund Freud, caregivers struggle to sublimate children's illusion that they are at the center of all that is important in the world. Humans tend to be revolted by the thought that they are but one twig on the mammal limb of the tree of life. More pleasing to the ego is the traditional notion, for example, that the Master Craftsman specially fashioned horses to carry loads for creatures made in the "image of God." Darwin raised consciousness about the way this mindset has often led to the abuse of the flora and fauna; Homo sapiens has been guilty of eliminating many species, aggressively and with impunity.

Freud perceptively commented that humans suffered two severe hits in history prior to his "psychological blow to man's narcissism."[84] The cosmological blow by Copernicus was an affront to earthlings who believed they lived at the hub of the universe. It took centuries before they could adjust to the thought of the earth as a ball of wet clay whirling in space amid other planets. Darwin then inflicted the biological blow by showing humans that nature no more revolves around them than the sun around the earth. He made many people painfully aware that God has not placed humans on a pedestal apart from other organisms, and that all are mixtures of H_2O and several other elements. Darwin's impact was greater than that of Copernicus, because the nonscientist, as Milton observed, is not greatly bothered by "whether the sun . . . rise on the earth or earth rise on the sun."[85] What has been intensely disturbing to most people is acknowledging that previously unacknowledged primate cousins have been discovered and accepting that nature is not headed toward solidifying the privileged position of humans on planet Earth. Consequently, in the name of religion, some leaders of society have scorned pioneering scientists—even when they have not been antagonistic toward religion. Copernicus, a consecrated churchman, was largely motivated by his religious devotion to investigate the movements of the planets. Galileo, Copernicus's later defender, was convicted of heresy even though he tried to prevent a rift between theology and science.

The outcry against those scientists was in large part caused by the psychological need for stability. At the dawn of modern science, traditionalists were so devoted to the alleged immovable earth that the concept of its rotation on its axis, or around the sun, was intolerable. Later, new security was found in the presumed fixity of our sun as a pivot for the circling planets, which caused Newton difficulty in proving the universal mobility of suns and stars. Some appealed in their presumed inerrant Bible to a psalmist who declared that the world cannot be moved.[86] Some were comforted by a heaven-to-earth scheme featuring a great unchangeable chain of being that placed humans in the link "a little lower than the angels."[87] First Copernicus, Galileo, and Newton in astronomy, then Darwin in biology, upset the common human craving for permanence.

Historian of science Benjamin Farrington writes sanguinely about those shattering the idol of an infallible book:

> Darwin in the nineteenth century was performing a service like that of Galileo in the seventeenth. He was forcing the orthodox to revise their attitude to their sacred books. The effect of the two men's work has been permanent. They brought to an end the practice of using the Bible as an authority on physical and biological science—a thoroughly wholesome development.[88]

◆ ◆ ◆

By looking with a wide-angle lens at the history of ideas since 1859, we can see the truth of White's thesis. In the preface to his classic study of the clash between science and theology, he wrote, "All untrammelled scientific investigation, no matter how dangerous to religion some of its stages may have seemed for the time to be, has invariably resulted in the highest good both of religion and of science." Supernaturalism is a case in point, which offended Darwin both scientifically and theologically. As evolutionary theory has become accepted, theologians have been more inclined to attribute to God the design they find in natural rather than in unnatural processes. When unaccountable things happen, the tendency to claim that they are breaches in the laws of nature has lessened. Paley's image of a miracle-mongering God now has little appeal to many people, but they find other images of God that allow for both order and chance more meaningful.

Some religious people were relieved to find that Darwin focused his attention on providing a scientific explanation only for the origin of species and not for the origin of life, leaving open the speculation that life could begin only by the infusion of a vital divine force. But Darwin, who knew little about genes or molecules and was totally unaware of DNA, the genetic roots of the tree of life, made a remarkable guess in 1866 that life arose from inorganic elements. A century later, biochemist

Stanley Miller set up a lab procedure simulating some assumed primordial conditions on Earth before there was any life. After a mixture of water, hydrogen, ammonia, and methane was disturbed by electrical discharges, amino acids were obtained from which the protein building blocks of life are formed. That experiment, along with subsequent modifications, convinced many that Darwin's speculations on the origin of life by chemical means was sound.

John Polkinghorne points out that primal forms are now called quarks, gluons, and electrons:

> All that marvellous tale, from big bang to *Homo sapiens* and on to whatever lies in the future, is the story of creation. . . . The matter revealed to the inquiry of modern science is neither inert nor formless. Its pattern-creating dance is in accordance with laws capable of astonishing fruitfulness in their consequences, laws which we have already claimed to be pale reflections of the faithfulness of the Creator who moment by moment ordains that they should be so.[89]

In the frontispiece of the *Origin*, Darwin quoted Francis Bacon's advocacy for serious study of "the book of God's word" as well as "the book of God's works," along with his warning against confusing the two disciplines. Much misunderstanding has resulted, on the one hand, from religionists who make declarations on scientific fact, and on the other hand, from scientists who pretend to speak definitively on religious matters. Since truth is one, the conflict over evolution is not between science and religion but between scientists and religionists who have difficulty living within their partial understandings. Religion and science travel together on the road to complete truth; one may from time to time outdistance the other, but it cannot go against the other. To think that one needs to choose between reasonable faith and reliable fact displays a lack of understanding of the purposes of religion or science.

Stephen Gould shares with Darwin the view that science and religion are not antithetical disciplines and that clashes only occur "when one domain tries to usurp the proper space of the other." Theology works with "who" and "why" questions about the ultimate origin and destiny of life. Science supplements, rather than supplants, with temporal and technological questions, such as "How, when, and where did humans evolve?" "Evolution studies the pathways and mechanisms of organic change following the origin of life," Gould points out.[90] Natural processes and phenomena alone are not able to explain human purposes and values. According to Gould,

The lack of conflict between science and religion arises from a lack of overlap between their respective domains of professional expertise—science in the empirical constitution of the universe, and religion in the search for proper ethical values and the spiritual meaning of our lives. The attainment of wisdom in a full life requires extensive attention to both domains.[91]

Echoing Gould's outlook, the National Academy of Sciences published this simple but profound statement in 1998: "At the root of the apparent conflict between some religions and evolution is a misunderstanding of the critical difference between religious and scientific ways of knowing. Religion and science answer different questions about the world. Whether there is a purpose to the universe or a purpose for human existence are not questions for science."[92]

The methodological *how* and temporal *when* queries of science, on the one hand, and the ultimate *why* and *who* queries of religion, on the other, are not only compatible but also complementary. Since science and theology occupy separate but overlapping spheres, there is no contradiction in claiming that humans are made both in the divine image in spiritual form and in a hominoid image in physical form. Scientists do not look through a telescope for God or through a microscope for the soul. Believing in interference by the supernatural can be fatal to both modern science and rational religion.

Darwin's account of evolution has probably changed our outlook on human and divine existence more than any other theory in the history of human thought. Accounts of presumed miraculous interventions by an omnipotent God have become a liability rather than an asset to theology. Darwin's critical vision was bifocal: his biological perceptions were supplemented by theological conceptions. His theory can be seen as pointing toward the patient wisdom of Deity. Order and change, cooperation and conflict are required for cosmic development.

Much rumbling is still being felt in both religion and science from the seismic cultural impact of Darwin's life and thought. Although volcanoes as well as earthquakes have generally been viewed by most people as unmitigated disasters with supernatural components, scientists do not interpret them as interventions of divine judgment but recognize their beneficial as well as their sometimes dire results for organisms. Prudent people try to understand their geological causes and make ample preparations for their occurrences. Likewise, both Newton and Darwin have provided understandings of natural law that are basic for apprehending "the book of God's works." I hope that during the third century since his birth, Darwin's theory will come to be as fully accepted as Newton's gravitational theory has become—after a lapse of centuries. Theologians and ethicists as well as biologists will then be better prepared for the next scientific revolution.

Notes

1. *Autobiography*, 87.

2. MLD, 1:321.

3. *Correspondence*, 8:389.

4. John Haught, *God After Darwin* (Boulder, Colo.: Westview, 2000), ix.

5. Kenneth Miller, *Finding Darwin's God* (New York: HarperCollins, 1999), 196.

6. Carl Zimmer, *Evolution* (New York: HarperCollins, 2001), 338–39.

7. Michael Ruse, *The Evolution War* (Santa Barbara, Calif.: ABC-CLIO, 2000), 37.

8. Michael Ruse, *Can a Darwinian Be a Christian?* (New York: Cambridge University Press, 2001), 112–13.

9. *Notebooks*, 350.

10. Loren Eiseley, *Darwin's Century* (Garden City, N.Y.: Anchor, 1961), 198.

11. Neal Gillespie, *Charles Darwin and the Problem of Creation* (Chicago: University of Chicago Press, 1979), 107.

12. Peter Bowler, *Evolution: The History of an Idea* (Berkeley: California University Press, 1984), 159.

13. David Strauss, *The Old Faith and the New* (New York: Holt, 1873), 1:205.

14. James Thomson, "The City of Dreadful Night" (1880), 14.

15. Andrew White, *A History of the Warfare of Science with Theology in Christendom* (New York: Appleton, 1898), 1:86.

16. Gertrude Himmelfarb, *Darwin and the Darwinian Revolution* (London: Chatto, 1959), 322–23.

17. Aristotle, *Politics* 1256b; Psalm 17:8.

18. Aquinas, *Contra Gentes* 3:22.

19. Alfred North Whitehead, *Science and the Modern World* (New York: Free Press, 1967), 276.

20. David McLellan, *The Thought of Karl Marx* (New York: Harper, 1971), 224; compare Acts 2:44–45.

21. *Westminster Shorter Catechism*, 1.

22. *Autobiography*, 90.

23. *Autobiography*, 57.

24. Quoted in Ronald Clark, *Einstein* (New York: World Publishing Company, 1971), 19.

25. Relis Brown, *Biology* (New York: Heath, 1956), 42.

26. *Autobiography*, 88–89.

27. Frank Brown, *The Evolution of Darwin's Religious Views* (Macon, Ga.: Mercer, 1986), 41.

28. Asa Gray, *Darwiniana* (Cambridge: Harvard University Press, 1965), 310–11.

29. Asa Gray, *Natural Science and Religion* (New York: Scribner's, 1880), 67.

30. Henry Osborn, *From the Greeks to Darwin* (New York: Scribner's, 1929), 106.

31. Osborn, *Greeks*, 109.

32. Quoted in Brown, *Biology*, 475.

33. Augustine, *Against the Manichees* 1:23.

34. Augustine, *On the Trinity* 3:8–9.

35. Augustine, *The Literal Meaning of Genesis* 4:33; 9:32.

36. Aquinas, *Summa Theologica* 1:69:2.

37. Aquinas, *Summa contra Gentiles* 3:69.

38. Aquinas, *Quaestiones de Potentia* 7.

39. Aquinas, *Summa Theologica* 1:69:2.

40. Aubrey Moore, *Science and the Faith* (London: Paternoster, 1892), 180.

41. John Greene, *Darwin and the Modern World View* (Baton Rouge: Louisiana State University Press, 1961), 36–37.

42. John Polkinghorne, *One World* (London; SPCK, 1986), 65.

43. William Phipps, *Genesis and Gender* (New York: Praeger, 1989), 1–66.

44. William Jennings Bryan, *Heart to Heart Appeals* (New York: Revell, 1917), 137.

45. William Jennings Bryan, *In His Image* (New York: Revell, 1922), 93.

46. Quoted by John Scopes, *Reader's Digest* (March 1961), 141.

47. Genesis 1:30; 2:7.

48. *Correspondence*, 7:398.

49. Moore, *Science*, 173.

50. *The Christian Century* (14 September 1983): 809–11.

51. 1 Kings 18:1–19:12.

52. Matthew 5:45; 7:24–27.

53. *Autobiography*, 87.

54. Geoffrey Rowell, *Hell and the Victorians* (Oxford: Clarendon, 1974), vii.

55. 1 Corinthians 15:22; Frederic Farrar, *Eternal Hope* (New York: Dutton, 1890), 64, 89.

56. William Phipps, *Paul Against Supernationalism* (New York: Philosophical Library, 1987), 18–22, 83.

57. 1 Corinthians 1:28.

58. William Phipps, *Muhammad and Jesus* (New York: Continuum, 1996), 165–69.

59. Ephesians 4:6.

60. Alfred North Whitehead, *Process and Reality* (New York: Macmillan, 1929), 533.

61. Alfred North Whitehead, *Religion in the Making* (New York: Macmillan, 1926), 94.

62. James Moore, "The Case of Charles Darwin," *Religion in Victorian Britain*, ed. Gerald Parsons (Manchester: Manchester University Press, 1988), 1:276–78.

63. Miller, *Darwin's God*, 197.

64. George Tyrell, *Essays on Faith and Immortality* (London: Longmans, 1914), 259, 264–65.

65. Frederick Temple, *The Relations Between Religion and Science* (London: Macmillan, 1884), 122–23, 165.

66. Aubrey Moore, "The Christian Doctrine of God," in *Lux Mundi*, ed. Charles Gore (London: Murray, 1921), 73–74.

67. James 1:17.

68. Moore, *Science*, 184–86.

69. Henry Ward Beecher, *Henry Ward Beecher in England* (New York: Fords, 1885), 94–95.

70. Henry Ward Beecher, *Evolution and Religion* (New York: Fords, 1885), 115, 46.

71. Quoted in Clark, *Einstein*, 19.

72. Lyman Abbott, *The Theology of an Evolutionist* (New York: Outlook, 1925), 57–60.

73. William James, *The Varieties of Religious Experience* (New York: Doubleday, n. d.), 440, 442, 444, 468.

74. Eiseley, *Darwin's Century*, 194.

75. George Trevelyan, *Autobiography* (London: Longmans, 1949), 23.

76. Michael Denton, *Evolution* (London: Burnett, 1991), 66.

77. *Correspondence*, 9:427.

78. William Gilbert, *Princess Ida* (1884), quoted in Stephen Gould, *Ever Since Darwin* (New York: Norton, 1977), 222.

79. George Gallup and Michael Lindsay, *Surveying the Religious Landscape* (Harrisburg, Pa.: Morehouse, 1999), 33.

80. George Gallup, *Religion in America* (Princeton: Religion Research Center, 1990), 50.

81. Malcolm Bowden, *The Rise of the Evolution Fraud* (Bromley, Kent: Sovereign Publications, 1982), 87.

82. Basil Willey, *Darwin and Butler* (London: Chatto, 1960), 31.

83. John Brooke, *Science and Religion* (Cambridge: Cambridge University Press, 1991), 305.

84. Sigmund Freud, *Collected Papers* (London: Hogarth, 1950), 5:173.

85. John Milton, *Paradise Lost*, 8, 161–67.

86. Psalm 93:1.

87. Psalm 8:5.

88. Benjamin Farrington, *What Darwin Really Said* (New York: Schocken, 1966), 95.

89. John Polkinghorne, *Science and Creation* (London: SPCK, 1988), 55.

90. Stephen Gould, *Bully for Brontosaurus* (New York: Norton, 1991), 408, 455.

91. Stephen Gould, "Nonoverlapping Magisteria," *Natural History* (March 1997): 22.

92. National Academy of Sciences, *Teaching About Evolution and the Nature of Science* (Washington: National Academy Press, 1998), 58.

Selected Bibliography

Aveling, Edward. *The Religious Views of Charles Darwin*. London: Freethought, 1883.

Barlow, Nora. *The Autobiography of Charles Darwin*. New York: Harcourt, 1958.

Barrett, Paul, ed. *The Collected Papers of Charles Darwin*. Chicago: University of Chicago Press, 1977.

————, and others, eds. *Charles Darwin's Notebooks 1836–44*. Ithaca: Cornell University Press, 1987.

Bowlby, John. *Charles Darwin*. New York: Norton, 1991.

Bowler, Peter. *Evolution: The History of an Idea*. Berkeley: California University Press, 1984.

Brooke, John. *Science and Religion*. Cambridge: Cambridge University Press, 1991.

Brown, Frank. *The Evolution of Darwin's Religious Views*. Macon, Ga.: Mercer, 1986.

Browne, Janet. *Charles Darwin*. New York: Knopf, 1995.

Burkhardt, Frederick, and Sydney Smith, eds. *The Correspondence of Charles Darwin*. Cambridge: Cambridge University Press, 1985.

Chadwick, Owen. *The Secularization of the European Mind in the Nineteenth Century*. Cambridge: Cambridge University Press, 1975.

[Chambers, Robert]. *Vestiges of the Natural History of Creation*. London: n.p., 1844.

Clark, Ronald. *The Survival of Charles Darwin*. New York: Random House, 1984.

Corsi, Pietro. *Science and Religion: Baden Powell and the Anglican Debate, 1800–1860*. New York: Cambridge University Press, 1988.

Darwin, Charles. *The Descent of Man and Selection in Relation to Sex*. London: n.p., 1874.

————. *The Expression of the Emotions in Man and Animals*. London: n.p., 1871.

————. *Origin of Species by Means of Natural Selection*. London: n.p., 1872.

————. *The Voyage of a Naturalist Round the World in H.M.S. "Beagle"*. London: n.p., 1839.

————, and Alfred Wallace. *Evolution by Natural Selection*. London: Cambridge University Press, 1958.

Darwin, Francis, ed. *The Foundations of the Origin of Species: Two Essays Written in 1842 and 1844*. Cambridge: Cambridge University Press, 1909.

———. *The Life and Letters of Charles Darwin*. 2 vols. New York: Appleton, 1888.

———, and A. C. Seward, eds. *More Letters of Charles Darwin*. 2 vols. New York: Appleton, 1903.

De Beer, Gavin. *Charles Darwin*. London: Nelson, 1963.

Desmond, Adrian. *Huxley*. Reading: Addison-Wesley, 1997.

———, and James Moore. *Darwin*. New York: Warner, 1992.

Dorsey, George. *The Evolution of Charles Darwin*. New York: Doubleday, 1927.

Durant, John, ed. *Darwinism and Divinity*. New York: Blackwell, 1985.

Eiseley, Loren. *Darwin's Century*. Garden City, N.Y.: Anchor, 1961.

FitzRoy, Robert. *Narrative of the Surveying Voyages*. London: Colburn, 1839.

Gillespie, Neal. *Charles Darwin and the Problem of Creation*. Chicago: University of Chicago Press, 1979.

Gray, Asa. *Darwiniana*. Cambridge: Harvard University Press, 1965.

———. *Natural Science and Religion*. New York: Scribner's, 1880.

Gray, Jane, ed. *Letters of Asa Gray*. 2 vols. Boston: Houghton, 1893.

Greene, John. *The Death of Adam*. Ames: Iowa State University Press, 1959.

Himmelfarb, Gertrude. *Darwin and the Darwinian Revolution*. London: Chatto, 1959.

Hull, David. *Darwin and His Critics*. Cambridge: Harvard University Press, 1973.

Huxley, Leonard, ed. *Life and Letters of Thomas Henry Huxley*. 2 vols. London: Macmillan, 1900.

Huxley, Thomas. *Darwiniana*. New York: Appleton, 1896.

———. *Methods and Results*. New York: Appleton, 1896.

———. *Science and Christian Tradition*. London: Macmillan, 1909.

———, and others. *Christianity and Agnosticism*. New York: Appleton, 1889.

Keynes, Richard, ed. *Charles Darwin's Beagle Diary*. Cambridge: Cambridge University Press, 1988.

Kohn, David, ed. *The Darwinian Heritage*. Princeton: Princeton University Press, 1985.

Kropotkin, Petr. *Mutual Aid, a Factor of Evolution*. Boston: Horizons, 1902.

Lightman, Bernard. *The Origins of Agnosticism*. Baltimore: Johns Hopkins University Press, 1987.

Litchfield, Henrietta, ed. *Emma Darwin*. 2 vols. New York: Appleton, 1915.

Livingstone, David. *Darwin's Forgotten Defenders*. Edinburgh: Scottish Academic Press, 1987.

Manier, Edward. *The Young Darwin and His Cultural Circle*. Dordrecht: Reidel, 1978.

Miller, Kenneth. *Finding Darwin's God*. New York: HarperCollins, 1999.

Moore, James. *The Darwin Legend*. Grand Rapids, Mich.: Baker, 1994.

———. *The Post-Darwinian Controversies*. London: Cambridge University Press, 1979.

————, ed. *History, Humanity and Evolution*. Cambridge: Cambridge University Press, 1989.

Newman, Francis. *Phases of Faith*. London: Manwaring, 1860.

Paley, William. *Works*. Philadelphia: Crissy, 1857.

Parsons, Gerald, ed. *Religion in Victorian Britain*. Manchester: Manchester University Press, 1988.

Powell, Baden, and others. *Essays and Reviews*. London: Parker, 1860.

Ruse, Michael. *The Evolution War*. Santa Barbara, Calif.: ABC-CLIO, 2000.

Stone, Irving. *The Origin*. New York: Doubleday, 1980.

White, Andrew. *A History of the Warfare of Science with Theology in Christendom*. 2 vols. New York: Appleton, 1898.

Whitehead, Alfred. *Science and the Modern World*. New York: Free Press, 1967.

Willey, Basil. *Darwin and Butler*. London: Chatto, 1960.

Wright, Robert. *The Moral Animal*. New York: Pantheon, 1994.

Index

Limited to cross-references of names and terms used more than once in different passages.